"Ollenburger has crafted an attentive portrait of God the Creator throughout the Old Testament, demonstrating that God's creative acts are not limited to origins. Rather, in freedom and love, God continues to maintain and sustain life, even through acts that *dis*order a false, life-threatening 'order.' Written with the wisdom of an accomplished teacher, scholar, and storyteller, this book will deeply enrich the theological imaginations of its readers."

—**Andrea D. Saner**, Eastern Mennonite University

"*God the Creator* is an exemplary account of doing biblical theology. Ollenburger creatively constructs a mosaic of the diverse views of what the Bible says about God the Creator. This eloquently written study overflows with thought-provoking insights gleaned from an impressive array of biblical texts. The fruits of the study stem from Ollenburger's hermeneutical wisdom, which combines literary sensibilities, historical knowledge, and theological imagination. God the Creator, whom Ollenburger animates within the biblical traditions, is dynamic, sovereign, and relational. The expansive understanding of God the Creator that is convincingly argued for in this book calls on faith communities to reflect on the implications of their belief in a God who established, sustains, and repairs this cosmos."

—**Safwat Marzouk**, Union Presbyterian Seminary

"This long-anticipated volume represents the distillation of a lifetime of exegetical reflection on the theology of creation in the Hebrew Bible. Ollenburger draws on a wealth of insight and engagement with generations of students and colleagues. But it is ultimately the wit and wisdom of the master theologian himself that marks these pages as a classic in the making. Covering every genre of relevant Old Testament literature, this book demonstrates the ubiquity and profoundly formative nature of creation theology—from ancient Near Eastern prototypes to apocalyptic texts and beyond. Ollenburger traces a creation that is ongoing and reveals something of the heart and soul of the God of creation."

—**Paul Keim**, Anabaptist Mennonite Biblical Seminary

"Ollenburger synthesizes and expands his career-long investigation of biblical concepts of creation. On display are the author's finest characteristics: keen attention to primary texts, breadth and depth of scriptural engagement, restraint of other scholars' overstatements, and the rare gifts of clarity and accessibility. Taking the Creator God as its touchstone, this book articulates a concise biblical theology: an assessment of divine-human interaction within the framework of the world's nature and structure. It comes most highly recommended."

—**C. Clifton Black**, Princeton Theological Seminary

"*God the Creator* is the magnum opus of a mature scholar and teacher, the loving product of years of study, teaching, and reflection. Ollenburger focuses on multifaceted ways that Old Testament and some New Testament texts portray God in the mode of Creator. He discusses forms of interpretation, reads passages closely, and uncovers nuances of language in a way that yields biblical theology of poetic power. This book is a must-read for seminarians, ecologists, pastors, church groups, and anyone seeking an encounter with the Creator God."

—**Kathleen M. O'Connor**, Columbia Theological Seminary (emerita)

"While much attention now rightly centers on how the Bible might speak to the precariousness of our ecosystems, this insightful work instead focuses on God as Creator. Exploring passages across the Old Testament before offering a brief look at Second Temple Jewish literature and the New Testament, Ollenburger spotlights the Creator's involvements since the beginning of all things and the responses of the faithful. A careful, informed study from a master theologian. A well-written gem."

—**M. Daniel Carroll R. (Rodas)**, Wheaton College and Graduate School

"Ollenburger skillfully weaves together the Bible's diverse portrayals of God as the maker of the cosmos. Combining scholarly acumen with inviting prose, Ollenburger serves as a trustworthy and engaging tour guide for specialists and laypeople alike. The book deeply engages the most famous creation stories in Genesis as well as lesser-known creation texts from prophetic, wisdom, and apocalyptic literature found in the Bible and beyond. In the introduction, Ollenburger laments the lack of a systematic work on God as Creator; this book capably begins to fill that void."

—**Jackie Wyse-Rhodes**, Anabaptist Mennonite Biblical Seminary

God the Creator

The Old Testament and the World God Is Making

Ben C. Ollenburger

BakerAcademic
a division of Baker Publishing Group
Grand Rapids, Michigan

Published by Baker Academic
a division of Baker Publishing Group
Grand Rapids, Michigan
www.bakeracademic.com

Printed in the United States of America

Library of Congress Cataloging-in-Publication Data
Names: Ollenburger, Ben C., author.
Title: God the creator : the Old Testament and the world God is making / Ben C. Ollenburger.
Description: Grand Rapids, Michigan : Baker Academic, a division of Baker Publishing Group, [2023] | Includes bibliographical references and index.
Identifiers: LCCN 2022030400 | ISBN 9780801048661 (paperback) | ISBN 9781540966469 (casebound) | ISBN 9781493440115 (ebook) | ISBN 9781493440122 (pdf)
Subjects: LCSH: Creation—Biblical teaching. | God. | Creationism—Biblical teaching. | Bible. Old Testament—Criticism, interpretation, etc. | Redemption.
Classification: LCC BS651 .O45 2023 | DDC 231.7/65—dc23/eng/20220810
LC record available at https://lccn.loc.gov/2022030400

Unless otherwise indicated, Scripture quotations are the author's translation.

Scripture quotations labeled KJV are from the King James Version of the Bible.

Baker Publishing Group publications use paper produced from sustainable forestry practices and post-consumer waste whenever possible.

23 24 25 26 27 28 29 7 6 5 4 3 2 1

To Janice Wiebe Ollenburger—the sunshine

Contents

Acknowledgments

This book's long gestation began with my dissertation on Zion theology at Princeton Theological Seminary and developed further in a course on war and peace in the Old Testament and in exegesis courses on Genesis and Isaiah. To my students in those seminars and courses at Princeton Seminary long ago, and to more recent students at Anabaptist Mennonite Biblical Seminary, I remain grateful. The insights and questions, often unanticipated, of generations of students contributed to my learning and, profoundly, to my joy in teaching. For them I acknowledge much gratitude.

The impetus to gather and present material related to the title and subject of this book came first from invitations to offer lectures in Japan at the Tokyo Anabaptist Center, Tokyo Biblical Seminary, Waseda University, and Kobe Lutheran Theological Seminary. The generosity of those who hosted my family and me in Japan and the stimulating theological conversations with pastors, faculty members, and students live in memory. I acknowledge in particular the pastors who came from Korea to Tokyo—they were expecting Stanley Hauerwas—and endured interpretation from English to Japanese to Korean. While the chapters of this book do not resemble those lectures of more than two decades past, they share a genetic connection I am pleased to acknowledge.

Heather Bunce of Great Lakes Christian College provided wise counsel and constant encouragement, along with editorial help on several chapters. I owe her many thanks.

Janice Wiebe Ollenburger, truly a woman of valor, an artist, a creator—to her this book is dedicated.

Abbreviations

General

BCE	before the Common Era
CE	Common Era
DSS	Dead Sea Scrolls
ET	English translation(s)
SBL	Society of Biblical Literature

Scripture Versions

CEB	Common English Bible
KJV	King James Version
LXX	Septuagint (Greek translation of the Old Testament)
MT	Masoretic Text
NJB	New Jerusalem Bible
NJPS	*Tanakh: The Holy Scriptures: The New JPS Translation according to the Traditional Hebrew Text*
NRSV	New Revised Standard Version
RSV	Revised Standard Version
Vulg.	Vulgate

Pseudepigrapha/Deuterocanonical Works

Bel.	Bel and the Dragon
1 En.	1 Enoch
Jdt.	Judith
Jub.	Jubilees
Tob.	Tobit
Wis.	Wisdom of Solomon

Secondary Sources

AB	Anchor Bible
ANET	*Ancient Near Eastern Texts Relating to the Old Testament*. Edited by James B. Pritchard. 3rd ed. Princeton: Princeton University Press, 1969.
BDAG	Danker, Frederick W., Walter Bauer, William F. Arndt, and F. Wilbur Gingrich. *A Greek-English Lexicon of the New Testament and Other Early Christian Literature*. 3rd ed. Chicago: University of Chicago Press, 2000.
BibInt	*Biblical Interpretation*
BZAW	Beihefte zur Zeitschrift für die alttestamentliche Wissenschaft
CBQ	*Catholic Biblical Quarterly*
CBQMS	Catholic Biblical Quarterly Monograph Series

DCH	*Dictionary of Classical Hebrew*. Edited by David J. A. Clines. 9 vols. Sheffield: Sheffield Phoenix, 1993–2014.
DDD	*Dictionary of Deities and Demons in the Bible*. Edited by Karel van der Toorn, Bob Becking, and Pieter W. van der Horst. Leiden: Brill, 1995. 2nd rev. ed. Grand Rapids: Eerdmans, 1999.
FAT	Forschungen zum Alten Testament
FRLANT	Forschungen zur Religion und Literatur des Alten und Neuen Testaments
GKC	*Gesenius' Hebrew Grammar*. Edited by Emil Kautzsch. Translated by Arthur E. Cowley. 2nd ed. Oxford: Clarendon, 1910.
HBT	*Horizons in Biblical Theology*
HTR	*Harvard Theological Review*
IBHS	*An Introduction to Biblical Hebrew Syntax*. By Bruce K. Waltke and Michael O'Connor. Winona Lake, IN: Eisenbrauns, 1990.
IBT	Interpreting Biblical Texts
IJST	*International Journal of Systematic Theology*
JBL	*Journal of Biblical Literature*
Joüon	Joüon, Paul, and Takamitsu Muraoka. *A Grammar of Biblical Hebrew*. 2nd ed. Rome: Gregorian and Biblical Press, 2009.
JSJSup	Journal for the Study of Judaism in the Persian, Hellenistic, and Roman Periods Supplement Series
JSOT	*Journal for the Study of the Old Testament*
JSOTSup	Journal for the Study of the Old Testament Supplement Series
KTU	*The Cuneiform Alphabetic Texts from Ugarit, Ras Ibn Hani, and Other Places*. Edited by Manfried Dietrich, Oswald Loretz, and Joaquín Sanmartín. 3rd enl. ed. of *KTU*. Münster: Ugarit-Verlag, 1995.
LHB/OTS	The Library of Hebrew Bible / Old Testament Studies
NIB	*The New Interpreter's Bible*. Edited by Leander E. Keck. 12 vols. Nashville: Abingdon, 1994–2004.
NICOT	New International Commentary on the Old Testament
OBT	Overtures to Biblical Theology
OTL	Old Testament Library
OTS	Old Testament Studies
RB	*Revue biblique*
SBTS	Sources for Biblical and Theological Study
SJT	*Scottish Journal of Theology*
VT	*Vetus Testamentum*
WBC	Word Biblical Commentary
WMANT	Wissenschaftliche Monographien zum Alten und Neuen Testament
ZAW	*Zeitschrift für die alttestamentliche Wissenschaft*

Introduction

In 1925 the already-famous attorney Clarence Darrow of Chicago joined a team of lawyers defending John T. Scopes against charges brought against him by the state of Tennessee. The state was prosecuting Scopes, a high school teacher, for violating a Tennessee law that prohibited anyone teaching the theory of evolution in its schools, a prohibition Scopes acknowledged violating. Assisting the prosecution as associate counsel was William Jennings Bryan, twice a presidential candidate and a renowned public speaker. Newspaper accounts at the time, and the oratorical skills of Bryan, helped ensure that people would remember this as "the Scopes monkey trial."

Darrow and his client, the defendant Scopes, lost at trial. While the legal issue turned on whether Scopes should suffer legal sanctions for violating Tennessee's laws, Darrow called Bryan to the stand as an expert witness and managed to put the Bible itself on trial. Under vigorous questioning from Darrow, Bryan professed to believe whatever the Bible says, including what it might say about creation. Darrow, in his turn, ridiculed *literal belief* in what the Bible says about creation. But what does the Bible say about creation? And what might it mean to read the biblical texts about creation *literally*? Addressing these questions will help in introducing this book and its title. Clarence Darrow and William Jennings Bryan will appear again below, by the way.

The question "What does the Bible say about creation?" may seem simple, but answering it can become complicated. It is not merely pedantic to ask a further question: What do we mean by *creation*? Contemporary references to creation tend to have in mind nature or the natural world and typically have as their context a concern for that world, our world, or the environment. A few decades ago, when I was a college student—when Elvis Presley and all four Beatles were alive and Richard Nixon was president of the United States—we learned to talk about ecology. We learned to think about ecology because we had become aware that the natural world is in fact a fragile system—an ecosystem considerably endangered by our exploitation of it and of its resources, including exploitation of its human and nonhuman inhabitants. More recently, it has become common in Christian circles to speak of "creation care," bringing the natural world under the category of (God's) creation and recognizing an obligation to care for that world, for this earth . . . to care for the natural world as God's creation. For example, in 2018 Douglas J. Moo and Jonathan A. Moo published a textbook titled *Creation Care: A Biblical Theology of the Natural World*. I have no objection at all to this understanding of creation. I have conducted courses on creation care. And I have no criticism of the authors—both well-credentialed and respected scholars—or their book; I would have adopted it as a textbook had I not retired from teaching the year it was published. I cite it simply as an authoritative example of the prevalent identification of *creation* with the natural world—the earth that God created.

While I will have occasion to refer to the natural world in the chapters that follow, my focus will be elsewhere: my focus will be on God the Creator, as the book's title implies. To be more precise and more accurate, my focus will be on what the biblical texts, and primarily texts from the Old Testament (more on this term below), say about God the Creator: how they depict or portray God acting as Creator in different ways and to various ends. These differences and this variety, which will be on display in this book's ten chapters, add another degree of complexity to the question "What does the Bible say about creation?"—and also to the question "What do we mean by *creation*?"

Clarence Darrow and William Jennings Bryan seem to have assumed that Genesis 1 and 2 exhaust "what the Bible says" about creation. But the Bible's rendering of God the Creator is too rich and complex to be limited to those two chapters. Much of that "rendering"—depicting God acting as Creator—is in verse, in poetry, pressing to the limit the resources of the Hebrew language in the service of artistic imagination and expression in praise and lament, urgent appeal and instruction in wisdom. Genesis 1 amounts to narrative poetry, a kind of litany, but its liturgical cadences of God creating differ almost violently from the thundering poetry of God the Creator's speeches in Job. In both Genesis 1 and Job 38–41, the natural world figures crucially, and in both texts, God speaks (or, in Genesis, is reported as speaking and acting) as the Creator. In Job, the creatures in God's created world are wild, dangerous, and beautiful, and sometimes beyond controlling. In the world of God's creation there be dragons. Genesis 1 describes God "creating [*bara'*] the great dragons" (v. 21), dragons exhorted to praise the Lord in Psalm 148:7. Psalm 74:13, by contrast, describes God smashing the dragons' heads primordially on behalf of God's created order and against forces inimical, hostile to it (vv. 12–14). These and other poetic and prophetic texts and the prose narratives in Genesis 2–11 on which this book will focus yield no systematic description of God the Creator—an indication, perhaps, that they offer authentic testimony to their dynamic subject.

The diverse ways in which God acts as Creator in texts of differing genres complicate any answer to a second question in the argument between Darrow and Bryan: What would it mean to read these texts literally? Debates about, and sometimes insistence on, literal versus figurative, allegorical, or symbolic interpretation have a long history. My first theological or hermeneutical argument—at perhaps ten years old—was with my father, a minister, over this issue. He insisted that we must interpret the Bible literally. As evidence to the contrary, I offered Psalm 6:6, which in the KJV (i.e., for us then, the Bible) reads, "I am weary with my groaning; all the night make I my bed to swim; I water my couch with my tears." No one can cry so much that their tears *literally* make their bed swim; that was my argument to my father, who chuckled. Even staunch literalists recognize that metaphors abound in the Bible—which is richly populated with poetry—especially in the Old Testament's references or allusions to God the Creator.

Poets, including biblical ones, sometimes refer to a heart of stone (e.g., Job 41:24; Ezek. 11:19; William Butler Yeats, "Easter 1916," stanza 4). Neither biblical nor other poets ask us to think of a rock-hard human heart, individual or corporate, in terms of mineral qualities, igneous or sedimentary. We recognize poetic references to hearts of stone, wind with wings, God with chariots, and God as a "rock" (Pss. 18:2; 19:14; Hab. 1:12). We know that these are metaphors, even if (like almost everyone else) we cannot offer a clear definition of metaphor. And we have a good sense of what these images, these metaphorical statements, *signify*. We know, more or less, how to take them. So, for example, we understand that biblical texts describing God as a rock urge us to understand God as, at least, solid, reliable, and unfailing—as worthy of trust. This interpretive skill does not come to us magically or from extensive knowledge of geology. It comes to us, rather, by way of reading—by way of reading the Bible, from which we may gain a new appreciation of rocks.[1]

1. By contrast, Sallie McFague claims that metaphors have "direct implications," so that from a particular metaphor "certain things follow." So, for example, royal metaphors have as their direct implication that "God is distant from the world" and "basically uninvolved with the world" (*Models of God*, 65, 66). This despite—it is contradicted by—Israel's address by its King and Creator, "You are precious in my sight and I love you" (Isa. 43:4, 15).

Discussion and debate about literal reading and interpretation began many centuries before my conversation with my father. Early in the fifth century CE, Augustine (354–430), the bishop of Hippo in North Africa, published a commentary titled *On Genesis Literally Interpreted*. In this commentary on Genesis 1–3, Augustine understands the creation story with only occasional appeal to allegory, while reading Genesis within the framework of Christian belief. Commenting on the creation of light in Genesis 1:3, for example, Augustine suggests that this has to do with illuminating the minds of the angels (*On Genesis Literally Interpreted* 4.21). What Augustine meant by "literal" was, thus, far from simplistic. For Augustine, a literal interpretation must speak truthfully of God, which meant that it must accord with convictions at the heart of Christian faith. In another work, *On Christian Doctrine*, Augustine writes that when we find something in Scripture that, understood literally, does not contribute to purity of life or soundness of doctrine, then it must be figurative (3.10.14). Centuries later, Thomas Aquinas (1225–74), while agreeing with Augustine, added something that seems almost modern. The literal sense, Thomas writes in his *Summa Theologiae*, is what the author intends. That interpretation of a work should be guided or determined by the author's intention(s) became controversial some decades ago. But Thomas regarded Scripture as a categorically different kind of work whose author is God (I-II, q.10, a.1). Thomas knew, of course, that people in all their humanity composed the biblical texts, but he joined long Christian tradition in insisting that, in the interpretation of Scripture, the author whose intention matters most is God. But how would someone, or some community, go about discovering what God's intention might be? Perhaps in something like the way we would come to understand what "God is our rock" and other metaphors signify—by locating them within other identifying descriptions of God in (the whole of) Scripture.[2]

In focusing on God the Creator, the chapters that follow in this book will employ a simpler understanding of *literal* in relation to the interpretation of biblical texts: they will assume that God is the subject of those acts that the texts ascribe to God, and they will seek to describe those acts within the framework of (or "the world within") those texts. This does not entail embracing the notion of God as the author of Scripture, but neither does it stand in tension with it. In any event, in a book—this one—professing to be about God the Creator, the author of the whole cosmos, belief that God is somehow the author of Scripture hardly seems daring.[3]

2. I have written more technically and with greater nuance on these and attendant matters in "We Believe in God."

3. For a way of thinking about God as authoring (or authorizing) Scripture, see Wolterstorff, *Divine Discourse*, and my essay "Pursuing the Truth of Scripture."

In his remarks at the conclusion of the Scopes trial, the presiding judge, John Raulston, expressed his own distaste for the arguments between William Jennings Bryan and Clarence Darrow. He suggested that their debate was so misplaced as to ignore both the character and the value of the Bible. In the course of his remarks, he described the Bible as "a waybill to the other world."[4] Judge Raulston's terms seem quaint so many years after the trial, and we would demur from his comparison of the Bible to a set of shipping instructions. But he was not entirely mistaken in associating the Bible with an "other world." Not many years before the Scopes trial, a young pastor in Switzerland spoke of the strange new world *within* the Bible. That pastor, Karl Barth, meant that the Bible presents us with a world in which "the chief consideration is . . . the doings of God."[5] The Bible presents us with a world of God's creation: God creating the heavens and the earth and all that is in them.

We know that there are very many things in the heavens and in the earth—more things than we could possibly name, more than we could even imagine. All of these *things* somehow fit together—not always in complete harmony and not without conflict, but they do fit together and work together within a universe, a *cosmos*, a word I used above. Our English word *universe* combines two Latin terms: *unus*, meaning "one," and *vertere*, meaning "to change (into)." Our universe is an unimaginable number of things turned into, formed into, one whole: a universe, or in Greek, a *cosmos*. A cosmos is not just a whole collection of things. In fact, the word in Greek means an "orderly arrangement," or a "just order." A *cosmos*, a world, is an ordered whole, beautifully arranged. It is "things in order," and not in any order but in good order: things as they should be, a just order. In the Old Testament, *order*—things as they should be—has a *natural* meaning; we could think of this as the world working as it should work, supporting and nurturing life, including human life. But in the Old Testament, order also has a *moral* meaning and a *political* one: think of this as "things as they should be" among people and among nations. This, too, is part of the ordered world, the cosmos, working as it should work. And in the Bible, of course, this *should* substitutes for "as God intends" or "as pleases or delights God"—as God desires (Isa. 46:10). God acts as Creator to establish, sustain, and on occasion repair that order: a dynamic, life-enabling order that can properly go by the name *creation*.

4. "Scopes Guilty, Fined $100, Scores Law," *New York Times*, July 21, 1925. My references to the trial depend on the newspaper account, which is archived here: https://archive.nytimes.com/www.nytimes.com/learning/aol/onthisday/big/0721.html.

5. Barth, "Strange New World," 38. The essay comprises the translated text of an address Barth gave in 1916.

In part because of the conjunction of these three dimensions of order into one—that is, as *creation*—my expansive attribution to God of the office "Creator" will elicit disagreement from scholars whose definition of *creator* is more restrictive.[6] In cultures and societies in ancient Israel's environment—and perhaps within ancient Israel itself—responsibilities and credits could be distributed and negotiated within a (sometimes competitive) community of deities. Psalm 82 may reflect this in Israel's case, as also Deuteronomy 32:8–9, differently. The Bible acknowledges other deities, other gods, but its texts do not apportion the formation of the world and the defense or repair of its order—or the creation, judgment, and restoration of a people—to other than the one Creator. In the Old Testament, God's *creating* is not limited to origins, much less to absolute origins.[7] God created—the Hebrew verb is *bara'*—the heavens and the earth (Gen. 1:1), and also the north and the south (Ps. 89:12) and the ends of the earth (Isa. 40:28). But God also promises to create (*bara'*) a well-watered and fruitful way in the wilderness for God's own return and the return of Israel from Babylon (Isa. 41:18–20), the same Israel that God created (Isa. 43:1; Mal. 2:10)—all who are called by God's name (Isa. 43:7). Indeed, the objects of God's actions as Creator are quite comprehensive, including light and darkness, well-being (*shalom*) and calamity, and salvation (45:7–8). The future itself—Israel's future in particular—is and will be God's creation (48:5–7). The Old Testament's own attribution of "Creator" to God seems to be as expansive as possible. The point was made by Eusebius of Caesarea (293–339 CE): "Such is the theology of the Hebrews, which first teaches that all things were constituted by a creative word of God, and then goes on to teach that the entire universe was not left abandoned . . . but that it is governed by the providence of God unto eternity, since God is not only creator and maker of all, but also savior, governor, king and chieftain, watching over sun and moon and stars and the entire heaven and world throughout the ages."[8]

Remarks on the Chapters That Follow

That God created the heavens and the earth is the Bible's opening affirmation in Genesis 1. And God's creating continues in Genesis 2, which initiates a narrative that continues in Genesis 3 and beyond. Because of the importance of Genesis 1 and 2–3 in the Bible's presentation and in contemporary understanding of God

6. E.g., Nevader, "Creating a *Deus Non Creator*."
7. As I argued in my essay "Isaiah's Creation Theology," 61.
8. Eusebius, *Praeparatio evangelica* 2.4, quoted in Timiadis, *Nicene Creed*, 35.

as Creator, and because of crucial, contested issues in the interpretation of these chapters, I have devoted a chapter each to Genesis 1, 2, and 3–11. The style and scope of Genesis 1 (1:1–2:3, to be precise) differ markedly from those of the chapters that follow. Its frame, in 1:1 and 2:1–3, mark it as a completed unit of text: the litany of creation was concluded (1:31), so God rested (2:3). Genesis 2:4 not only begins a new creation story but creates the possibility of drama by introducing characters, agents, all of whom God created: a man, a woman, and a serpent. The latter two agents converse about what God said and, according to the serpent, about God's actual purpose concealed under what God said. The narrative beginning in Genesis 2 continues without interruption through Genesis 4 and has echoes especially in 6:1–4, preceding the flood narrative, and in 11:1–9, the tower of Babel story. These accounts narrate the possibility and actuality of creation-threatening rivalry with God, and God's action in defense of creation.

While the Bible's first verse says that God created the world, its second verse describes something prior to, or in the midst of, or in the way of—obstructing—the creation of a cosmos: the earth as *tohu wabohu* (Gen. 1:2), which sounds menacing. In Genesis, God does only verbal battle with the menace (1:3). But the creation and flood accounts in Genesis have as their wider milieu texts from Mesopotamia and Egypt that narrate the world's creation and a great flood. In chapter 4, for example, I briefly describe *Enuma Elish*, in which the deity Marduk does engage a menacing force in battle. In some literature from Israel's neighborhood (Syria) poetic texts tell of a deity's battle with the menacing Sea and a sea monster, Leviathan (*lotan*), and the dragon. These narrative-poetry texts from the ancient city of Ugarit, in a language closely related to the biblical languages of Hebrew and Aramaic, feature deities and powers whose names also appear in the Bible.

The discussion of literature from Israel's environment provides context for chapter 5 on the Psalms. There the Sea itself is menacing, personified as Leviathan or Rahab—a force hostile to creation that God vanquishes in defense of it. God's undeniably violent action against the Sea, Leviathan, and the dragon in defense of creation, recalled in retrospect (Ps. 74:12), was at the same time an appeal to God to act again as Creator on behalf of Zion and God's people. In Psalm 89, Babylon's destruction of Jerusalem and desecration of the temple seem to call into question God's faithfulness or power, power celebrated in the memory of God's calming of the sea and crushing of its monster, Rahab. God's action in securing the order of the world was the grounds for God's promises of enduring faithfulness to David and David's house. In the Psalms (for example, Ps. 77) God's action as Creator has both cosmic or primordial dimensions (prevailing over the Sea and the deep) and historical ones, reminiscent of God's deliverance of Israel in the exodus. But the Sea does not uniformly appear as a hostile power in the Psalms, and neither does Leviathan. God did need to put the waters in their place, Psalm 104 says, but then God could enjoy watching Leviathan play in the sea.

The Psalms are profound and beautiful poetry. Genesis 1–11 is narrative prose, but it is poetic in its own way. The term *poetry* comes from a Greek word, *poieō*, which means "to make" or "to create." God is the Creator, of course, and thus the supreme poet. It should not surprise us that God chooses poetry, literary artistry, as a biblical mode of divine self-expression. Poets, including biblical ones, make things—they create—with words. Israel's poets lived in a world full of gods, and those poets, divinely inspired no doubt, took up this world into their poetry and employed it in testimony and in appeal to God the Creator.

Leviathan also makes an appearance in Job, within the broad and strained category of Israel's Wisdom literature, the subject of chapter 6. God the Creator is certainly in focus in Job, whose protagonist longs to put God in the witness dock so that he can accuse the Creator of malfeasance. A young woman from Indonesia, a seminary student newly arrived in Elkhart, Indiana, walked out of her apartment one icy but unusually brilliant (for far northern Indiana) January morning and asked, "Why isn't the sun working?!" Job protests that God isn't making the world work as it should, and he envisions the reversal of creation itself. Then God exposes Job to the wild and volatile world that is a marvel even to God, who brought it about—a dangerous but inhabitable world that doesn't yield to the demand that God and cosmic order should ensure justice for the righteous. Proverbs, in which God, creation, and wisdom are closely joined, presents a different view. The book does not so much articulate—despite Wisdom's speech in Proverbs 8:22–31—as it assumes a creation theology. In Ecclesiastes, Qoheleth joins Job in observing that neither divine purpose nor divine justice are perceptible. Job, Proverbs, and Ecclesiastes acknowledge God's creation of the world. Job and Ecclesiastes observe, each of them at first and at length, that this fact is far from unambiguously to God's credit. Each of them—Job, and Qoheleth in Ecclesiastes—concludes with a profession, a confession . . . a confession of faith. In both instances, it is a confession and a profession of God the Creator made in resignation: Job resigns from his suit against the Creator, and Qoheleth resigns from his campaign to gain all wisdom empirically. By virtue of the providence that guided Jews to include and Christians to retain Job and Ecclesiastes as Scripture, the Bible presents us with *critical* reflection on the claim or conviction that God is this world's Creator.

God as Creator in Isaiah is the subject of chapter 7. The book of Isaiah portrays God acting as Creator, claiming to have acted as Creator, and claiming to *be* the Creator—of the heavens and the earth (42:5), of Jacob/Israel (43:1, 15), and of all humankind (45:12). Isaiah also draws on the ancient poetic tradition of God's conquest of the dragon and the Sea to recall God's deliverance in the exodus in an appeal for a new exodus (51:9–11). Isaiah's references to God as Creator recall Genesis 1—especially in light of Isaiah's repeated use of the term *bara'* (to create), which appears seven times in Genesis 1:1–2:4. But the resonance between Isaiah and Genesis goes beyond this. Genesis 1–3, of course, presents us with no context, no milieu, but for the one the text constructs. The book of Isaiah, by contrast, sets itself within a particular context, or rather several contexts—social, geopolitical, and military ones—clearly alluded to or explicitly named. Even so, the emphasis in Genesis 1–11 against rivalry with God and insistence on the creation-constitutive distinction and difference between Creator and creature have their echoes in Isaiah's insistence on God's exclusive prerogative as Zion's (Creator) King and Defender. Isaiah is unyielding in its condemnation of injustice, dependence on armaments, and reliance on military alliances as incompatible with trust in God.

While references to creation and to God as Creator are most extensive in Isaiah, they appear in other prophets as well—the subject of chapter 8. In Amos, those references serve the book's predominant note of judgment against Israel. But Amos makes the arresting claim that God's juridical reach extends to other nations as well, ones near to and others distant from Israel. This divine "reach" extends cosmically: the God who pronounces judgment on other nations for violating norms of justice and humanity, and on Israel for systemic injustice and infidelity, is the God who made the constellations—the Creator of the heavens. In Jeremiah and Ezekiel, too, God the Creator can be the executor of judgment. But each book envisions a new creation beyond judgment, destruction, and exile: God's creation of a renewed—a resurrected and re-created—Israel with a new heart, a new mind, and a new covenant.

While Jeremiah and Ezekiel envision the restoration of Israel and Israel's reunion with Judah, Zechariah and Daniel foresee a more decisive reordering of current, disordered arrangements. Both Zechariah (chaps. 1–6) and Daniel receive disclosures of the future, revelations—Zechariah through an interpreting angel and Daniel through his dream and Nebuchadnezzar's, through a vision and an interpreting angel, and by direct revelation, the Greek term for which is *apokalypsis*. These features already suggest an apocalyptic mode, as I claim in chapter 9. Further, Zechariah 2:1–4 (1:18–21 in English translations) compresses imperial history—the series of nations that oppressed Judah—into a single image, anticipating Daniel's representation of imperial history in the form of a statue composed of metals declining in value from head to toe: from gold to clay, from the past to Daniel's present. Neither Zechariah nor Daniel envisions the end of time, but they do envision God bringing about, creating, a world dramatically different from one in which tyrants and rulers who worship power and force claim to be its lords.

Chapter 10, the final chapter, begins with a pair of Old Testament texts, Exodus and Zephaniah, that have little in common apart from references to creation. In the case of Zephaniah, God performs a strange work of "un-creation" in what seems to be a reversal of God's acts of creation in Genesis. In Exodus as well God performs a strange work, introducing in the plagues distortions of the natural world over which God claims to be sovereign as Creator against the competing claims of Pharaoh. The plagues are, of course, preparatory to God's deliverance of Israel from Egypt at the sea—not only *at* the sea but *with* the sea as God's instrument against the horses and riders and chariots of Pharaoh's army. The sea in Exodus 15, far from being the creation-hostile force God vanquishes in some Old Testament texts, serves God's purposes for Israel's salvation.

Zephaniah retrieves parts of Genesis 1–11 and appropriates them in service of announcing catastrophic judgment and then of promising restoration and repair. Zephaniah serves as precedent for later Jewish texts, such as 1 Enoch, Jubilees, and Tobit, which draw from Genesis in speaking of God the Creator. Other Jewish texts, such as Judith and the Wisdom of Solomon, continue the biblical tradition without reference to Genesis. At the same time, Exodus 15 serves later texts, including the New Testament's Synoptic Gospels, in identifying Jesus closely with God the Creator. Both Judaism and the newly born Christianity drew heavily and creatively, if differently, on scriptural resources and tradition in speaking of creation and its Creator.

Finally, in chapter 10 I briefly address "creation out of nothing"—*creatio ex nihilo*—which becomes a topic in early Christian theology (hence the Latin). I also discuss its putative origin in Jewish and New Testament texts. I first mentioned "creation out of nothing" at the beginning of chapter 2, in relation to the first verses of Genesis 2, which begin with a description of the earth as "virtually nothing." I conclude with God's creation "out of nothing" as a gift.

In the above paragraphs and in the chapters that follow, I refer consistently to the Old Testament. I do so not to be provocative, and certainly not to be offensive, but to be honest. I write as a Christian for whom the Bible comprises two Testaments, one of which is historically—and crucially—prior to the other. In consideration of this historical priority, John Goldingay retains "the politically incorrect terms B.C. and A.D.," because his *Old Testament Theology* "is a work of Christian theology."[9] I use the terms BCE and CE—"before the Common Era" and "Common Era." Nothing of theological significance, so far as I can tell, attaches to the BC/AD terminology, especially since its origin was medieval, and AD first referred to the years after Diocletian became the Roman emperor (284–305 CE)—the Diocletian whose persecution of Christians was the last and most severe. AD as *anno domini*—"the year of the Lord"—was adopted by medieval Christians. Although Goldingay refers to the New Testament, he avoids "Old Testament"—except in the book's title—in favor of "First Testament."[10] Other scholars refer to First and Second Testaments, as if they were two volumes of a *festschrift*, without regard to the temporal—and one might say, foundational—priority of the Old Testament. "Hebrew Bible," the term of choice in academic circles in the past several decades, owes its wide adoption to the admirable intention of providing common ground in biblical studies on which people of different faith traditions or none at all might collaborate. Jews and Christians could "bracket their traditional identities," as Jon D. Levenson put it, in working on a Hebrew Bible that was neither the Tanakh nor the Old Testament—not the Scripture of either Jews or Christians.[11] In this book, I have not bracketed my traditional, Christian—even more specifically, Mennonite—identity. While I have read and interpreted the texts, and written about them, from inside that identity (which has more dimensions than those named, of course), what I have written remains in all its details subject to criticism, academic or otherwise. I have tried not to impose on the texts what other readers, interpreters, could not find there.

You will find in this book very little discussion of critical matters such as the composition and dating of Old Testament texts. The pursuit of those and other critical questions, common to the guild of biblical studies, is entirely unobjectionable and can be interesting and also profitable, depending on the kinds of questions an inquiry poses to and about the texts. My inquiry here is oriented to the question "What do the texts say about God the Creator?" In some instances, as in discussion of Genesis 2–3, I engage other scholars, for two reasons. First, scholarship on those chapters, and on Genesis 1–11 altogether, has been influential in shaping contemporary understanding of God as Creator. And second, my interpretation of those chapters disagrees, at what seem to me crucial points, with a kind of consensus within some current scholarship. Generally, I have tried to keep footnotes and technical matters to a minimum, hoping that the book will be accessible to a wide range of readers interested in the subject.

9. Goldingay, *Old Testament Theology*, 13.
10. Goldingay, *Old Testament Theology*, 15.
11. Levenson, *Hebrew Bible*, 105.

Unfortunately, English translations of the Old Testament do not always match the versification of the Hebrew text (the NJPS is an exception). For example, Zechariah 2:5 in Hebrew is 2:1 in the NRSV. In such instances, I will give the Hebrew or Aramaic reference followed by the NRSV reference in brackets—for example, Zechariah 2:5[2:1]. All translations are my own unless otherwise credited.

Finally, the Hebrew and Aramaic texts of the Bible use several words or names for God, the God of Israel, including *Yhwh*, the name introduced to Moses in Exodus 3:14–15 and 6:2–6, and the name upon which people began to call according to Genesis 4:26.[12] In Genesis 1, the God who creates is *'Elohim*, a common, plural noun adopted to designate "God"—the same God, surely, whom Genesis 2–4 names *Yhwh*. In chapters beyond those treating Genesis 1–11, I will use "God" and "Yhwh" interchangeably. They refer to and name, as I believe, the same God the Creator who summoned into being the world and all that is within it.

12. In accord with Jewish prohibition of pronouncing the divine name, the MT provides the consonants *yhwh* but supplies vowels for pronouncing another name, such as *'adonai*, "Lord," or *hashem*, "the name."

1

God's World at Peace

GENESIS 1

Darkness covered the face of the deep. . . . Let there be light.

Genesis 1:2–3 NRSV

The year 1968 was tumultuous and violent. In February, police fired into a crowd protesting racial segregation in Orangeburg, South Carolina, killing three young African Americans. Two months later, Martin Luther King Jr., a champion of civil rights, social justice, and peace, fell victim to an assassin's bullet in Memphis, Tennessee. His assassination provoked massive riots in several cities, including the US capital, Washington, DC. Just two months after King's death, Robert F. Kennedy Jr. was assassinated in Los Angeles, California. Kennedy was campaigning for the Democratic presidential nomination less than five years after his older brother, President John F. Kennedy, had been assassinated in Dallas, Texas. The racial violence and the assassinations of Martin Luther King Jr. and Robert "Bobby" Kennedy—these coming so close together and not long after JFK's death—left people mourning and wondering what kind of world they inhabited.

Violence seemed to have infected the whole world, while global attention directed itself to the conflict in Vietnam. In January 1968, the North Vietnamese launched the Tet Offensive in a war that would grow in intensity until fifty-eight thousand Americans and millions of Vietnamese had lost their lives. In August of that year, in Chicago, during the Democratic National Convention, tensions between anti-war protestors and police exploded into violence—violence that included politicians, reporters, and bystanders among its victims. But protests and riots did not remain within the US or have Vietnam as their only focus. In many countries around the world, students and others mounted protests, sometimes violently. In 1968, the world seemed to have become unhinged, disordered, chaotic.

Intervening in the pervasive darkness, near the year's end, three astronauts aboard Apollo 8—William Anders, Frank Borman, and James Lovell—became the first humans to orbit the moon. From the distant reaches of dark space, they viewed the earth and photographed it for the first time.

From that uniquely distant perspective, the world appeared perfectly ordered and beautifully arranged—a spherical island of color and light in a sea of darkness. On Christmas Eve, in a broadcast heard around the world, Anders

Public Domain / Wikimedia Commons

Figure 1. The good earth

read these words from the vast darkness of space: "In the beginning God created the heaven and the earth. And the earth was without form, and void; and darkness was upon the face of the deep. And the Spirit of God moved upon the face of the waters. And God said, Let there be light: and there was light" (Gen. 1:1–3 KJV).

With pictures of the earth and the moon displayed on television, all three astronauts aboard Apollo 8 read from Genesis 1, through verse 10, on Christmas Eve 1968. It seemed possible, despite all the darkness and violence of that year, to believe Borman when he referred, in closing, to "the good Earth."[1] The term *good* appears seven times in Genesis 1, each time referring to what God has created. And each time, the assessment "good" is God's. Borman likely had in mind the title of Pearl S. Buck's 1931 novel, *The Good Earth*, but both Buck and Borman echoed God's assessment in Genesis 1.

First, God

The creation of heaven and earth in Genesis 1 occurs entirely at, and as, God's initiative. The narrator who speaks in Genesis 1 supplies no reason for, assigns no motive to, why God began this work of creation. The Bible's first verse states, simply, that there was a beginning in which God created heaven and earth. Nothing precedes this beginning; nothing else of which we can speak or know comes first or comes before. First was God, and God created. In his *Confessions*, Augustine addresses the question of what God was doing before creating the world (12.14). The North African bishop reports, and dismisses, the answer someone before him had offered: God was preparing hell for those who probe illicitly into mysteries. Augustine refuses to mock in this way those who ask probing questions. He prefers instead to acknowledge that he cannot know what cannot be known.[2] The classic rabbinic midrash on Genesis, *Genesis Rabbah*, addresses the issue differently. The story of creation in Genesis 1 opens with the Hebrew word *bere'shit*, traditionally translated "in the beginning." In Hebrew, the word's first letter (*b*) is written ב. The rabbis debated the question "Why was the world created with a ב?" Hebrew is written from right to left (the opposite of English and European languages), and one answer to the question assumed this: "Just as the ב is closed at the sides but open in front"—open to the left, that is, and to all that follows—"so you are not permitted to investigate what is above and

1. "The Apollo 8 Christmas Eve Broadcast," NASA, last updated September 25, 2007, http://nssdc.gsfc.nasa.gov/planetary/lunar/apollo8_xmas.html.

2. Augustine, *Confessions*, 11.12.

what is below, what is before and what is behind" (*Gen. Rab.* 1.10).[3] What is not possible to know, according to Augustine, may not be investigated, according to the rabbis. What can be known is that God created and that nothing preceded.

Neither does the narrator in Genesis 1:1 provide us background information about the subject of creation, about God, about this *'Elohim* (in Hebrew) who began to create. The Bible's first verse introduces God but provides no identifying description preceding "God created." Who, then, is this "God"? We cannot read behind Genesis 1:1 to find out, for the preceding pages are not only blank; they are absent. The same is true, of course, of other books, more recent ones. Flannery O'Connor's *The Violent Bear It Away* (1960) begins with the name "Francis Marion Tarwater." Sinclair Lewis's 1927 novel begins with the name "Elmer Gantry," and Melville's *Moby-Dick* (1851) offers us, in its first sentence, the name "Ishmael." We cannot read behind these opening sentences to discover something about Tarwater or Gantry or Ishmael, even though readers familiar with the Bible will recognize the name Ishmael. Who they are, their identities, unfold before our eyes as we read. Sometimes we need not read far to learn something more about them: we learn in O'Connor's first sentence that Tarwater is drunk, and in Lewis's that Gantry is as well. Ishmael's character unfolds more slowly and more mysteriously. After reading all of *Moby-Dick*, we cannot again read its opening sentence or regard the name Ishmael with the naivete of a first reader. Every story begins, as it were, with a *b*, open to what follows while foreclosing investigation of, but inviting by that fact, speculation about what may have preceded.

We need not read far in the Bible, or in Genesis, to learn something about God: God created heaven and earth. As we shall see, God created the world at peace. But as with Melville's Ishmael or Captain Ahab—Ahab being another biblical allusion—God's identity unfolds as we read further and encounter God's speakings and makings, and God's involvement with different characters and places. Most of us are familiar with the larger story or with parts of it. We know that the deity introduced as *'Elohim* in Genesis 1:1—and acquiring the name *Yhwh Elohim* in Genesis 2, and then *Yhwh* alone in Genesis 4—will have a particular relationship with Israel, a relationship often troubled. Having read further, we may wonder if that relationship, with all its ramifications, was not the reason God created heaven and earth. Was it to receive Israel's worship, and not Israel's alone? The story that begins in Genesis 1:1 continues in later parts of Genesis but also in Exodus. In Exodus we read that God delivered the Hebrews from slavery in Egypt but also that God brought them to Sinai (Exod. 1–19) and, through Moses, spoke to them . . . at great length (Exod. 20–40). That speaking continues

3. Freedman and Simon, *Midrash Rabbah*, 1:9.

through Leviticus and Numbers, books we sometimes read with difficulty (if we read them at all), given their attention to minute details of worship and holiness. Many of those details have to do with a fractured relationship between Israel and God and with its repair; they have to do with atonement (e.g., Lev. 16:29–34). Atonement, or the repair of a fracture in Israel's relationship with God, may seem far removed from "God created heaven and earth." It may seem even further removed from any association with peace. But atonement, like creation itself, is at God's initiative. And it restores peace between Israel and God the Creator (Lev. 26:1–6; Ps. 85:8); it repairs creation.[4] All of God's great historical acts, narrated in the Bible, including especially the exodus (Ps. 81:10), have their foundation and their horizon in creation—in God the Creator of heaven and earth, introduced first in Genesis 1:1. *This* God brought Israel out of slavery to Sinai and to Canaan. *This* God provided for atonement, for restored peace—on Israel's behalf and ultimately on behalf of the world God created, a world that is, from beginning to end, God's (Ps. 24:1–2). To put it another way, the one whom the New Testament calls "the God of peace" (Rom. 15:33; 16:20; Phil. 4:9; 1 Thess. 5:23; Heb. 13:20) is the God who, as Genesis 1:1 declares, created heaven and earth.

Having read *Moby-Dick*, we know that Ishmael will narrate a troubled relationship between Captain Ahab and the white whale Moby-Dick. We also know that Ishmael, Captain Ahab, and Moby-Dick are imaginative inventions of Herman Melville. They have no existence, no reality, beyond *Moby-Dick* the novel. What we can say about Captain Ahab remains bound to what Melville tells us about him. What we can say and have to say about the person Genesis 1:1 calls *'Elohim*, and about this God's creating, is bound to the Bible, apart from which we would have nothing to say on the subject. But Genesis 1, and whoever may have written it, did not invent God. God's reality preceded, and it exceeds, the text of Genesis and of the Bible, which speaks often of "the living God" (e.g., Deut. 5:26; Josh. 3:10).[5] This is a confession of faith. Genesis 1 is itself a confession of faith, testimony to God the Creator of heaven and earth.

God Created Heaven and Earth

This is the announcement with which the Bible begins: God created heaven and earth. And as I mentioned above, the word introducing that announcement, the Bible's first word, is *bere'shit*. This term certainly designates a first, or a beginning.

4. Barker, *Creation*, 151.

5. In Bel and the Dragon, one of the "additions" to the book of Daniel found in the LXX, Daniel declares, "I worship the living God, the creator of heaven and earth" (Bel. 1:5).

But does it refer to *the* beginning, as English translations have traditionally rendered it: "In the beginning . . . "? These translations thus understand Genesis 1:1 to be a superscription to, or summary statement of, the entire first chapter. Or does the word *bereʾshit* have a temporal sense—"When God began . . ."—as the NJPS translates? It may even be possible to understand Genesis 1:1 in this way: "As his first [best?] work, God created heaven and earth."[6] Scholars have debated the matter for generations, and the debate remains unresolved. The issues of grammar and syntax are too technical for extensive discussion here.[7] I will return to 1:1 below, but for now we can turn attention to heaven and earth.

In Genesis 1:1, "heaven and earth" encompasses everything; it designates the whole cosmos, as, for example, in Genesis 14:19, 22; Deuteronomy 4:26; and Isaiah 37:16.[8] Literary scholars call this a *merism*: the two nouns and the conjunction between them designate a totality. In this case, it is a cosmic totality. In other words, this first verse announces that God created the entire cosmos. Later in Genesis 1:7–10, the Hebrew words translated "heaven" (*shamayim*) and "earth" (*ʾerets*) in verse 1 have a narrower reference. In these latter verses, the heavens and the dry land (*yabbashah*) are created, or made to appear, individually on different days, and they are named "sky" (*shamayim*), on the one hand, and "earth" (*ʾerets*), on the other (vv. 8, 10). These are the sky we see above us and the dry land on which we live. This sky and this earth, rather than designating the totality of God's creative work (the whole cosmos), form the visible, material arena—the sky above us and the dry land beneath our feet—in or over or under which lives every created thing produced, day by day, in 1:3–31.

Genesis 2:1 then provides a summary of that production: "So were completed heaven and earth and all their host." "Their host" here refers to all and everything that God had brought about and brought into being in Genesis 1. In this way the summary statement in 2:1 returns us to the beginning, to 1:1, which it interprets as a rubric or an introduction that sets the stage:

> In the beginning that [in which] God created heaven and earth . . . (1:1)
>
> Then were completed heaven and earth and all their host. (2:1)

What the first verse of Genesis sets the stage *for*, of course, is God's six-day work of creation, a work whose completion Genesis 2:1 announces. God's crea-

6. Cf. Oswald, "Das Erstlingswerk Gottes."

7. The linguistic issues are discussed in Holmstedt, "Restrictive Syntax of Genesis 1:1." Holmstedt informs my interpretation of Gen. 1:1 below.

8. Bauks, *Die Welt am Anfang*, 108.

tive work begins in 1:3, when God speaks light into existence: "Let there be light, and there was light." But intervening between the stage-setting announcement of verse 1 and God's first creative, ordering word in verse 3, verse 2 offers this description:

> The earth was wildness and waste,[9]
> and darkness was over the face of the deep,
> while the wind [spirit/power] of God was sweeping over the waters.[10]

The earth was wildness and waste; it was *tohu wabohu*, or "without form, and void" in the KJV's still familiar terms. In Deuteronomy 32:10 *tohu* describes a desert, a place without life and hostile to life—a *no* place (Job 12:24; 26:7). This condition of the earth was not the product of God's creative work. God did not create the earth *tohu*, Isaiah 45:18 declares. Rather, Genesis 1:2 continues setting the stage for creation by describing what the earth then *was*: not a cosmos but a "precosmic condition" before God's creative speech.[11] Genesis 1:2 continues with reference to an encompassing darkness over *the deep* and the wind (spirit/power) of God sweeping over *the waters*. The terms in italics name entities that we will encounter again, later in this book, as powers. Here in Genesis 1:2, they exert no independent power but stand in the way of creation, including the creation of earth as an inhabitable space and place, a place of and for life. They stand in the way, not as powerful enemies—Genesis 1:2 doesn't describe a chaos that actively opposes God and creation—but as elements to be ordered and incorporated within the cosmos of God's creation and constituent within the good and beautiful order that is, not a hostile *tohu* but peace.

Genesis 1 does not concern itself with questions about the origin of matter, of subatomic particles, of the elements. Genesis 1 has nothing interesting to say about creation if we understand creation as having only or primarily to do with such questions. Genesis 1 assumes the presence of darkness and the deep and the waters, and of the precosmic earth as wildness and waste, and it presents these as the stage for God's creative work. To be sure, the darkness, the deep, the waters, and the earth as *tohu wabohu* do amount to a no-thing, with neither space nor place. It would not be mistaken to say that God, beginning in 1:3, created out of nothing—created *ex nihilo*, in the language of the Christian tradition. But this nothing, this absence, is not the absence of matter or of

9. Modifying the translation of E. Fox, *Five Books of Moses*, 13.
10. On the "wind of God" (*ruach 'elohim*), see Mark Smith, *Priestly Vision of Genesis 1*, 52–57. And see further below.
11. The term is Walton's in *Genesis 1 as Ancient Cosmology*, 139.

power; it is the absence of form, function, and space. Sweeping over this nothing, in 1:2, is the wind, the spirit, the power of the God named in verse 1. In the next verse, this wind, this power, takes verbal form and issues in the poetry of creation.

The Poetry of Creation

Above, I described Genesis 1 as testimony to God the Creator. This testimony takes poetic form. The poetic character of Genesis 1 may not be obvious at first glance. English versions do not lay out the text in verse as they do the Psalms, most of Job, Proverbs, and large portions of the prophetic books. Indeed, the chapter lacks several of the features by which we tend to identify poetry, by way of meter and parallel lines (couplets), for example. And Genesis 1 certainly does not rhyme! Rather, it achieves its poetic effect by the use of cadence or rhythm, repetition, and overall structure. One element of that structure is obvious and well-known: creation proceeds by way of temporal progression through a sequence of six days. Day seven (2:1–3) brings the movement, God's movement, to rest—God's rest. The sequence begins, of course, with day one in 1:3–4.

Two other, related patterns intersect this six-day temporal progression. We can think of the first as liturgical and the second as spatial. Together, the temporal progression and the liturgical and spatial patterns intersecting it—these components of the literary artistry of Genesis 1—reflect the art and craft of God's work as Creator.

A Liturgical Pattern

Consider first the liturgical pattern. Liturgical worship typically includes a litany with refrains: for example, "Lord, have mercy; Christ, have mercy" among Christians, or *avinu malkenu* (our Father, our King) among Jews. The constant refrain in Psalm 136, "for his steadfast love endures forever" (NRSV), provides an example from the Old Testament itself. Refrains also serve to structure Genesis 1, beginning with the first day. "God said . . . and so it was" (v. 3). "God saw that the light was good. . . . And there was evening and there was morning, the first day" (vv. 4–5 NRSV). Concluding each of the six days in Genesis 1 is the refrain "there was evening and there was morning, the . . . day." And six times we encounter the statement "God saw that . . . was good." These two refrains appear together, the first of them in expanded form, in the summary and climactic verse 31: "God saw all that he had made [all that he had done], and assuredly, it was very good." The refrains form a liturgical pattern that is part of Genesis 1's structure and contribute to the chapter's poetic character. For example:

Day 1: Light (1:3–5)
  God *said*, "Let there be . . ."
  God *saw* that it was good.
  God *named* the day and night.
Day 3: Dry land and vegetation (1:9–13)
  God *said*, "Let the waters . . ."
  God *saw* that it was good.
  God *called* the dry land earth.

Each of the six days follows a pattern close to this one.

God's speaking dominates this liturgical pattern and also opens it. God speaks and light appears (Gen. 1:3). The repeated "God said . . . and so it was" (e.g., 1:9, 11) displays the intimate connection between God's spoken word and creation. Creation by fiat this has been called, following the Latin Vulgate's rendering of Genesis 1:3, *fiat lux*: "Let there be light." We can observe this intimate connection between God's word and creation in the Psalms as well. Psalm 33:6a declares that the heavens were made by the word of Yhwh. The verse continues: "And all their host by the breath of his mouth [were made]" (v. 6b NRSV). The Hebrew word the NRSV here translates as "breath"—*ruach*—is the same as in Genesis 1:2, which speaks of the *ruach 'elohim*, which I rendered above as "the wind [spirit/power] of God." The word is often translated, correctly, as "spirit," while sometimes it means simply "wind" (e.g., Exod. 10:19). But especially when it is God's attribute or gift, *ruach* can have the sense of power (1 Kings 18:12), God's empowering presence (Isa. 63:11–12), God's creative intention and design (Isa. 40:13), and even the gift of human creative power or skill (Exod. 31:3). In Genesis 1:2, the wind (spirit/power), the *ruach* of God, was sweeping over the waters, while the earth was not yet an ordered creation, as a preface to God's speaking light into existence. In Psalm 33 we may see an intimate connection not only between God's spoken word and creation but between the wind (spirit/power) of God of Genesis 1:2 and the spoken, creative word of God in 1:3 and in all of Genesis 1.[12]

While God's speaking may dominate the liturgical pattern of Genesis 1, God does not only speak. God also makes (*'asah*) and creates (*bara'*) what God's speaking calls into being. After saying "Let there be a vault," God *makes* the

12. Mark Smith, *Priestly Vision of Genesis 1*, 54–55.

vault or dome (vv. 6–7). After saying "Let there be lights," God makes those lights, the luminaries: sun, moon, and stars (vv. 14–16). In other words, God's speaking is joined, or conjoined, with God's fashioning the components of a world, making them into an ordered, lively world. Sometimes God's *creating* seems to be much the same as *making*. So in verses 20 and 21, God speaks as before—"Let the waters swarm with living swarmers, and let birds fly"—but then God creates (*bara'*) the sea creatures and birds, just as God had made (*'asah*) the lights. These verses also introduce another of God's actions: blessing. In verse 22, God *blesses* the sea creatures and issues an injunction: "Be fruitful and become numerous, and fill the waters in the seas." And in verses 26–28, God's determination to *make* humankind precedes the notice that God *created* them. Then follows the same blessing given the sea creatures and a similar injunction: "Be fruitful and become numerous, and fill the earth" (v. 28). God's blessing is more than merely an endorsement or a "good luck" wish; it is empowerment. God's blessing—because it is *God's*—empowers the sea creatures and humans to fulfill the injunction to be fruitful.[13]

God's active involvement in creation, even following God's speaking, has its complement in the responsiveness of created reality itself. While God alone creates, the objects of God's creation themselves become subjects. They actively participate in the emergence of an ordered world. For example, rather than simply speaking animals into existence, God assigns this function to the earth: "Let the earth bring forth . . ." (Gen. 1:24). And to the waters God speaks similarly: "Let the waters swarm with swarms of living creatures" (v. 21). Both the earth and the waters are productive but only in response to God, who alone creates. What God instructs the waters and the earth to bring forth, God creates (*bara'*, v. 21) and makes (*'asah*, v. 25). The waters and the earth are not cocreators with God. In all of Genesis 1, God alone is the purpose-forming agent in creation. For their part, the earth and the waters respond productively to God's creative initiative. Created reality is alive to God's purposes, and it responds immediately, vitally, to them. Michael Welker is surely right in calling into question conceptions of creation in Genesis 1 as "pure production and causation." As he puts it, "Genesis 1 and 2 describe the entire creation as in many respects having its own activity, as being itself productive, as being itself causative."[14] But creation is all of these things in response to God's creative initiative.

Along with speaking, creating, making, and blessing, in Genesis 1 God also draws distinctions—or imposes them; God divides and separates. God is the

13. See, in brief, Martens, "Intertext Messaging."
14. Welker, *Creation and Reality*, 10.

subject of the several active, transitive verbs in Genesis 1—that is, God says *something*, creates and makes and blesses *something*, and now also divides or separates *things*. But we should not assume that these verbs designate different discrete acts on God's part. Above, I observed that creating (*bara'*) and making (*'asah*) seem to be more or less equivalent. In its biblical instances, *bara'* has only God as its subject, but creating may encompass making and almost always does. Creating also encompasses—it may even consist in—separating or imposing distinctions (the Hebrew term is *hibdil*).[15]

This should come as no surprise, since Genesis 1:2 portrays a condition, a state, void of crucial distinctions and, thus, *void*. Into this mess of *in*distinction and darkness, into this uninhabitable void, this *tohu wabohu*, God first speaks light into existence. But the creation of light remains incomplete until God *separates* light from darkness (vv. 3–4). Similarly, in verse 6, God speaks the vault or the dome (the KJV's term is "firmament") into existence, at the same time speaking its purpose into existence: the purpose of *separating* among the waters. The following verse (v. 7) then reports that God *made* the vault, which *separates*—or, on some interpretations, divides—the waters above the vault (the sky) from the waters beneath it. Finally, in verses 14–18, the light God spoke into existence in verses 3–4, and its designated function of *separating* light from darkness, is assigned to the lights in that sky—the sun and moon, with an added mention of the stars.

All these distinctions and separations involve darkness and water, including the deep—elements named in Genesis 1:2. These provide, we may say, the raw elements of the lively world God brings into being by intervening verbally in the unordered condition described in verse 2, an intervention that involves speaking and making, separating and creating, and blessing. All the acts Genesis 1 ascribes to God are integrated within its temporal sequence and within the poetic, liturgical, and spatial patterns of the chapter.

A Spatial Pattern

Within the liturgical pattern of Genesis 1 is a second, spatial pattern, which also contributes to the artistry of the chapter. This spatial pattern organizes the day-by-day temporal sequence of creation into three pairs or panels.[16] Figure 2 illustrates this spatial pattern.

15. Wolde, *Reframing Biblical Studies*, 184–200; see also Walton, *Genesis 1 as Ancient Cosmology*, 127–39.

16. B. Anderson, "Stylistic Study of the Priestly Creation Story," 157; McBride, "Divine Protocol," 12–13.

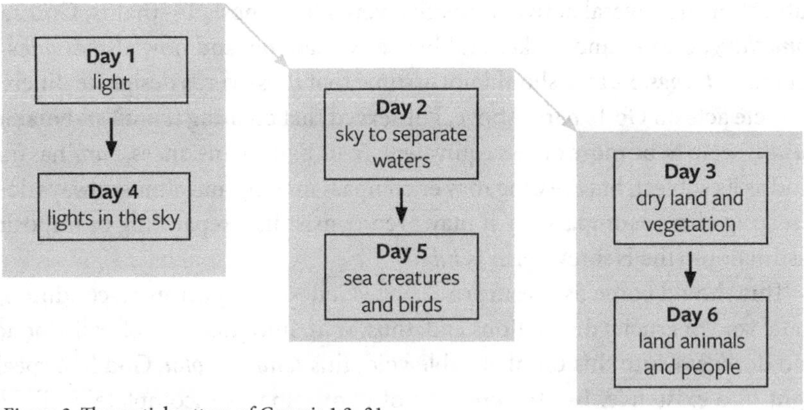

Figure 2. The spatial pattern of Genesis 1:3–31

The correspondence of days within each of these panels, and the relation of each panel to the next, displays an artistic arrangement and a functional order, but not always what we would recognize as a natural one. In the first panel, God creates light before fashioning lights, including a sun! While God sets the lights in the sky on day four in the first panel, forming the sky itself is God's initial act in the second panel, on day two. And the lights serve to illumine the earth, which does not appear until the third panel. These anomalies with what we know of the natural world make functional and poetic sense, and they make sense theologically. The sun and other luminaries are related to light, of course, but not as its ultimate source; this, for the Priestly narrator, can only be God. The luminaries, rather, sustain and govern the *separation* of light from darkness (Gen. 1:18) that was part of God's initial speech act. They also serve to distinguish the festal seasons while exercising a delegated dominion (*memshelet*) over day and night (vv. 14, 16). Similarly, the sky functions to provide a place for the luminaries but also to sustain the *separation* of waters that God brought about on the second day—and thereby to provide a habitat for the sea creatures and birds. Moreover, precisely this *separation* of the waters has a functional relation to the third panel, since it provides for the appearance of dry land. Dry land, in its turn, provides the grounds, literally and functionally, for vegetation. And this vegetation functions to sustain the creatures that God creates on the sixth day.

I have described this three-paneled pattern of Genesis 1 as spatial. We may even say that, from this perspective, Genesis 1 narrates the creation of space. Space requires separation, distinction, differentiation; these God brings about, day by day. At the beginning, before God's first word, the earth was void of distinctions, of space, and of place. Without space, there is no light. God's first action, then, after speaking light into existence, is to *separate* the light from the darkness (v. 4), creating a space for light. Creation then proceeds through a series of separations or distinctions (vv. 4, 6, 7, 14, 18), creating space and place for life. Indeed, creation in Genesis 1 amounts largely to separation, distinction, and differentiation.[17] The creation of space, and of place, contrasts dramatically with the state of things prior to creation, at the (precosmic) beginning, when *nothing* was distinct. In Genesis 1, God creates space and place for created life—earthly space and place for earthly creatures that are distinct from God, and an earth that is not heaven.

The three-paneled spatial pattern of Genesis 1, with its dynamic movement, narrates an increasing distinction of heavenly realms from earthly ones. The initial "days" across the three panels move from light to sky and then to earth. Likewise, the subsequent days across the three panels move from luminaries to sea and sky creatures and, finally, to creatures who inhabit the earth. A vital distinction involves the separation of the waters so that the earth, the dry land, may appear. But separation and distinction do not imply annihilation. In creating, according to Genesis 1, God does not destroy darkness, the waters, or *the deep*—the abysmal sea. Rather, darkness and the waters become ingredients of the earth's dynamic vitality.[18] God incorporates them within the ordered world of heaven and earth, of God's creation.

Finally, two features of this spatial pattern bear mentioning or repeating. First, God not only makes and creates space for life but also populates this space—fills the sky, the water, and the dry land with birds and sea creatures, plants of every kind, and animals, including dragons (*tanninim*, Gen. 1:21). Second, the movement from one panel to the next, from heavenly to earthly realms, reflects and narrates a critical, definitive distinction between Creator and creature. God, in Genesis 1, precedes and governs the entire sequential, liturgically cadenced spatial arrangement of this chapter's cosmology, eliciting the responsive vitality of the earth and the waters, fashioning the sky and the dry land—creating heaven and earth. God remains sovereign over creation and distinct from it, even while intimately related to it. In two instances, God delegates dominion to creatures. On day four (panel 1; vv. 16, 18), God delegates to the sun and moon dominion over day and night. And on day six, God assigns a ruling function to the last of the creatures God makes and creates: humans.

17. Beauchamp, *Création et Séparation*.
18. DeRoche, "Isaiah XLV 7 and the Creation of Chaos?"

Male and Female

Prior to God's final creative act on the sixth day, God deliberates, takes internal counsel, in the first-person plural: "Let *us* make . . ." This deliberate pause in the midst of the sixth day—a day on which God has already made wild animals, cattle, dragons, and all kinds of ground-dwelling creatures, and has blessed them (Gen. 1:22)—marks the following act as unique. It was the earth that God called to bring forth the animals, which God then made (vv. 24–25). But now, in verse 26, it is with God's own self that God takes counsel for the making and creating of *'adam*—humans. The pause, the deliberation, the taking counsel foreshadow the uniqueness of what God then creates. In the case of *'adam*, God does not utter a "Let there be . . ." or "Let the waters/earth bring forth . . ." Rather, God deliberates, and then God makes and creates a creature as God's own image and likeness—a creaturely icon of God, a creature with a special status among God's creatures.

The terms *image* and *likeness* suggest a physical representation (Gen. 5:3; 2 Kings 16:10; Ezek. 16:17; 23:14). But while Genesis 1:26–28 does have to do with representation—humankind (*'adam*) as God's creaturely representative—physical resemblance is not the point here. Rather, humanity's creation in (or as) the image of God, and on the model of God's likeness, has as its purpose the designated responsibility of humans. Humans are to rule—to exercise, on God's behalf, an administrative authority over the earth and other creatures: "Let us make humankind in [as] our image, according to our likeness, *so that* they may rule [*radah*] over the fish . . . , birds . . . , cattle . . . , over the whole earth, and over all creeping things that creep on the earth" (v. 26).[19]

The language here is royal, as with the dominion-granted luminaries in Genesis 1:16, 18. The verb translated "rule" (*radah*) always means just that: to rule, as in Psalm 72:8, where the king shall rule from sea to sea. In Genesis 1:26, the image and likeness of God distinguishes and establishes humankind as God's icon, God's royal representative in the world of God's creation. God's subsequent command—"Be fruitful, become abundant, and fill the earth"—follows God's blessing and thus God's empowerment to carry out the command (v. 28). In verses 21–22 God had also commanded and blessed the creatures of the sea and air. But to humankind God gives a further assignment. They are to "subdue the earth" (v. 28 NRSV)—that is, to take possession of the earth or to domesticate it. The following verses (vv. 29–30) stipulate that God has given the earth's vegetation to humanity, and also to the animals, for food. In other words, subduing the

19. See McBride, "Divine Protocol," 15–16. On the translation, here and in what follows, see also my essay "Creation and Peace."

earth, possessing it, domesticating it serves to benefit humans, who are to fill the same earth, and also to benefit the nonhuman creatures over which humankind exercises dominion or administrative authority (cf. 1 Kings 5:30[5:16]). The command to "subdue the earth" should be understood as instruction to engage in agriculture, for which God has prepared the earth, and agriculture requires some governance of creatures.[20] At the same time, God has also provided the earth's vegetation to all the living creatures, including domestic animals and those that fly or creep (Gen. 1:30). Among these, humanity, created in the image of God and according to God's likeness, serves as God's royal representative.

The creation of humans as God's image, on the model of God's likeness, echoes a theme common in the ancient world. But in most other ancient texts, the king himself, and only the king, is the divine image and likeness. This authorizes the king's sovereignty over peoples and lands as the deity's earthly representative.[21] Genesis 1 subverts and redefines this ancient royal theology, democratizing it by assigning God's image to collective humanity. Further, while kings who are said to be the image of a deity rule lands and people, no political domain and no people(s) fall within the scope of humankind's representatively royal dominion. Neither will any conquest be required. The dominion God has delegated to humankind as God's representatives, and the possession or domestication of the earth ("subduing") that God assigns them, follow what God has already accomplished in creation. They are by no means a charge, or a license, to conquer and exploit. Humans, in Genesis 1, are to maintain "order and peace on God's behalf," as Annette Schellenberg has put it.[22]

I stressed earlier the significant role of distinction, separation, or differentiation in the creation account of Genesis 1. In creating *'adam*, God makes a further distinction, one between male and female. The term *'adam* in some contexts designates an individual male (e.g., Exod. 13:13), and it will later serve as the name of one man: Adam. But in Genesis 1:26–28, among other places, *'adam* refers to humankind:

> God created humankind [*'adam*] in his image,
> in the image of God he created them;
> male and female he created them. (v. 27 NRSV)

In the first two lines of Genesis 1:27, *'adam* is a collective noun, following the plural noun and verb—that *they* may rule—in verse 26 and preceding the

20. Middleton, *Liberating Image*, 59–60.
21. In general, see Brett, *Genesis*, 27–28; Walton, *Genesis 1 as Ancient Cosmology*, 74–86.
22. Schellenberg, "Humankind as the 'Image of God,'" 102.

plural verbs and pronouns in verse 28. In the third line of verse 27, the plural pronoun "them" has *ʾadam* as its antecedent. In other words, *ʾadam* encompasses both male and female. The distinction of the sexes facilitates—it makes possible—fulfillment of the command to be fruitful, of course.[23] But the preceding verses mention no male/female distinction when nonhuman creatures are commanded to be fruitful and are blessed, thus empowered, to be fruitful. So why is the distinction necessary for humans? Here in verse 27, the text states that the unique function and status of *ʾadam*—humankind as God's image and royal representative—includes both male and female. While we should not attribute to the narrator egalitarian views that may mirror our own, neither should we overlook the liturgical, poetic, and visionary character of Genesis 1. Liturgy, like poetry, not only offers descriptions of the world, its past, or its origin but also envisions a world, commends it to us, reminds us of it as lost (sometimes well lost), and encourages us to hope for it and sometimes to work toward it. Genesis 1 projects a vision of the world that corresponds to the world of Israel's (and our) experience only at a tangent. For example, it envisions humans and animals alike, but also birds and creeping things, as vegetarian (v. 30). Genesis 9:2–3 refers to that vision, after the flood, by way of granting humankind a new license: to use animals for food. After the flood, the world of Genesis resembles more nearly the one we inhabit. But even after the flood, the vision of *ʾadam* as the image of God, male and female, is never abrogated.

Cosmos as Temple

The entire cosmology of Genesis 1—its "creation account"—projects a vision of the world corresponding to God's creative, and verbally expressed, intention. Each feature of creation, from light through humankind, came to be as it should be, as God intended. God's spoken intention corresponded to an extension in the world that came to be day by day. This correspondence receives affirmation in God's repeated observation of what God has made and God's evaluation that "it was good." The Hebrew word *tob*, usually translated "good," conveys a range of meanings that include "fitting" and "in order," even "beautiful." The first chapter of Genesis reflects such order and beauty, both in its composition and in God's creation of heaven and earth, which it narrates. It reflects a world, a cosmos, at peace. God proclaims it, on a final observation, "very good" (v. 31). That observation and evaluation conclude the Bible's first chapter, but its narrative of creation continues into chapter 2. The notices in 2:1–3 that God completed

23. Bird, "'Male and Female He Created Them.'"

the creation of heaven and earth "and all their host" on the seventh day and that God then "ceased" (*shabat*) from the work of creation are not incidental. They include, of course, God's consecration of the seventh day, which foreshadows the Sabbath, the hallowed day of rest. This does not exhaust the significance of Genesis 2:1–3.

People sometimes speak of a poet building a poem. Aristotle, for example, compared building or making a poem with building or making a boat.[24] The poem that the author of Genesis 1 built both narrates and mirrors God's building the cosmos. In fact, 1:1–2:3 portrays God building the cosmos as if building a house. In the first three days—as illustrated in figure 2—God prepares the cosmic house and provides for its sustenance, while in days four through six, God populates this house and provides for its maintenance.[25] Finally, as noted above, 2:1 reports that the cosmos (the world-building project announced in 1:1) was completed, including its "host"—that is, the abundance of created things populating this house, this world.

Scholars have noted that Genesis 1:1–2:3 resembles other ancient texts that describe a king constructing a building. For example, the Assyrian king Esarhaddon reports *building* a palace, *completing* it, and *filling* it "with abundance."[26] Kings also gave themselves credit, citing divine authorization, for building or restoring a temple—the *house* of a deity. Often in the Bible, the temple, or the sanctuary, is called God's house (e.g., Exod. 23:19; 1 Kings 8:10). Genesis 1, with its conclusion in 2:1–3, calls to mind the building of a temple, a cosmic temple. In poetic cadences, it narrates God's building a cosmic house "by a process of royal commands and separations" and then both filling this cosmic house and instructing creatures, including humans, further to fill it (1:22, 28).[27] But there is a difference to be noted between Genesis and other ancient accounts of house/temple building. Kings and deities in the ancient world furnished houses and temples with provisions for their own use and benefit. But in Genesis, these provisions are not for God's use or benefit, and neither do they provide for God's dwelling within this cosmic house. Rather, God the Creator provides the earth's produce for the use and benefit of the creatures, human and nonhuman alike, that God created on the fifth and sixth days (vv. 29–30).

God's work of cosmos/temple building ceases on the seventh day. But God does not yet take up residence *within* this cosmic temple in which God has assigned humankind a representative dominion and responsibility. In the

24. Aristotle, *Poetics* 1, p. 67.
25. Van Leeuwen, "Cosmos, Temple, House."
26. Hurowitz, *I Have Built You an Exalted House*, 240.
27. Van Leeuwen, "Cosmos, Temple, House," 408.

Priestly vision animating Genesis 1:1–2:3, the distinction between Creator and creature, God's differentiation from creation, remains crucial. Provision for God's presence within the cosmic temple of God's creation requires further differentiation—of a people, Israel, from among the nations; of a consecrated priesthood from among the Israelites; of sacred rites and seasons from ordinary time; and of a sacred space, a sanctuary, from "profane" space. The book of Exodus narrates these further differentiations, a narration whose language sometimes echoes that of creation. For example, in Exodus 31, which concerns the building of the tent or tabernacle and the making of the ark of the covenant, among other things, God announces to Moses, "I have called by name Bezalel . . . and have filled him with the spirit of God" (vv. 2–3). This is the same spirit of God—the *ruach 'elohim*, the wind/power of God—named in Genesis 1:2 (see above). Here in Exodus, God's spirit empowers a certain Bezalel with the wisdom, understanding, and knowledge necessary for building not the cosmos but the sanctuary and its furnishings, not the macrocosm but the microcosm: the "world" of God's presence.[28] "Make me a sanctuary, so that I may dwell among you" (25:8).

Further, in the same chapter (Exod. 31) God concludes the instructions that began in chapter 25, with Moses on Sinai, by commanding Sabbath observance and linking it expressly to creation: "It is a sign between me and the people of Israel forever: [over] six days Yhwh made heaven and earth, but on the seventh day he ceased and was refreshed" (v. 17; see also 20:11). Yhwh's refreshment on the seventh day in turn echoes the humane purpose of the Sabbath: "Six days you shall perform your work, but on the seventh day you shall cease [*shabat*], so that your ox and your donkey may rest [*yanuach*] and your maid and the resident alien may be refreshed" (23:12).

The Sabbath, which is holy to the people (Exod. 31:14), and which is for the benefit of both the people and those who serve them—including animals—is also holy to God (20:10; Deut. 5:14), for whose presence all the instructions and building in Exodus 25–31 and 35–40 prepare. It is finally God's "glory"—God's presence—that *fills* the tabernacle, the "work completed . . . according to all that Yhwh commanded Moses" (39:32; 40:33–34). God's work of cosmic "house" building, furnishing, and filling was completed in Genesis 2:1–3, but God's completing this work of creation, and so ceasing from it, was not yet God's dwelling within it. This required the further building and filling and completing—of the sanctuary and its furnishings—carried out by Moses and Israel in response to instructions that seem an echo of those God issued in Genesis 1.

28. Levenson, *Creation and the Persistence of Evil*, 78–99.

Conclusion as Prologue

In Genesis 2:1 the narrator concludes the Bible's first account of creation by referring back to 1:1, marking all the intervening actions and events, and creation itself—heaven and earth and their host—as completed. Genesis 2:2–3 then gestures toward the institution of the Sabbath in the book of Exodus. As in 1:21 (marine life and birds) and 1:28 (humankind), so in 2:3 God pronounces a blessing. This time God blesses the seventh day and also consecrates it, because God ceased on the seventh day. While the day is blessed and consecrated—declared holy, set apart—nothing is yet said about this being a day of rest or about a Sabbath. Here in Genesis, God hallows the seventh day because God's work of creation is completed. Nothing more remains to be done. All is in order, the order God intended, and thus at peace. The poem is completed. God's world, God's cosmic "house," corresponds to God's repeatedly expressed intention: "God said . . . and so it was." God's work of creating and making and differentiating is accomplished with the world of heaven and earth in cosmic, lively, dynamic order. All is (at) peace but not (at) rest, in this new, vital world of God's creation.

Like a king building a temple, in the poem of Genesis 1 God builds a world and creates humankind—a creature among creatures but with royal responsibilities as God's representative. Is it then significant that the creation of humans and their commissioning in 1:26–28 are *not* followed by the otherwise routine divine observation and assessment "and God saw that it was good"? The concluding, comprehensive observation and superlative assessment—"God saw all that he had made, and assuredly, it was very good" (1:31)—surely includes the creation and commissioning of humankind (*'adam*) as God's royal representative. Surely?

Within the compass of Genesis 1, *'adam*—the male and female icon and representative of God—is addressed and blessed and commissioned but does not yet act . . . is not yet a subject, not yet an agent. The chapters of Genesis that follow invest this creature, humankind, with agency and subjectivity, with the capacity to decide and to conceive of and pursue its own projects. In consequence, *'adam* becomes an actor in a drama that imperils creation and its peace. It is a long and fractured story, and also, eventually, one of redemption, to which Genesis 1 is a good—a very good—prologue.

2

From Virtually Nothing to the Garden of God

GENESIS 2

"All poetry is creation, and it is creation *ex nihilo* (out of nothing)."[1] What Valentin Husson says here of poetry also describes traditional Christian beliefs about God's creation of the world. In the previous chapter I pointed to the poetic character of the creation story in the first chapter of Genesis, a chapter that not only narrates God's creating but also serves as an example of poetic artistry. In this regard, following Husson, Genesis 1 counts as a "creation *ex nihilo*." But does its poetry describe God's creating the world out of nothing—*ex nihilo*? I will return briefly to this theological question in chapter 10. But with respect to the Old Testament and Genesis, our concern here, the prevailing opinion seems to be no—that is, biblical scholars today tend to deny that the Old Testament expresses or assumes the idea of creation out of nothing: *creatio ex nihilo*.[2] After all, even Genesis 1 says nothing explicit about the existence, or not, of *something* before creation—what some biblical scholars and theologians call "pre-existent

1. Husson, "Building and Dwelling in *Inception*," 272.

2. Westermann, *Genesis 1–11*, 174; Levenson, *Creation and the Persistence of Evil*, 121–22; Löning and Zenger, *To Begin With, God Created*, 10; B. Anderson, *Contours of Old Testament Theology*, 87. For a contrasting view, see G. Anderson, "Creation."

matter."[3] The Bible evinces no interest in or understanding of such a notion, much less in countering it. But our commonsense conceptions of matter, and of nothing, may be naive. Things may be more complicated than we have imagined. When physicists talk about virtual particles, are they talking about *matter*?[4] Does what we may have thought of as *nothing* make up most of the universe?[5]

Already in antiquity people found these concepts perplexing. The fourth- and fifth-century North African bishop and theologian Augustine of Hippo wrote in his *Confessions* of his struggle to attain a correct understanding of matter. His insistence on creation from nothing (*de nihilo*, in his terms) was explicit and consistent. Yet Augustine inherited and transmitted a tradition that spoke of "formless matter" (*materia informi*), as in the book of Wisdom, which describes God's all-powerful hand creating the world "out of formless matter" (Wis. 11:17). The term goes back as far as Plato, though Augustine supplies his own Christian understanding of it, consistent with creation from nothing. The ancient notions of unformed matter may be nearly as perplexing as contemporary physicists' references to matter and nothing and mass. Augustine employed the notion of unformed matter in order to interpret the early verses of Genesis 1. Verse 2 of that chapter refers to "the deep," which the Greek and Latin translations render as "the abyss," another term with resonance in classical literature. Augustine describes "the abyss," the deep of Genesis 1:2, as "almost nothing" (*prope nihil erat*).[6] Today, we might say "virtually nothing" or "for all practical purposes, nothing." Those terms fit well the state of affairs that verse 2 describes.

"Virtually nothing" also fits the description of the state of things at the beginning of the Bible's second creation story in Genesis 2. The chapter concludes with Eden, God's verdant and fruitful garden, at peace, populated with a pair of humans, an abundance of other creatures, and two exceptional trees.

God Forms a Farmer and Plants a Garden

The Bible's second chapter announces that, like Genesis 1, it will recount the creation of heaven and earth. As I suggested in the previous chapter, the first part of Genesis 2:4 serves as both a conclusion to what precedes and an introduction to what follows: "These are the generations of [or: this is the account of] heaven and earth when they were created" (v. 4a). The second part of the

3. E.g., Watson, *Chaos Uncreated*, 18; McGrath, *Christian Theology*, 198.
4. Folger, "Virtual Particles."
5. Folger, "Nothingness of Space."
6. Augustine, *Confessions*, 12.7 and 12.8. The Latin text is from http://www9.georgetown.edu/faculty/jod/latinconf/latinconf.html.

verse, however, inverts the order: "On the day Yhwh Elohim made the earth and the heavens" (v. 4b). This inversion signals that the earth will be the focus of attention, and it is to the earth that the story immediately turns. Like 1:2, 2:5 describes an uninhabitable earth—describes it in terms of lack or absence: "On the day God made the earth and the heavens, when there was no . . ." or "before there was . . ." (vv. 4b–5a).[7]

Also, as in Genesis 1, the description of virtually nothing sets the stage for God's action that follows. The subject or agent of that action has a different or extended name in the second story. While Elohim—"God"—acts in 1:1–2:3, the actor in the remainder of chapter 2 and in chapter 3 is Yhwh Elohim—"the Lord God," as English translations render the names. The book of Exodus introduces the name Yhwh in two places: 3:13–15 and 6:2–6. These texts identify Yhwh as the God who is Israel's Savior and Lord of its history. In using the combined name Yhwh Elohim, Genesis 2–3 joins the story of creation with Israel's story while at the same time identifying God the Creator of Genesis 1 with the Yhwh on whose name people began to call at the birth of Enosh (4:26)[8] and who brought Israel out of Egypt generations later. It will be Yhwh Elohim, then, who acts in this story that begins when the earth is, for all practical purposes, nothing.

Here is the opening scene, Genesis 2:4–7, set out according to its syntax in Hebrew:

> This is the account of heaven and earth when they were created.
> In the day when Yhwh Elohim made the earth and the heavens,
>   (and) all pasture grasses—before they were in the earth,
>   (and) all field crops—before they grew
>   because Yhwh Elohim had not made it rain on the earth,
>   and there was no *'adam* to serve the *'adamah*—
>   but moisture went up from the earth
>   and watered the surface of the *'adamah*—
> then Yhwh Elohim formed the *'adam* from dust of the *'adamah*.

The story these verses tell compresses the seven days of Genesis 1:2–2:3 into one: *the day* when God made the earth and the heavens. On this day of God's creating, the earth remained virtually nothing. It was marked by lack and absence. First, despite the presence of a water source to irrigate the fertile soil, the earth lacked vegetation, whether pasture grasses or field crops—cereals (2:5–6).

7. Ellen van Wolde notices the "lack" or "deficiency" that Gen. 2:4–5 describes in *Words Become Worlds*, 13.

8. The word *'enosh* can mean "a man" or "humankind."

Second, there was no one to till the soil, no one to be a farmer. The absence is emphatic: "A man, there was none, to till the soil."[9] God's remedy for this lack was to form an *'adam* from the *'adamah*—a human from the humus, a man from the dust of the soil[10]—to till the soil. In Genesis 1, God created *'adam*—humankind—male and female (vv. 26–27). In 4:25, *'adam* will become "Adam"; the first man will acquire a name. But in Genesis 2 and 3, *'adam* refers to an individual man, yet unnamed, a tiller of the soil, a farmer.[11]

Yhwh Elohim created the man to be a farmer, and in the narrative flow of Genesis 2:5–7, this seems to be the decisive moment in the movement from virtually nothing to an ordered, fruitful world. The list of what was absent from the earth on the day Yhwh Elohim made it—pasture grasses, field grains, rain—finally includes the absence of a farmer, a man to till the soil. And for that absence God provides the remedy, forming the *'adam* from the *'adamah* to till it. We might expect, then, that the narrative would go on to tell us that this newly formed farmer tilled the soil and tended field crops producing cereal grains, and that the abundant world of plants and animals followed. Instead, and abruptly, the text announces a new divine initiative: Yhwh Elohim planted a garden. Attending this unexpected planting of a garden is the displacement of the man from the soil to the new garden: "Yhwh Elohim planted a garden . . . and there he put [*sim*] the man whom he had formed" (v. 8). That this was a displacement of the man, not only from his "place" but also from his agricultural vocation, Genesis 3:23 makes explicit: "Yhwh Elohim expelled the man from the garden to till the soil from which he had been taken [*laqach*]." The man will be responsible "to watch and to keep"[12] the garden where God now placed (*nuach*) him (2:15),[13] but tilling the soil remains his original—and will be his future—vocation.

The Eden Narrative, Part 1: Genesis 2:5–25

The narrative framework that Genesis 2:5–7 and 3:23 provide—God first forms a man for a vocation as a farmer and then returns him to it—sets the Eden

9. Joüon, #160i; GKC, #152k.

10. On the grammar, see Joüon, #125v2. The meaning of *'aphar*—dust—is illustrated by Num. 5:17, which refers to the dust on the floor of the tent. Ziony Zevit argues for the translation "a clod of soil." *What Really Happened in the Garden of Eden?*, 80.

11. For *'adam* as "a man" in this context, see Chapman, "Breath of Life," 243. Phyllis Trible argues that, in Genesis 2:7, *ha'adam* is sexually undifferentiated. *God and the Rhetoric of Sexuality*, 80–81.

12. E. Fox, *Five Books of Moses*, 20.

13. Schellenberg, *Der Mensch, das Bild Gottes?*, 206.

narrative apart. Ellen van Wolde describes the man's garden tenure as "this intermediate period."[14] The man whom God formed continues his life beyond Eden, but the continuity will be agricultural, not horticultural. The entire Eden narrative, in 2:5–3:24, constitutes a kind of set piece. It is integrated within the larger story of Genesis 1–11 but as a discrete unit within that story. Two of its features set the Eden narrative apart. First, 2:8 locates the garden in Eden somewhere in an unspecified east (*miqqedem*, translated as "eastward" or "to the east"[15]), which does not point to a known location; rather, it serves here as a gesture of dislocation. The garden and Eden—they may be the same thing—wherever they may be, are not *here*; they are somewhere distant from the perspective of the narrator . . . and of the reader. Second, in addition to the dislocation of Eden to the east, verses 10–14 interrupt the Eden narrative to describe a river, flowing from Eden, that divides into four rivers. The river irrigates the garden (v. 10), but the four rivers that follow serve no obvious purpose beyond circumscribing a series of known and unknown places. I maintain, however, that the passage—Genesis 2:10–14—has significance within the Eden narrative, especially for its readers.

An Excursus on Eden's Four Rivers

The description of four rivers branching out from one river in Genesis 2:10–14 intrudes in a narrative that would otherwise proceed from the account of what God formed, planted, and made to grow—the man, the garden, and beautiful trees (vv. 7–9)—to God's settling the man within the garden and offering instruction about eating, and not eating, from the garden's trees (vv. 15–17). Verse 9 piques our interest in the two trees that, among all the garden's lovely fruit-bearing trees, receive special mention. But the verses that follow (vv. 10–14) interrupt the narrative with information not obviously related to the story.[16] Verses 10–14 do not advance the narrative. Rather, they slow its pace and draw the reader's attention away from the two remarkable trees that have just been named: the tree of life and "the tree of the knowledge of good and bad."[17] About those trees, and especially the latter one, I will have more to say below. First, though, the four rivers require comment.

14. Wolde, *Words Become Worlds*, 14.

15. I translate *miqqedem* here as "to the east" following *IBHS*, 11.12.11b, example #4. The identical term appears also in Gen. 3:24 and 11:2.

16. The interruption is marked syntactically in Hebrew by a disjunctive clause at the beginning of v. 10.

17. The traditional translation of *tob wara'* as "good and evil" remains common (e.g., the NRSV and the CEB), but the term *ra'* (whether as an adjective or a noun) covers a range of meaning

Both the syntax of Genesis 2:10–14 and its contents—the rivers themselves—offer hints about its function within Genesis 2. First, the text surrounding verses 10–14 describes action that took place in the past: for example, "Yhwh Elohim formed" and "Yhwh Elohim planted" in verses 7 and 9. And in verse 15, following the river excursus, "Yhwh Elohim took the man and settled him. . . ." In Hebrew, these are *wayyiqtol* verbs—verb forms that advance the narrative by telling us what happened and in what sequence. They relate something about the past. By contrast, verbs within the river excursus, verses 10–14, do not express action in the past; they describe continuous action: "A river flows . . . it flows around . . ." (vv. 10, 11, 13).[18] According to these verses, Eden, the garden, and the four rivers are not something that once was but is no more; rather, they endure. They endure somewhere "eastward," at a place Kathleen M. O'Connor describes as "at once of the earth and not of it."[19] Access to Eden—to the garden and its tree of life—remains forever foreclosed.

In addition to the syntax of these verses, and their interruption of the surrounding narrative, the rivers themselves—their names and their descriptions—distinguish Genesis 2:10–14. Two of the rivers, the Tigris and the Euphrates, the text mentions in one verse (v. 14). Both rivers were familiar in antiquity and remain so today. Verse 14 reports that the Tigris flows on the east side of Assyria, more or less in the same space as today's Iraq. These are mundane rivers, in a known place, associated with a familiar political and geographical space. The other two rivers, the Pishon and the Gihon, are unknown, as are the lands of Havilah and Cush that they circumscribe. These two rivers are decidedly not mundane; they are not of the known world. Scholars have sought to identify the rivers Pishon and Gihon and the places associated with them (Havilah and Cush), suggesting Arabia and Ethiopia-Nubia, south of Egypt, for example, or perhaps Anatolia (Turkey).[20] But in verses 10–14, the narrator does not try cryptically to *locate* Eden for us, perhaps at some coordinate between

---

broader than the moral connotations of "evil." My translation follows the NJPS. On the infinitive construct with article (*hadda'at*) preceding an object, see GKC, #115d; Joüon, #124j.

18. Verses 10–14 consist largely of circumstantial clauses (Hamilton, *Book of Genesis, Chapters 1–17*, 168). The verbs here are all participles (*yotse'*, *sobeb*, *holek*), except for one infinitive and one imperfect *niphal*. Gordon J. Wenham points to the verb forms drawing "attention to the continuity of the actions." *Genesis 1–15*, 46n10b, 46n10d.

19. O'Connor, *Genesis 1–25A*, 50.

20. Theodore Hiebert discusses several such proposals in *Yahwist's Landscape*, 53. He proposes the Jordan Valley as the location Gen. 2–3 has in mind for Eden (53–58). Victor P. Hamilton proposes rivers in Assyria for Pishon and Gihon (*Book of Genesis, Chapters 1–17*, 169). "Gihon" names a spring in Jerusalem; obviously, it is not in view here. A place or nation Havilah is mentioned several times in the Bible. Cush usually means Ethiopia-Nubia, and the LXX translates it that way, as does the KJV. But the description of the river in v. 13 makes this identification improbable.

what are now northern Iraq and Sudan. Rather, this intrusion in the narrative *dislocates* Eden. While the Tigris and Assyria are part of the world's familiar features, and the Euphrates is so familiar it requires no description, the first two rivers and their lands (vv. 11–13) move Eden beyond the familiar. Within its broader context, 2:10–14 describes Eden as the source of rivers that still flow, in places we can find on a map, and also of rivers unknown—unknown to us and to the first readers of Genesis—that flow in lands that cannot be mapped.[21]

By way of its syntax and its contents, then, Genesis 2:10–14 situates Eden in a unique space, one that shares in the world's known geography but is not wholly contained within it. Above, I wrote that the location of Eden "to the east" in verse 8 serves as a gesture of dislocation. Genesis 3:24, in narrating the man's expulsion from the henceforth inaccessible Eden, uses the same term ("to the east," *miqqedem*) to describe the position of the winged sentries (cherubim) and the flaming sword that prevent access to Eden's tree of life. The entire Eden narrative guards Eden's location.

What role, then, does this literary intrusion play—this excursus on four rivers—within the larger narrative? The interruption of Genesis 2:10–14 provides a medium, a lens, through which to read the Eden narrative (2:5–3:24). The entire narrative is refracted through those verses. We have all seen how, for example, a drinking straw seems to bend, to assume a different angle, when we insert it in water. That is refraction at work. The analogy may be crude, but Genesis 2:10–14 serves as a medium that bends the angle of the Eden narrative. Its effect within that narrative is to lead readers to understand Eden, the garden, as contiguous with the world whose history began before Genesis 2:8 and continues beyond Genesis 3—and beyond Genesis 9 and 11—but also to understand that the events of Genesis 2 and 3 happen in a refracted space, part of the familiar world and, at the same time, a place apart from it. Within this space, Yhwh Elohim plants trees of extraordinary character (2:9), an animal of the field practices a hermeneutics of suspicion while discussing theology

---

Claus Westermann summarizes the matter: "We cannot then identify the first two rivers with any rivers known to us." *Genesis 1–11*, 218.

21. Other scholars disagree with this claim. Detlef Jericke, e.g., proposes that the Pishon and Gihon rivers of Gen. 2:11–13 represent the Blue Nile and the White Nile of Africa (*Die Ortsangaben im Buch Genesis*, 27). "With the two pairs of rivers [Tigris and Euphrates, Pishon and Gihon] the 'Paradise' geography attempts to delineate the two great cultural regions of the first millennium BCE's known world" (28). While my interpretation differs from his, Manfried Dietrich offers a rich study that draws on comparative material from Mesopotamia. He acknowledges—both in that material and in Genesis—a "space inaccessible and invisible" in which the human (*der Mensch*) was formed. "Das biblische Paradies," 320.

(3:1–5),[22] and Yhwh Elohim goes about in Eden during the breezy part of the day (v. 8),[23] asking the whereabouts of the first and still only man (v. 9). The world in which these extraordinary things take place occupies space continuous with the familiar world that Genesis 4—the story of Cain and Abel and the (entirely human) creation of civilization (4:16–24)—begins to narrate. But Genesis 2:10–14 also locates them in a place beyond our finding out, an unknown place and a dramatic space. Genesis 2 and 3 refer to a definite place, Eden, but that reference is refracted through the river excursus.[24]

The story into which Genesis 2:10–14 intrudes features two trees, beginning in verses 8–9 with the report that Yhwh Elohim planted a garden in Eden, moved the man there, and brought it about that every tree of pleasing appearance and good for food grew from the soil. Two of Eden's trees are named: the tree of life and the tree of the knowledge of good and bad.[25] As noted above, after the interruption of the river excursus (vv. 10–14), the story resumes: "Yhwh Elohim took the man and settled him [*wayyannichehu*] in the garden of Eden to till it and to care for it" (v. 15). One tree—the tree of life—frames the narrative, in 2:9 and 3:22–24, while the other plays a central role in the drama that Genesis 3 will narrate.

The Tree of Knowledge

Two divine initiatives animate the drama that Genesis 3 will narrate. First, within a generous grant of freedom, Yhwh Elohim places a single limitation, in the form of a prohibition: "You are free to eat of any tree in the garden. But from the tree of the knowledge of good and bad you must not eat, for on the day you eat from

22. Paul Ricoeur coined the term in *Freud and Philosophy*, 32.

23. Some versions (e.g., the LXX [*peripateō*] and the Vulg. [*ambulare*]), translations (e.g., the NRSV), and commentaries (e.g., Wenham, *Genesis 1–15*, 45) have God walking in the garden. That rendering may be overly literal, but it is grammatically possible. Jeffrey Niehaus argues that Gen. 3:8–9 actually describes God appearing in a storm theophany, with much thunder ("In the Wind of the Storm"). But in no biblical theophany does God walk about. And the deity's thunderous appearance in a storm theophany, in the deity's own garden, would be odd. Theophanic thunder would be incompatible with the probing divine-human conversation that takes place in vv. 9–13.

24. Tryggve N. D. Mettinger claims that the Eden narrative has no "referential ambition, in the sense that it purports to tell the truth about some extralinguistic reality" (*Eden Narrative*, 67). In my view, the claim is too strong by half: Eden is not simply a mundane reality but, on the terms of Gen. 2–3, as refracted through 2:10–14, does exist.

25. Some translations of Gen. 2:9 locate the trees "in the middle" of the garden (e.g., NJPS, CEB), but the trees' specific location in the garden seems irrelevant. The noun with preposition *betok*, in 2:9, often simply means "within" (e.g., 9:21; 18:24; 42:5).

it you will surely die" (Gen. 2:16–17). Second, Yhwh Elohim notices another lack in the created world. While in verse 5 the narrator mentions the lack of a man, a lack God remedied by forming one from the soil's dust, in verse 18 Yhwh Elohim judges the man's being alone to be "not good": "Not good is it for the man to be by himself." God offers no explicit reason why a tree with lethal fruit should be in the garden, a tree whose beauty and (it would appear) nutritious fruit mirror those of the garden's other trees. Neither does God explain why the man's being alone is not good. That God's remedy for the man's loneliness turns out to be a woman serves the purpose of continuing the human story into Genesis 4 and beyond. Her subsequent procreative function, however, plays no role in Genesis 2 and 3, where the woman enters into theological discussion with the serpent, a product of God's failed first attempts to find for the *'adam* a suitable counterpart by forming candidates from the *'adamah* as the *'adam* had been formed.[26] Perhaps the dust-formed man was not suited to theological discussion. In any event, the ensuing conversation between the smart serpent formed of soil and the woman—the first creature formed, like every human since, from another human and not from soil—concerns the tree, the only tree on which God had pronounced a limitation, a prohibition, and a sanction: the tree of the knowledge of good and bad.

Consideration of this tree begins with the conclusion of the Eden narrative, with Yhwh Elohim recognizing, in counsel, that the man (*ha'adam*), having already "become like one of us," retains access to the tree of life (Gen. 3:22). The reappearance of the tree of life here, with its first and only other mention in 2:9, frames a story in which the tree of the knowledge of good and bad figures centrally and crucially (2:9, 17; 3:1–6), first in its inclusion among the garden's attractive and nutritious trees (2:9), then as the object of the divine prohibition "you must not eat" (2:17), and finally as the subject of dialogue and contradiction (3:1–6). This dialogue, between the serpent and the woman, concerns the prohibition of eating from the tree and the lethal sanction attending its violation: "You will surely die" (2:17). The serpent's denial amounts to a direct contradiction of Yhwh Elohim's sanction, which the serpent quotes and then nullifies: "'You will surely die' is not true" (3:4). But the serpent also interprets God's statement suspiciously—I referred above to his hermeneutics of suspicion—and proposes God's motivation for the prohibition: "Elohim knows that on the day you eat from it your eyes will be opened and you will be like Elohim, knowing

26. The adjective *'arum*, which the NRSV translates in Gen. 3:1 as "crafty," has that negative connotation in Job, but Proverbs gives the term a positive valence and commends the quality. The LXX translates *'arum* in Gen. 3:1 in a positive sense, with *phronimos*, as "sensible, thoughtful, prudent, wise" (BDAG, s.v. "*phronimos*").

good and bad."[27] Yhwh Elohim acknowledges the consequence: *ʾadam* has indeed "become like one of us, knowing good and bad" (3:22). In other words, knowing good and bad means, in the context of the Eden narrative, being like Yhwh Elohim. And this acknowledgment, which assumes and responds to a violation of the first (and only) divine prohibition, serves as a preface to the prevention of another way in which *ʾadam* could be like God—living forever. Articulating my understanding of "the knowledge of good and bad," as Genesis 2 and 3 use this language, will serve the characterization of God the Creator in these early chapters of Genesis.

On Being like God

Recent discussion of "the knowledge of good and bad," or the knowledge of good and evil, has argued or assumed that the story in Genesis 2 and 3 concerns not a fall into sin in a traditional Christian sense but a kind of maturation. Consistent with this assumption, the first humans, in eating from the prohibited tree, began the practice of discernment, including moral discernment, that marks mature and responsible human life. In both a literal and a metaphorical sense, on this interpretation, the first man and woman left the paradisiacal realm of Eden and entered the mundane realm, where, for example, society and culture required, as do most of ours, the wearing of clothes. Attaining the knowledge of good and evil, then, would simply mean attaining adulthood and the kind of adult discernment that children lack. Konrad Schmid summarizes the conclusions of this line of interpretation well. The knowledge of good and bad, he writes, "indicates a differentiation between life-supporting and life-damaging knowledge, which . . . is especially characteristic of adults."[28]

This reading of Genesis 2 and 3 seems to gain support from the literary context, in which God assigns the woman and the man roles and responsibilities, and challenges, that resemble those with which an early reader of Genesis would have been familiar; some of them remain familiar today: farming is beset with difficulties, and labor—childbearing, especially combined with farm work—is onerous (3:16–19).[29] Moreover, the first chapters of Genesis move the reader from an Edenic world to one in which human achievement and inven-

27. "Elohim," usually referring to Israel's God in the Old Testament, is plural in form and can also refer to multiple deities (e.g., Deut. 32:37; Josh. 22:22). Whether the narrator has the serpent referring to (the) one God or to multiple deities need not concern us; in Gen. 3:22, it is Yhwh Elohim who echoes the serpent in acknowledging that the *ʾadam* has "become like one of us."

28. K. Schmid, "Ambivalence of Wisdom," 282. Schmid's essay provides a comprehensive bibliography on the subject. See also the summary of views in Mettinger, *Eden Narrative*, 4.

29. Meyers, "Gender Roles and Genesis 3:16 Revisited."

tion (4:16–24)—human creativity—do not involve God in any way; they are the productions of an adult, autonomous humanity whose achievements receive no immediate assessment, positive or negative, from God. But while Schmid describes the knowledge of good and evil as characteristic of "adult differentiation" between knowledge that supports life and knowledge that damages it, the earliest adult differentiation proved catastrophic: the first fratricide—Cain killing Abel—led to the multiplication of retributive violence (4:24), and then came the deluge (6:13). What turns out to be characteristic of adult knowledge, early in Genesis, is wrecking the world.

I maintain that understanding "the knowledge of good and bad," then, requires reading the prohibition of Genesis 2:17, and its violation in chapter 3, within the larger context of Genesis 6–9 and 11:1–9. This larger context includes both the strange episode of divine beings ("the sons of God") marrying and reproducing with humans ("the daughters of mortals," 6:1–4) and the tower of Babel story (11:1–9). These texts, which I will describe further in the next chapter, narrate instances of God's defense of creation against threats to it, threats constituted by God-rivaling human knowledge, unending human life, and unlimited human power. Our attention here turns to places in the Old Testament where "knowing good and bad" describes not "a universal human trait"[30] but uniquely comprehensive, godlike knowledge. In the Eden narrative (Gen. 2–3), I argue, this amounts to God-rivaling knowledge, as the serpent says expressly in 3:5 and as God acknowledges in 3:22.

We can gain insight into the use of the opposite terms "good [*tob*] and evil [*ra'*]" by considering other biblical texts that pair these terms. Scholars have long recognized that Biblical Hebrew sometimes uses pairs of opposite terms to express totality. Carl Friedrich Keil pointed to this in his commentary on the Minor Prophets (Book of the Twelve), first published in German in 1866.[31] English speakers are familiar with this use of opposites: "They searched high and low," which means, of course, that they searched everywhere. We already encountered an example of this—scholars call it a merism—in Genesis 1:1, where "heaven and earth" refers to everything.[32] Second Samuel 14 provides another biblical example; it describes King David's son Absalom as the picture

30. K. Schmid, "Ambivalence of Human Wisdom," 282. Wolde refers to "the ability of discrimination" (*Words Become Worlds*, 37). It should be noted that the woman possessed keen powers of discrimination prior to eating the prohibited fruit (Gen. 3:6).

31. Keil and Delitzsch, *Twelve Minor Prophets*, 2:449–50. The German original was published by Keil in 1866. For the grammar of opposites expressing totality, he refers to F. E. C. Dietrich, *Abhandlungen zur hebräischen Grammatik*, 197–210.

32. For "good and bad" as a merism in Gen. 2 and 3, see also Soggin, "'And You Will Be like God'"; Mettinger, *Eden Narrative*, 67; Botterweck, "*yada'*," 5:465.

of physical perfection: "From the sole of his foot to the crown of his head he was without blemish" (v. 25; cf. Job 2:7).[33] Absalom or David figures in two other instances of merism with "good and evil" (or "good and bad") as the opposite terms. In the first, despite learning that his half-brother Amnon had raped his sister Tamar, Absalom says nothing to Amnon. "Absalom spoke not at all with Amnon, neither bad nor good [*lemera' we'ad-tob*]" (2 Sam. 13:22). Here the opposites bad (or evil) and good serve to stress Absalom's complete silence—he said nothing at all—in the face of Amnon's crime against Tamar. The first clause of the verse already reported Absalom's silence; the modifying phrase "neither bad nor good" states emphatically that Absalom's silence was total. Absalom soon showed what he thought about the matter and what he thought of Amnon: he murdered him. But in this case, the pair of opposites—"good and bad"—has to do not with Absalom's moral assessment of the event or of Amnon but with the completeness of his silence to Amnon.

In the second instance David's general, Joab, enlists a wise woman from Tekoa to flatter David and convict him into returning Absalom to Jerusalem, after David had sent Absalom into exile for the murder of Amnon. The woman tells David that he is "like the angel of God, understanding [*lishmoa'*] good and bad" (2 Sam. 14:17).[34] Earlier, the king of Gath, Achish, who provided David refuge in his flight from Saul, declared David to be "like an angel of God" with reference to David's integrity (1 Sam. 29:9). The anonymous but wise Tekoan woman applies the comparison expressly to David's wisdom (*chokmah*). She further identifies this angelic capacity of David's as wisdom that amounts to "knowing everything in the earth" (2 Sam. 14:20).[35] The woman of Tekoa engages in hyperbole and flattery, of course, acting on behalf of Joab and as his agent, but the associations she draws are instructive: associations among "the knowledge of good and bad," wisdom, being like an angel of God, and knowing everything, even if "everything" in the context of 2 Samuel 14 refers especially to David's judicial acumen.

Such wisdom, even if in a hyperbolic speech, of course calls to mind the wisest of all, Solomon—no one was wiser before or after him (1 Kings 3:12). Offered his choice of divine gifts, Solomon asks God for "an understanding mind to govern [God's] people, discerning between good and bad" (v. 9). The verse has

33. Wolde, *Stories of the Beginning*, 46.

34. I follow the CEB and the NJPS in translating *lishmoa'* here as "understanding." P. Kyle McCarter translates it as "attending to" (*2 Samuel*, 336). Note that 1 Kings 3:11 has the identical Hebrew construction (see further below).

35. The prepositional phrase could be translated as "in the land." Linguistic considerations alone cannot decide the matter.

verbal and conceptual links with 2 Samuel 14, including the opposites good and bad and the ascription of angelic or godlike wisdom to the characters, David and Solomon.[36] In both texts, the opposites good and bad refer to something far beyond what Ellen van Wolde has described as "a general capacity for discernment one gets when one is grown up."[37] In some places, of course, knowing good and bad does refer to maturation or growing up. At Qumran, the Rule of the Congregation stipulates twenty years of age as "when a young man knows [good] and bad" (1QSa 1:10–11). Deuteronomy 1:39 observes that youngsters "do not know good and bad" (NRSV: "do not yet know right from wrong"). Isaiah 7:16 also associates knowing good and bad, or distinguishing right from wrong, with maturity. In 2 Samuel 19:36[19:35], David's friend Barzillai complains that, at eighty years of age, he can no longer tell whether food and drink taste good or bad. All of these latter examples involve maturity, whether not enough or too much. None of the examples comprises an analogy with Solomon.

Expressly, in Solomon's case, the wisdom corresponding to discerning good and bad came as a unique, divine endowment (1 Kings 3:15; 5:11[4:31]), one he received *after* he had been mature enough to secure his throne with strategic shrewdness and violence (2:13–46). But the story of Solomon and his greatest-ever, godlike wisdom ended badly: 1 Kings 3–11 narrates his catastrophic judgments, which placed Israel's very existence in peril (9:6–9). His devotion to the Canaanite deity Astarte and his construction of shrines for the Moabite deity Chemosh, the Ammonite deity Molech (or Milcom), and many others (11:5–8) soon brought disaster. Solomon's autonomous exercise of extraordinary, godlike wisdom serves within the Bible itself as a cautionary tale. It does so especially when read together with Genesis 2 and 3. And as Peter T. Lanfer has illustrated, when read together with 1 Kings 3–11, the Eden narrative "presents the possession of unchecked god-like wisdom as a serious threat," specifically a "threat to proper boundaries between divinity and humanity."[38]

Threats to the boundary between divinity and humanity—or, more precisely, threats to the constitutive difference between God and God's creation, and thus to creation itself—provide a leading theme for all of Genesis 1–11, as I suggested above. The story Genesis 2 and 3 tells does involve a kind of maturation on the part of the first couple. But the serpent announces, and God acknowledges, that eating from the tree of *prohibited knowledge* will place (and then does place) the first couple on a plane with their Creator: "like God, knowing good and

36. Mordechai Cogan notes the links in *1 Kings*, 187.
37. Wolde, *Stories of the Beginning*, 47. She is referring here to Gen. 2 and 3.
38. Lanfer, "Solomon in the Garden of Eden," 1:715, 1:715n2.

bad" (3:5), and "like one of us, knowing good and bad" (3:22). God's "knowing good and bad," of course, is not simply—or anything—like that of anyone who has grown up; it is not a matter of God's maturation. As other biblical texts have helped to confirm, the knowledge of good and bad in Genesis 2 and 3 is knowledge proper to God alone.[39] The prohibition in 2:17 was not simply about moral discernment or human maturation. It warned against the acquisition of human knowledge that breaches the definitive distinction—"the line of demarcation"—between divine and human, between Creator and creature.[40] That breach would threaten creation itself.

Peace in the Garden of God

Beginning from virtually nothing—an earth lacking even vegetation—God formed a man from the soil's dust to farm the soil. God then postponed the man's farming vocation, planted a verdant garden, and placed (Gen. 2:8), then settled (2:15), the man there, in Eden, a place touching the mundane world—and God's history with Israel—at a tangent. This garden of God, with its beautiful and nourishing trees, including two trees of special character, stands in the starkest contrast with the description in 2:5 of an earth marked by absence. The Septuagint calls the well-ordered world of Eden a paradise (*paradeisos*). Helping to shape the way Christians have thought about paradise is Jesus's statement to one of those crucified with him, that on that day he would be in paradise (Luke 23:43; cf. 2 Cor. 12:4; Rev. 2:7). The word derives from Persian, where it referred to the gardens of Achaemenid (early Persian) kings, beginning with Cyrus (Isa. 45:1).[41]

Gardens and parks (the Hebrew word *gan* can refer to either one) have been associated with royalty for millennia. Contemporary examples remain, like the Imperial Gardens in Tokyo and the Gardens of Buckingham Palace in London. In the United States, formal events often take place in the Rose Garden. Gardens in antiquity, royal gardens, held greater symbolic power. The Hanging Gardens of Babylon, built by Nebuchadnezzar II (605–562),[42] remain the most famous of these. They were described, according to Kathryn L. Gleason, "as being in

39. "This knowledge is proper to the divine world: it is a mark of deity." Humans acquire this knowledge "only as a result of a deliberate act of disobedience." Machinist, "How Gods Die," 211.

40. Mettinger, *Eden Narrative*, 27.

41. Three late Old Testament texts transliterate the Persian term as *pardes*: Neh. 2:8; Eccles. 2:5; Song 4:13.

42. Or perhaps by Sennacherib in Nineveh. So argues Stephanie Dalley in *Mystery of the Hanging Garden of Babylon*.

imitation of the alpine landscape of Media."[43] Media was located in the northwestern part of what is now Iran. Its alpine landscape stood in stark contrast with the alluvial plain of Babylon, Nebuchadnezzar's capital. Or perhaps the contrast was with Nineveh, which Sennacherib (705–681) built as his capital on the banks of the Tigris River in what is now Iraq.[44] With their gardens, kings like these created an enclosed environment whose order and beauty—including exotic plants from distant regions—bore witness to the capacity of the kings to bring good order to their realm, surrounded by an unruly and disordered, largely unknown world. Royal gardens represented the king's imperial rule and his creation of peace in the natural world, just as the king's military victories had done in the political realm, victories that the gardens also celebrated. Judah's kings, too, had gardens, though we have no descriptions of them (2 Kings 21:18, 26; 25:4).

Gardens also accompanied temples in antiquity. These gardens provided produce for sacrifices to the deity or, in ancient understanding, food to nourish the gods.[45] Indeed, the garden could serve as the deity's dwelling. The Old Testament itself reflects the picture of God's dwelling as a garden. The temple in Jerusalem—the site of God's earthly dwelling—constructed with Phoenician artistry under Solomon's direction (1 Kings 7), was furnished with abundant arboreal, garden-park images, including lilies and pomegranates (vv. 13–22).[46] At an even smaller scale, the lampstand or menorah in the tabernacle, symbolizing God's presence, was the image of a tree, with branches and leaves (Exod. 25:31–36; cf. Zech. 4:2–3). In a different literary environment, Ezekiel identifies Eden as the garden of God (Ezek. 28:13),[47] perhaps supporting the idea of Eden as God's dwelling—Eden as temple, as Zion—in Genesis. Indeed, scholars have identified temple symbolism in the Eden narrative of Genesis.[48] But the Eden narrative itself undermines the idea of the garden as temple or divine dwelling.[49] Its trees were beautiful and good for human food (Gen. 2:9), and their fruit was all but universally—only one tree excepted—offered for human enjoyment and nourishment, not for a king's banquet or a god's offerings. "The garden

43. Gleason, "Gardens," 2:383. Zevit, *What Really Happened in the Garden of Eden?*, 114–19.

44. Dalley, *Mystery of the Hanging Garden of Babylon*. The ruins of ancient Nineveh are by the city of Mosul in Iraq.

45. McDowell, *Image of God in the Garden of Eden*, 142–44.

46. See Smith and Pitard, *Ugaritic Baal Cycle*, 60–66, with bibliography and discussion of comparative material.

47. Greenberg, *Ezekiel 21–37*, 581. Ezekiel 31:9 refers to "the trees of Eden that were in the garden of God."

48. An early example is Wenham, "Sanctuary Symbolism in the Garden of Eden Story."

49. Block, "Eden."

was planned only . . . as a gift of God's gracious care for the man he created," Gerhard von Rad writes.[50]

Von Rad's "only" here exceeds what the text says. The garden was indeed a gift to the man and then to the other creatures God formed, like the man, from the soil—and then also to the woman God built. But God's garden plan included both an assignment ("to watch and keep" the garden) and a singular prohibition ("do not eat" of this one tree). The Hebrew term translated "to keep" (*shamar*) has a range of applications, from keeping sheep (1 Sam. 17:34) to keeping commandments (Exod. 20:6; Deut. 5:1). Here in Genesis 2, the application of "keeping" to tending a garden merges with that of keeping a commandment or obeying a single prohibition. Von Rad was right: the man's tending the garden seems to amount to enjoying it and its nourishment. But if it is appropriate to speak of God's plan for and with the garden, then God's plan also included a test, in the form of a prohibition.[51]

Beginning from what amounted to nothing, God created an Eden, a verdant realm apart and a place of peace. And God populated that peaceful park, God's own garden, with creatures formed from the soil: "every living creature" (Gen. 2:19; 9:12). From the first such creature, a man, God built a woman, an act of creation that repaired the one remaining lack in this world of God's creation, the absence that had provoked God's assessment "not good" (2:18). Genesis 2 concludes with God having filled every lack, every absence. The garden is a picture of peace, and the two human creatures enjoy an untroubled peace between them. Nothing in Genesis 2 foreshadows the drama and the broken peace that Genesis 3 narrates. Nothing except "You shall not . . ."

50. Von Rad, *Genesis*, 78.

51. "With the prohibition of one of the two trees (Gen. 2:17), God confronts man with a test." Mettinger, *Eden Narrative*, 23.

3

From God's Peaceful Garden to Peace Divinely Disturbed

GENESIS 3:1–11:9

Beginning in the middle of the past century, the literary critic and philosopher René Girard proposed that human culture, including religion and its rituals, had its origins in mimetic or imitative desire, envy, and rivalry. He argued that our desire for something, for some object, is provoked by someone else—"a model"—who desires that object. Our desire then imitates that of the model, who becomes our rival, both of us desiring the same object. This rivalry leads to violence. Within a society, it leads to a contagion of violence, which culture—especially religion—aims to contain.[1] We first encounter rivalry in the Bible expressly in Genesis 4, the story of Cain and Abel. Cain, the firstborn of Adam and Eve, murders his brother and rival, Abel. Cain's fratricidal anger grows from the favor Yhwh shows toward Abel's sacrifice from his sheep over Cain's offering of produce from the ground (Gen. 4:1–5). Girard draws formatively on this account, in which mimetic desire, rivalry, and violence form the plot.[2]

1. Girard's most accessible works remain *Things Hidden since the Foundation of the World* and *Violence and the Sacred.* Chris Fleming provides a good introduction to Girard's thought in *René Girard.*

2. Girard, *Things Hidden since the Foundation of the World*, 144–49.

Regardless of the merits of Girard's theory, it cannot be denied that rivalries constitute much of the drama in Genesis. Abraham's magnanimity defuses a rivalry with his nephew Lot (Gen. 13), while his unspeaking acquiescence to a request for surrogate fathering contributes to a rivalry between his wife, Sarah, and her Egyptian maid, Hagar (Gen. 16; 21). Those unions produce the rivals Isaac and Ishmael, who (with Rebekah) precipitate a rivalry between their sons, Jacob and Esau (25:23; 27–33). Jacob's wives, Leah and Rachel, are rivals (Gen. 29), and their father, Laban, briefly becomes Jacob's rival (Gen. 30–31). Jacob's sons enter into a rivalry with Shechem and his father, Hamor, over Dinah, daughter of Jacob and Leah. Two of Leah's sons, Simeon and Levi, then slaughter the men of the city of Shechem (Gen. 34). All these rivalries produce some form of violence, with fratricide—executed in Genesis 4 and attempted in chapter 37—framing the stories. In Genesis 37 Jacob's sons plot to kill or enslave their brother Joseph in a violent reflex of the rivalry between their different mothers—Leah and Rachel—provoked by their father, Jacob, and emanating from their grandparents Rebekah and Isaac.

Rivalry's pedigree and the violence regularly attending it reach back at least to the progenitors, Abraham and Sarah and Hagar, and extend forward beyond the book of Genesis. David's rivalries with Saul and then with Absalom are narrated in detail in 1 and 2 Samuel. Much earlier there arose in Egypt a rivalry between Moses and Pharaoh, a rivalry that, as narrated in Exodus 4–15, was in fact between Yhwh and Pharaoh. Egypt's Pharaoh was infused with divinity as the "Son of Ra," the sun-god and creator, and was empowered to establish and maintain justice and order while defeating injustice and disorder.[3] When Moses declares, "Thus says Yhwh," Pharaoh responds, "Who is Yhwh, that I should obey Yhwh?" (Exod. 5:1–2). The rivalry between Yhwh and Pharaoh, Son of Ra, then plays out through a series of plagues that precedes Israel's exodus from Egypt, plagues and an exodus that prove liberating for the Hebrews but disastrous for the Egyptians.

I wrote above that rivalry's pedigree reaches back at least to Abraham and Sarah. In fact, it reaches back to the first couple, Adam and Eve. At the end of Genesis 2, Eden, God's garden, is at peace, with every lack and every absence filled. At the end of Genesis 3, God—Yhwh Elohim—observes that humans have become like God, having eaten prohibited fruit from the tree of the knowledge of good and bad (3:22). As I argued in the previous chapter, the prohibition preserved what Tryggve Mettinger calls the "line of demarcation" between Creator and creature, divinity and humanity.[4] The humans' violation of this prohi-

3. Assmann, *Ma'at*, 206–7. See also Ephron, "Royal Ideology and State Administration."
4. Mettinger, *Eden Narrative*, 27.

bition was a breach of that "line" and constituted, in Peter T. Lanfer's words, a "threat to proper boundaries between divinity and humanity."[5] In other words, their violation of Yhwh Elohim's prohibition made the man and woman God's rivals in a way that threatened creation. But another, even earlier (indeed, the initial) rivalry anticipated and fomented this divine-human one. It involved the serpent—the most astute of the nonhuman creatures Yhwh Elohim had formed from the soil (3:1)—and the woman who satisfied God's effort, as the serpent did not, to find a suitable counterpart to the man (2:22–24).[6]

In this chapter, I explore further the threats to creation narrated in Genesis 3–11 and God the Creator's actions in response to them, actions in defense of creation and of creaturely flourishing. The section titled "On Being like God" in the previous chapter introduced the issue addressed in narrative fashion, as I contend, in these early chapters of Genesis. There I discussed the issues of (illicit) godlike knowledge and godlike endless life presented as a threat to the constitutive distinction between Creator and creature. Both of these matters of concern appear in Genesis 3, as I noted in "The Eden Narrative, Part 1" in the preceding chapter. Here I turn to Genesis 3 once more.

The Eden Narrative, Part 2: Genesis 3:1–24

Genesis 2 concludes with the observation that the man and the woman—"the husband and his wife"—are naked but not ashamed (v. 25). The Hebrew syntax suggests that the narrator finds this state of affairs—nakedness without shame[7]—remarkable, even though the couple was joined as husband and wife in 2:23–24. Their absence of shame in each other's presence is remarkable, though, only in light of their imminent life outside of Eden. The narrator's remark about nakedness immediately precedes the notice in 3:1 that the serpent is the smartest of all the nonhuman creatures God formed from the soil. As readers of the Hebrew text have noticed, the words for "naked" (*'arom*, 2:25) and for "smart" (*'arum*, 3:1) look and sound strikingly similar, suggesting that the couple's unashamed nakedness bears some relation to the serpent's astuteness. This proves to be the

5. Lanfer, "Solomon in the Garden of Eden," 1:715, 1:715n2.

6. Here and in what follows, I draw on material explored in my earlier essay "Creation and Peace." There I suggest a rivalry between the serpent and the woman. See also Barr, *Garden of Eden*, 62. Wisdom of Solomon 2:24 says that death entered the world through the devil's envy or jealousy. Mark Smith, *Genesis of Good and Evil*, 29.

7. The root *bosh*—"to be ashamed"—here appears in a reflexive form; it does so nowhere else in the Old Testament. On this and other interpretive issues in Gen. 2:25–3:24, see Turner-Smith, "Naked but Not Ashamed."

case, as we will see. First, though, some features of the biblical text's presentation of the serpent bear mentioning.

The serpent appears in the narrative without warning or introduction, except for the narrator's comment that he is the smartest of the nonhuman creatures. God formed the serpent and all the other creatures, of course—and formed them from the soil, as Yhwh Elohim had formed the man. The man recognized and named the other God-formed creatures, each one a candidate to be his counterpart.[8] But in the Eden narrative, the only other "named" creatures, the man and the woman, God specifically formed or built and gave place and purpose (Gen. 2:8, 15, 18, 22). The serpent simply appears. He evidently appears on his own initiative and immediately speaks.

The serpent speaks to the woman, addressing her with a question about what God had or had not said. Of course, in terms of what we can know from the narrative, neither the woman nor the serpent existed when God spoke (Gen. 2:16–17); only the man did. I suggested above that the serpent addresses the woman as her (unsuccessful) rival. His first words suggest as much: "Elohim did not really say . . . , did he?"[9] The serpent's words constitute a challenge, as a prosecutor interrogating a witness might challenge a testimony: "You don't expect me to believe . . . , do you?" What the serpent rhetorically asks the woman to deny turns the expansive freedom and permission God earlier granted the man, with a single restriction, into a wholesale prohibition.[10] Yhwh Elohim had said, "You are free to eat of any tree in the garden. But from the tree of the knowledge of good and bad you must not eat, for on the day you eat from it you will surely die" (2:16–17). The serpent asks only about the prohibition and exaggerates it: "Did Elohim really say that you may not eat from *any* of the garden's trees?" (3:1).

The serpent here engages the woman in a theistic argument, an argument about what "god" (*ʾelohim*) may have said and what *ʾelohim*'s motive had been. The woman's reply, too, speaks of *ʾelohim*, not the Yhwh Elohim who otherwise speaks and is spoken of in Genesis 2–3.[11] In the woman's subsequent testimony, accepted by Yhwh Elohim, she says that the serpent deceived her (3:13–14). Her reply to the serpent corrects him: "We may eat the fruit from the garden's trees" (v. 2). But she adds her own exaggeration: *ʾelohim* prohibited even touching the tree "in the midst of the garden, lest you die" (v. 3). The woman's "lest you die

8. J. Dietrich, "Sozialanthropologie des Alten Testaments," esp. 224–26.

9. For the Hebrew syntax, see Ronald Williams, *Hebrew Syntax*, #385.

10. Levinson, *"Right Chorale,"* 40–47.

11. Ellen van Wolde observes the appearance of *ʾelohim* in the conversation between the serpent and the woman and draws connections with Gen. 1:26–28. *Words Become Worlds*, 39–40.

[*pen-temutun*]" (v. 3) lacks the definitive "on the day you eat from it, you will surely die [*mot tamut*]" (2:17). The serpent restores the strong, definitive form of Yhwh Elohim's earlier prohibition in order to negate it: *lo'-mot tamut*. As if to say, "'You will die' is false." The implication of his further statement—"*'elohim* knows that on the day you eat from it, your eyes will be opened and you will be like the gods, knowing good and bad" (3:5)—is that God's threatened sanction, death, is but a ruse, intended to prevent the man and the woman from becoming "like *'elohim*": like gods. Both Yhwh Elohim and the serpent say "on the day . . . ," but the serpent, contradicting Yhwh Elohim, promises her that the day on which the man and woman eat from the tree will bring likeness with the gods, the *'elohim*: the possession of open-eyed perception.[12] She does eat.

The woman eats from the tree because "she saw that the tree was good for food, that its appearance was pleasing, and that it was desirable for gaining insight [*lehaskil*]" (Gen. 3:6). In this she echoes the narrator's own description of the garden, which contains "every tree that is pleasant to the sight and good for food, the tree of life also in the midst of the garden, and the tree of the knowledge of good and evil" (2:9).[13] The woman eats from the tree, and she gives some "to her husband with her, and he ate" (3:6). And the eyes of both are opened.

Just as the smart (*'arum*) serpent predicted, with opened eyes, the couple perceives—they know (*yada'*)—that they are naked (*'arom*), and they proceed immediately to cover themselves (Gen. 3:7). Repeatedly in the Old Testament, God's opening someone's eyes enables them to perceive what had been hidden: Hagar in the wilderness (21:19); Balaam and an angel (Num. 22:31); the king of Aram and his troops (2 Kings 6:17). In the garden, it is not God—not Yhwh Elohim (at least not directly)—who opens the couple's eyes. As the serpent had suggested it would do, their eating the fruit yields a capacity for knowledge they had not possessed. The narrator does not inform us how the serpent understands "the knowledge of good and bad" and what makes such knowledge godlike—or how he may have come by this understanding. Neither does the narrator let readers know how the serpent and his intentions (as the woman interpreted them)—not to mention the entire conversation between the serpent and the woman—somehow escape God's attention. Instead, the narrator says only that God strolls in the garden's evening breeze.

The woman does eat from the prohibited tree, as does the man. Yhwh Elohim's assessment, at the end of Genesis 3, is that "the man has become like one

12. I understand the second occurrence of *'elohim* in this verse to mean "gods," with the following plural participle *yod'e*. See Machinist, "How Gods Die," 211, 211n59.

13. On the vocabulary of Gen. 2:9 and especially 3:6, see Mark Smith, *Genesis of Good and Evil*, 56–59.

of us, knowing good and bad" (v. 22). But from all the narrator tells us, the knowledge the couple gained from violating the prohibition amounts to their perceiving, knowing (*yada'*), that they are naked. Knowledge of a more intimate kind will wait, so far as we are told, until the first verse of Genesis 4. But the continuation of the narrative in Genesis 3 discloses the consequences of this new knowledge that they are naked.

Shame, Nakedness, Fear, and Sin

The first couple is shamelessly naked (Gen. 2:25). Then their eyes are opened, and they *know* they are naked. The narrative itself may hint at matters of sexuality, between "they were naked but unashamed" (2:25) and "they knew they were naked" (3:7), but any such hints remain only that.[14] That the couple immediately makes fig-leaf belts for themselves suggests shame and, in that respect, a "fall" from the condition the couple enjoyed at the end of Genesis 2. Indeed, *shame* has been commended as a category for understanding the narrative in Genesis 3, by Simon Cozens and Christoph Ochs, for example.[15] This even though the prevailing term in the chapter is *fear*.[16] Cozens and Ochs claim, "Their fear is the fear of being seen by one another."[17] The text seems to say otherwise, however. In response to Yhwh Elohim's first question—"Where are you?"—the man replies that he was afraid and hid because he is naked. God's second question, "How did you know you were naked?" immediately precedes a third and final one: "From the tree I commanded you not to eat from did you eat?" My awkward translation strictly follows the Hebrew word order, which places emphasis on *the* tree and God's command, God's explicit prohibition. The fear that led the man (presumably also the woman) to hide derived from (1) the searching presence of God; (2) the man's knowledge that he is (they are) naked; (3) the man's recognition (presumably, also the woman's) that the knowledge of their nakedness came as a consequence of their violation of a quite specific and singular prohibition: a "thou shalt not." That shame was a component of this fear seems more than likely. But their direct violation of a divine prohibition generated the fear that led them into hiding and led in turn to God's responses in Genesis 3:14–24 . . . which led them out of Eden.

Traditional Christian interpretation of Genesis 2–3 speaks of (original) sin and the fall.[18] Questions about the fall that depend on the New Testament

14. Turner-Smith discusses the matter thoroughly in "Naked but Not Ashamed."
15. Cozens and Ochs, "'Have You No Shame?'"
16. Mark Smith, *Genesis of Good and Evil*, 59.
17. Cozens and Ochs, "'Have You No Shame?,'" 193.
18. On the issue from a scholarly and Christian-theological perspective, see G. Anderson, "Biblical Origins and the Problem of the Fall." After listing the conditions of the world in Gen. 3:12–24,

can here be left aside. But contemporary biblical scholars have argued for the inappropriateness of describing as "sin" what transpired in the garden as Genesis 3:1–6 narrates it. Mark S. Smith brilliantly represents and advances these arguments in a book devoted to Genesis 2–3. Among Smith's principal arguments is that the Eden narrative makes no mention of sin (*chatta't*), which first appears in 4:7, in the story of Cain and Abel.[19] But the absence of a term for "sin" hardly means that sin cannot be at issue in Genesis 3. That classical Hebrew does not know the word *misogyny* does not make it illicit to cite instances of it in the Bible, for example, in Judges 19.[20] In Genesis 3, Yhwh Elohim says to the man, "Because . . . you ate from the tree I commanded you, 'you shall not eat from it,' cursed is the ground because of you; in hardship you shall eat from it" (v. 17). The text makes explicit that God issues a command, the couple violates that command—that is, they transgressed it—and God imposes sanctions for those transgressions. We would not go amiss in understanding this sort of thing—this kind of transgression or trespass—as sin, even in reading the Eden narrative.

Death and Life

The sanction God first announces for eating of the tree of the knowledge of good and bad is death, "on the day you eat from it" (Gen. 2:17). Obviously, the couple continues to live after eating from the tree. Much ink has flowed in debate over whether the serpent or Yhwh Elohim told the truth in this matter.[21] I incline toward agreement with Claus Westermann, who describes the difference between God's announced sanction and God's subsequent action in terms of "inconsequence"[22] in light of a new situation. Examples come readily to mind of lethal threats God made and subsequently rescinded, even if the "new situation" lay substantially within God's own self. In Exodus 32, God "repented [*wayyinnachem*] of the disaster [*hara'ah*] he had said he would bring on his people" (v. 14). This statement is repeated, almost verbatim, in Jonah: "Elohim repented of the disaster he had said he would bring on them"—the people of Nineveh (Jon. 3:10). In Exodus, God's repentance follows Moses's intercession.

Mark Smith says, "In other words, we might say, the world has fallen." But, he goes on: "Genesis 3 is not the story of original sin or the Fall." *Genesis of Good and Evil*, 62.

19. Mark Smith, *Genesis of Good and Evil*, 59–60.

20. Kuja, "Remembering the Body."

21. Gordon, "Ethics of Eden." Gordon assesses a debate between James Barr and R. W. L. Moberly on this question.

22. Westermann, *Genesis 1–11*, 225. Westermann places this term in scare quotes. Victor P. Hamilton explores the grammar and syntax of Gen. 2:17, with examples from other Old Testament passages, tempering the absoluteness of "on the day . . . you will surely die." *Book of Genesis, Chapters 1–17*, 172–74.

In Jonah, God's repentance follows the repentance of Nineveh's people. God's threatened annihilation of Israel in Deuteronomy 8:19–20 is reduced to exile from the land (28:63).[23] In both Jeremiah and Ezekiel, God recognizes that Israel's obedience and thus continued existence require God's own intervention in the form of a new covenant (Jer. 31:31–34) or a "new heart of flesh" instead of stone (Ezek. 36:24–28)—prior to any repentance on exiled Israel's part. In Genesis 3, no one intercedes or repents, but God does commute the death sentence attached to eating from the tree. Otherwise, God would have no more story to tell or anyone—at least not any of us—to hear it.[24] Sanctions seem still to apply, even so. "By the sweat of your brow you will eat food, until you return to the soil, because from it you were taken; for you are dust," Yhwh Elohim tells the man, "and to dust you shall return" (Gen. 3:19; cf. 2:7). But is death—mortality—which is here in view, a sanction?

Did Yhwh Elohim form the man and build the woman as immortal? The difficulty in answering the question depends in part on the presence in the garden, and in the Eden narrative, of the tree of life, mentioned along with the tree of the knowledge of good and bad (Gen. 2:9).[25] Peter Machinist concludes that the "pattern of occurrence" of the tree of the knowledge of good and bad and the tree of life in Genesis 2–3 "suggests not simply that 'life' in the tree of life means immortality, but that originally Adam and then his spouse possessed this immortality before they ate of the tree of life."[26] Konrad Schmid insists, to the contrary, "there are far too many problems for . . . a thesis of an original immortality in Genesis 2–3 to be maintained."[27] One of the "problems" Schmid mentions is Yhwh Elohim's statement in 3:22, that the man has already "become like one of us, knowing good and bad, and lest he reach out his hand and take also from the tree of life, and eat, and live forever."[28] As I argued in the previous chapter, "being like God" with respect to knowledge constituted a breach, a violation of the constitutive distinction between Creator and creature. Eating from the tree did not bestow on the woman the capacity to make discriminating judgments.[29] She already had that capacity, which she demonstrated in her remarkable

23. Lohfink, "Der Zorn Gottes und das Exil," 36.

24. As R. W. L. Moberly remarks, commenting on Gen. 2–3, "The relationship between human disobedience and divine judgment is to most appearances ambiguous." *Theology of the Book of Genesis*, 85.

25. On the tree of life in Genesis, see Heard, "Tree of Life in Genesis." Michaela Bauks argues that, in Gen. 2:9, the tree of life "defines the tree of knowledge more precisely" ("Erkenntnis und Leben in Genesis 2–3," 23). Her appeal to an explicative *waw* here lacks justification in my view.

26. Machinist, "How Gods Die," 214.

27. K. Schmid, "Loss of Immortality?," 62.

28. K. Schmid, "Loss of Immortality?," 62–63.

29. Bauks, "Erkenntnis und Leben in Genesis 2–3," 22.

perception regarding the tree (3:6). In consequence of her taking fruit from it, giving some to her husband with her, and their eating, Yhwh Elohim observes that the human "has become like one of us." David M. Carr refers in this context to "the vulnerability of the divine-human boundary."[30] This vulnerability God acknowledges by foreclosing access to the tree of life and thus foreclosing the possibility of godlike endless life . . . beyond Eden.

Above, I asked whether God's announcement to the man (that he was dust and that he would return to dust) amounted to a sanction—a judgment and punishment—and whether God created the first humans immortal. The text permits no certainty regarding the questions, as the disagreement between Schmid and Machinist illustrates (see notes 26 and 27). Interpreters have noted, of course, that Yhwh Elohim's initial instruction to the man does not prohibit eating from the tree of life (Gen. 2:16–17). Foreclosure of access to it follows the couple's eating from the tree of knowledge and their consequent becoming "like God." Immortality, then, was an initial possibility if not a reality. Christopher Heard's conclusion seems judicious: "Until they ate from the tree of knowledge and were subsequently expelled from the garden, their deaths were only possible, not certain. . . . After the humans ate from the tree of knowledge the deity expelled them from the garden, after which, due to lack of access to the tree of life, their deaths were assured, though not immediate."[31]

Robert P. Gordon writes in this regard of "humanity's forfeiture through its first parents of the chance of immortality."[32] If it was a chance forfeited, it was also one they evidently did not seek, at least not before eating from the tree of knowledge and perhaps learning then what *death*—as in "you will surely die"—meant. Death had not been part of Eden's environment, so far as the narrative discloses. Following their transgression, neither were the first humans part of Eden's environment.

Back to the Soil

God formed the man from the soil—from the dust of the soil—to till the soil, to be a farmer, but then God displaced him to care for the garden and enjoy its fruit. As I maintained in the previous chapter, God reverses this displacement, re-placing the man on the soil as a farmer: "Yhwh expelled [the man] from the garden to till the soil from which he had been taken" (Gen. 3:23)—from which Yhwh Elohim had taken him. Of course, the conditions of the soil and

30. Carr, *Reading the Fractures of Genesis*, 237.
31. Heard, "Tree of Life in Genesis," 94–95.
32. Gordon, "Ethics of Eden," 31.

of farming it have both become grievous (vv. 17–19); life for the woman has become even more severe (v. 16). Moreover, following Yhwh Elohim's initial questioning of the man (v. 11), relations between the woman—Eve, named in 3:20—and Adam (first named in 4:25) have become strained. Upon first seeing Eve, Adam had said, "Finally, bone of my bone, flesh of my flesh" (2:23). Now, he distinguishes himself from her: "The woman you [God] gave me, she gave me . . ." (3:12). The rivalry displayed in the serpent's conversation with Eve now infects the relationship between Eve and Adam—the *'adam* who was formed from the *'adamah*, the soil, soil that God curses (3:17) and from which the first couple's firstborn, Cain, brings an offering. His younger brother, Abel, offers some of the fat from the firstborn of his sheep (4:3–4), fat that will become essential in Israel's sacrificial rites—for example, "as a soothing aroma to Yhwh" (Lev. 17:6).[33]

When the story beyond the Eden narrative moves into the mundane world, the name of God moves from Yhwh Elohim to Yhwh alone, as the Eden narrative itself had moved from Elohim in Genesis 1 to Yhwh Elohim. Still, the story that begins in Genesis 4 exhibits parallels with what preceded in Genesis 3. Desire, for example, affecting the relationship between Eve and Adam has echoes with sin's desire for Cain in Genesis 4:7.[34] Yhwh's questions for Cain—"Where is Abel, your brother?" (4:9) and "What have you done?" (4:10)—echo the questions Yhwh Elohim posed to Adam and Eve: "Where are you?" (3:9)" and "What is this you have done?" (3:13). Yhwh Elohim cursed the *'adamah*—the soil—because of Adam (*ha'adam*, 3:17), and Yhwh declares Cain to be cursed from the *'adamah*, which has received his murdered brother's blood (4:11). The man's—*ha'adam*'s—hardship in wresting food from the *'adamah* as its tiller (3:18) becomes even worse for Cain, "a tiller of the *'adamah*" (4:2), who leaves the soil to wander (4:12) and to build a city. Cain's city-building and the cultural inventions of his descendants—animal husbandry, musical instruments, metallurgy (4:20–22)—proceed without any divine involvement, and with neither endorsement nor censure.[35] Neither farming nor the soil is again mentioned until Noah's birth and naming are taken as hope for relief from the soil's curse in 5:29: the verse interprets the name "Noah" as deriving from the word *nacham*, meaning "to provide comfort or rest." Farming (or viniculture) resumed with

33. Whether God's preference for Abel's animal offering reflects this sacrificial context or that God disregarded Cain's vegetable offering because it came from the cursed soil (as I claim in my essay "Creation and Peace") cannot be known.

34. Mark Smith comments extensively on the theme of desire in the Eden narrative in *Genesis of Good and Evil*, 55–63 and elsewhere.

35. Despite claims such as those of Robert S. Kawashima in "Violence and the City."

Noah, "a man of the soil" (9:20), after the flood had covered the earth—after violence had filled the earth (6:11).

The Flood of Violence

In the narrative framework of Genesis 1–11, Cain's act of fratricide signifies an innovation. God had threatened death in Genesis 2, and the serpent had denied the threat in Genesis 3, but neither the threat nor its denial made death's agent explicit. In the new world of Genesis 4, no longer refracted by the dislocating effect of Eden's placement "to the east" and at the source of four rivers (2:8, 10–14),[36] death's agent bears the name Cain. God had promised to protect Cain, who worried about retribution for murdering Abel, by imposing sevenfold vengeance on anyone who killed Cain (4:15). Lamech, Cain's descendant who killed a young man for striking him, lamented that his own death in retribution for his act of killing would be avenged seventy-sevenfold (vv. 23–24). Here the implication is clear that the agents of both retribution and vengeance would be human, as were Cain's and Lamech's acts of lethal violence.

In Genesis 1, God commands and occupies the narrative. In Genesis 2 and 3, the narrative includes independent agents besides God. In Genesis 4, humans take full control of the narrative: following God's dialogue with Cain (4:6–16), God no longer speaks or acts—save for God "taking Enoch" (5:24)—an inactive silence amounting to many hundreds of years, according to the linear genealogy in Genesis 5. Humans also assert command over life and death, beginning with Cain and culminating with Lamech. To Lamech, God makes no promise protecting him from retribution, as God had done for Cain. As Victor P. Hamilton writes, "Unlike his ancestor several generations earlier who felt the desperate need of divine protection, Lamech feels he is his own security."[37] And with the calculus of vengeance God explained to Cain multiplied by Lamech, the world is filled with violence.

"The earth had become corrupt in God's [Elohim's] sight; the earth was filled with violence [*chamas*]" (Gen. 6:11).[38] The Hebrew word for "to corrupt" or "to become corrupted" (*shachat*) occurs five times in Genesis 6:11–13, 17. The earth had become corrupt, or ruined, as the narrator reports (6:11). God

36. As I argued in chap. 2 under the heading "An Excursus on Eden's Four Rivers."

37. Hamilton, *Book of Genesis, Chapters 1–17*, 241.

38. On the subject of violence in the early chapters of Genesis, see Schüle, "And Behold, It Was Very Good," esp. 107–11.

saw that the earth had become corrupt because "all flesh" had corrupted its way upon the earth (6:12). God decided to bring all flesh to an end, because "the earth is filled with violence because of them." God says, "I am going to destroy [corrupt] the earth" (6:13) "and destroy [corrupt] all flesh in which there is the breath of life" (6:17). The Hebrew words for "violence" and for "corrupting" or "destroying" (*chamas* and *shachat*) occur for the first time in 6:11. This corrupting violence—the corruption that *is* violence—has left the earth corrupted, ruined (6:12). God determines to meet and does meet this corruption with massive, cosmic violence: a flood, destructive of all life, that amounts to the "un-creation" of God's own creation, to borrow Joseph Blenkinsopp's term.[39] God's determination to bring about such an un-creation comes as a narrative consequence of God's regret—Yhwh's repentance (*wayyinnachem*)—and grief at having made humankind in the first place (6:6–7), since human wickedness had become pervasive in the earth, and everything people planned was only evil all the time (6:5).

Seeing how humanity has corrupted itself and the earth, God regrets (repents of) the entire creation project and intends to return the earth to the conditions that Genesis 1:2 describes: before the waters were separated and gathered so that the dry-land earth could appear (1:7–9) and before creatures of any kind existed (6:7). With the flood, God performs a comprehensive act of un-creation, scouring the earth of life and submerging it. But, as in 2:17, where God's sanction—"on the day you eat from it, you will surely die"—does not issue in the immediate extinction of Adam and Eve, so here God makes exceptions: Noah, his immediate family, and two of every kind of animal (or seven, if they are ceremonially clean) will survive the flood, and they will do so aboard an ark (6:18–21; 7:1–9). Not coincidentally, while an ark (*tebah*) bears Noah's family and the animals above the flood after God regrets—repents of—creating life because of human violence and wickedness, an ark (*tebah*) also bears to safety the infant Moses (Exod. 2:3–5), through whose entreaties God repents of a decision to annihilate Israel (32:14). Only in reference to Noah and Moses does the Old Testament mention an ark—a floating box (*tebah*). In Exodus 32–34, Israel's existence is at stake, and in Genesis 6, all of human and animal life is imperiled. God's repentance and pardon (*salach*) spare Israel (Exod. 34:9). In Genesis 6 and 7, God determines to continue the human project, even while acknowledging—at the flood's end—that the human heart's inclination to evil is ingrained (Gen. 8:21; cf. 6:5).[40]

39. Blenkinsopp, *Creation, Un-creation, Re-creation*.

40. R. W. L. Moberly reflects exegetically and theologically on these two verses and, in particular, the "evil thought" clause in Gen. 8:21 in "On Interpreting the Mind of God."

An Illicit Union and Cosmic Threat: Genesis 6:1–4

Human life will continue, but its extent will be limited. Already in Genesis 3, as mentioned above, Yhwh Elohim took measures to prevent the first couple from eating from the tree of life and living endlessly. Those measures followed Yhwh Elohim's recognition that the couple had already breached the divine-human, Creator-creature distinction by eating from the tree of the knowledge of good and bad and becoming "like one of us" (Gen. 3:22). As Richard J. Clifford summarizes, unending life or "immortality is one of the two great differences between heavenly and earthly beings, the other being super-knowledge. Genesis 2–3 . . . told how human beings were not meant to have the knowledge proper to heavenly beings, and its conclusion alluded to, but did not develop, the other great distinction between gods and humans—living forever (Gen. 3:22)."[41]

Situated between the story of rivalry and escalating violence in Genesis 4 and the flood narrative beginning in 6:5, Genesis 6:1–4 develops further the matter of life without limits. The actors in this unique passage are "the sons of God," encountered elsewhere in Job 1:6, 2:1, 38:7, and in Psalm 29:1 and 89:7[89:6].[42] These beings, evidently possessing immortality themselves, observe that "the daughters of mortals" are "good" (*tob*, Gen. 6:2), echoing Elohim's observation that light is good in 1:4,[43] and they marry those "whom they chose." The Hebrew text of 6:3 is difficult, but it seems clear enough that, in response to this illicit union of divine and human beings, Yhwh imposes a limit of 120 years on human life. The divine immortals—"the sons of God"—will not be permitted to bequeath, through sexual union, their gift of endless life to mortals.[44] In this way, God preserves a crucial distinction between divine and human and prevents the fundamental order of creation—"the demarcation of divine and human spheres"[45]—from coming into crisis.

God pronounces no judgment on the actors in Genesis 6:1–4.[46] Judgment on the women would be entirely misplaced, since they are not described as actors, except perhaps in giving birth to the beings described in verse 4. But neither do the actions of "the sons of God" receive any comment, despite the

41. Clifford, "Divine Assembly in Genesis 1–11," 1:281–82.

42. Here I also draw from material in my earlier essay "Creation and Peace," 153–55.

43. The Hebrew syntax of the clauses in Gen. 6:2 and 1:4 is identical. See Joüon, #157d.

44. Clifford, "Divine Assembly in Genesis 1–11," 1:288. The narrative does not make explicit whether such a bequeathal was in fact the intention of the divine immortals.

45. Bührer, "Göttersöhne und Menschentöchter," 508.

46. Bührer, "Göttersöhne und Menschentöchter," 508. So also Bachmann, "Illicit Male Desire or Illicit Female Seduction." Contrast Claus Westermann, who writes of "*people's* attempt to transcend the human by means of raising humanity's status . . . by union with the divine" (*Genesis 1–11*, 382, italics mine). But the text ascribes no such attempt at all to the "people."

threat those actions pose. Neither God nor the narrator announces, much less *de*nounces, a motive, beyond the observation on the part of "the sons of God" that the women are, in an undefined way, "good." As I mentioned above, their observation echoes God's own about light in 1:4—that it is good.

Observation—observation and assessment—plays a significant role in these early chapters of Genesis. Elohim, of course, repeatedly observes and assesses as good—and, finally, very good (Gen. 1:31)—the world of God's own creation. Eve, before she is named, observes that the tree of knowledge is good (3:6). "The sons of God" observe that the women are good. Unlike God's, the observation of the divine beings and of Eve is acquisitive: "She saw that it was good, and she took . . ." (3:6); they "saw they were good, and they took . . ." (6:2).

Typically, interpreters have understood Eve's act (and with her, Adam's) of eating from the fruit of the tree of knowledge as grasping at divinity. Gerhard von Rad, for example, writes that the couple was "wanting to be like God,"[47] and William P. Brown describes the couple as "grasping to *gain* power and wisdom."[48] The text itself does not support this view. As I pointed out above, the woman observes that the tree is nutritious, lovely, and good for gaining insight (Gen. 3:6). Becoming like God, or the gods, is no part of her expressed motivation, and what we are warranted in saying about her motivation does not exceed what the text tells us. The only part of the serpent's counsel she evidently attends to is the part about not dying, since she does eat. Even so, and regardless of the presence or absence of any intention, the couple's transgression—their trespasses—brings creation under threat and leads to their banishment from Eden. And regardless of any intention on the part of "the sons of God," their action—their "blurring of the divine-human boundary"[49]—threatens "cosmic disorder"[50] and leads to the imposition of a humanizing limit on the span of human life.

Despite any problems translating Genesis 6:3—specifically, the words *yadon* and *beshaggam*—the verse makes clear enough that embodied human existence is life in the *flesh*, distinct from God's divine *spirit*, which is life-giving. "Flesh"—*basar*—is mentioned before Genesis 6 only in the context of Yhwh Elohim's building the woman from the side or rib of the man, the surgical wound closed with flesh (2:21). In the verses immediately following, "flesh" assumes a less literal, more significant meaning: the man recognizes the woman as bone of his bone and flesh of his flesh, and the two become one flesh (2:23–24). Being

47. Von Rad, *Genesis*, 101–2.
48. Brown, *Seven Pillars of Creation*, 88.
49. Carr, *Reading the Fractures of Genesis*, 239.
50. Clifford, "Divine Assembly in Genesis 1–11," 1:288.

flesh, in the context of Genesis 2, is part of what defines humanity—a defining quality, an attribute that the couple shares as humans and as their identity: one flesh. Within the narrative of Genesis 2, the couple has no need to be reminded that they are not *spirit*. Circumstances reflected in Isaiah 31 differ dramatically: there Judah's leaders require an emphatic reminder of the contrast between humans and God, flesh and spirit (v. 3). In both Genesis 2 and Isaiah 31, flesh serves as a metaphor for humanity and dependence—dependence on God the Creator for existence itself (in Genesis) and dependence on God the Creator in facing the threat of defeat and subjection (in Isaiah). This dependence on God and the weakness that accompanies being flesh deprive humanity of neither freedom nor initiative but are the foundations of both.[51]

In Genesis 6:1–4, God disarms the threat that "the sons of God" pose by uniting with mortal women. The divine beings do not receive punishment from God for crossing this "significant boundary . . . between the divine and the human,"[52] and neither, of course, do the women. Limiting mortal life span to 120 years may seem to be punishment in light of the centuries-long lives of the forebears listed in Genesis 5, several of whom lived more than nine hundred years, with Noah himself living five hundred years before becoming the father of children who, with him, survive the flood (v. 32). Nevertheless, 120 years amounts to a generous allotment to Noah's postdiluvian descendants like us.

In Genesis 2 and 3, becoming like God with respect to the knowledge of good and bad constitutes a threat to creation. In response, Yhwh Elohim prevents a subsequent threat by denying access to the tree of life, lest the first couple gain (or preserve) endless life. In Genesis 6, God acts to prevent the illicit union of divine beings and mortal ones from becoming a grant of divine immortality to mortal flesh. In these episodes, God acts in defense of creation. Creation, in these early chapters of Genesis, is defined by the unprecedented and unconditioned action of God creating, making, dividing, forming, building, calling into being, and summoning into production a world—a creation—that is constitutively and beneficently *not* God and not (a) god, thus with the possibility of a nonrivalrous relation to God.

The Tower of Babel: Genesis 11:1–9

Yet one more threat to creation—the possibility of unlimited human power—remains. After the flood, and thus after God's determination never again to perform such an act of un-creation (Gen. 9:11, 15), humans flourish and spread

51. See Bauckham, *God and the Crisis of Freedom*.
52. Klaiber, *Schöpfung*, 129.

abroad, according to Genesis 10. But Genesis 11 describes humanity united in place, in language, and in purpose.

The united people journey "eastward"—*miqqedem*—the term Genesis 2:8 used to locate or *dis*locate Eden.[53] They come to a valley or plain in the land of Shinar. According to Genesis 10:10, Shinar includes Babylon, and Zechariah 5:11 and Daniel 1:2 make explicit the association of Shinar with Babylon, which in Hebrew is *babel*. From its beginning, then, with its mention of Shinar, Genesis 11 evokes Babylon, that great devastator (Ps. 137:8) and oppressor (Isa. 14:4) whom God promises to destroy (Jer. 51:11, 37).

In Shinar, the united people collaborate on a construction project: "Come, let us make bricks . . . , and let us build a city and tower reaching to the sky"—or "whose top is in the heavens [*wero'sho bashamayim*]" (Gen. 11:3–4). This is not a project designed to "reach unto heaven" (KJV) as if to invade God's domain, efforts that Isaiah 14:12–14 describes (cf. Ezek. 28:1–2). But the story in Genesis 11 may well be mocking the royal pretensions of kings like the one Isaiah 14 mocks. Andrew Giorgetti has made this argument, showing that the building project in Genesis 11:1–9 resembles Mesopotamian building accounts; he quotes Hayim Tadmor as describing these as "official documents of self-praise."[54] Giorgetti argues that 11:1–9 mocks those hubristic Mesopotamian accounts. And he points to details in Genesis that echo those in the Mesopotamian documents, including the emphasis on "the whole earth" and "one people" and the intention not to be scattered (v. 4) but "to make a name for ourselves."[55] Victor Hurowitz, in a comprehensive study of building accounts in Mesopotamia—a study on which Giorgetti draws—lists the structural elements of those accounts, which typically include molding bricks, as in Genesis 11:3.[56] The account of King Gudea (2164–2144 BCE) building the temple Eninnu for the deity Ningirsu in Lagash (near the confluence of the Tigris and Euphrates) describes it as "grown up 'twixt heaven and earth" and "like a great mountain abutting heaven,"[57] language anticipating that of Genesis 11:4. Gudea's is an example of "official documents of self-praise."[58] It seems reasonable to entertain the notion that Genesis 11:1–9 mocks such accounts and the hubris of royal ideologies they reflect.

53. See chap. 2 under the heading "An Excursus on Eden's Four Rivers."

54. Giorgetti, "'Mock Building Account,'" 3.

55. On this point, see also Rose, "Nochmals."

56. Hurowitz, *I Have Built You an Exalted House*; see, e.g., p. 69.

57. Hurowitz, *I Have Built You an Exalted House*, 66. Hurowitz quotes another text: "Brickwork rising out of the shining plain . . . city grown (high) between heaven and earth" (67), language analogous to that in Gen. 11:3–4. It would be nonsense, of course, to suppose that Gen. 11 reflects a Hebrew author's reading of the actual late-third-millennium Gudea cylinders.

58. Giorgetti, "'Mock Building Account,'" 3, quoting Tadmor, "History and Ideology," 14.

Certainly, God disapproves of the project of united and univocal humanity gathering on Shinar's plain, a project—like the inventions named in Genesis 4:20–22—that neither seeks nor receives divine authorization. Yhwh, a stranger to the Shinar developments, "went down to see what these mortals [sons of men] had built" (11:5). The report was ominous. As I wrote in an earlier essay, "Here, in Genesis 11, God intrudes into the narrative and into a world from which he is alienated. And God offers an interpretation of the human project at Shinar. Because they have one language and the same vocabulary, this city and tower, this construction project, is but the beginning of their projects. They will not be prevented from doing anything they may propose to do (11:6)."[59]

The vocabulary and syntax of Genesis 11:6—"This is the beginning of their doings. Now, nothing they plan to do will be thwarted"—have their counterparts in Job 42:2: "I know that you [Yhwh] can do anything. No purpose of yours will be thwarted."[60] Job's confession follows God the Creator's thunderous speeches "out of the whirlwind" (38:1). A chastened, powerless Job demurs from being God's rival (42:3). In Genesis 11:6, after going down to inspect the Shinar project, Yhwh recognizes the God-rivaling power of the people.

The people's "*come, let us* make bricks" (Gen. 11:3) now has its counterpart in Yhwh's "*come, let us* go down"[61]—a second descent, after verse 5—"and mix up their language, so that they will not understand one another's speech" (v. 7). By this measure, Yhwh scatters the people over the whole earth, and they abandon the project (v. 8). The city earns the name Babel (v. 9). The name is a wordplay on *balal*, which means "to mix up" or "to confuse," and a mocking reference to Babylon (*babel* in Hebrew). Babylon, that proud, arrogant city (Jer. 50:29; 51:41; cf. Isa. 13:19), serves as a symbol of the hubris that the tower of Babel story mocks in a narrative portraying God's defense of creation against a final universal human threat: the God-rivaling power of all humanity on Shinar's plain.

In Genesis 3, the threat was God-rivaling human knowledge and God-rivaling immortality, which threatens again in Genesis 6, with the illicit union of divine and human beings. In Genesis 4 and 6, men assert themselves over life and death, the earth becomes full of violence, and God nearly un-creates the world with a flood. Finally, in Genesis 11, God-rivaling power threatens creation, and God responds.[62] In none of these instances do the people involved—from

59. Ollenburger, "Creation and Peace," 156.

60. Ollenburger, "Creation and Peace," 156. See Giorgetti, "'Mock Building Account,'" 15–16.

61. In both instances, *habah* (an imperative) precedes a cohortative.

62. Theodore Hiebert takes as the text's principal issue the people's desire to remain one people in one place with one language and culture ("Tower of Babel"). For an earlier, similar view, see Wolde, *Words Become Worlds*, 84–109. William P. Brown's claim seems closer to the mark: "Multiculturalism

Adam and Eve to all humanity at Shinar—express the intention to rival God or betray envy of God, and every last thing we know of their motivations we can know only from the biblical text. Even so, the threats their decisions and actions pose do not depend on their motivations, whatever these may be. The people may not recognize the threats they pose, but God does—and acts in defense of creation in Genesis 3–11.

The tower of Babel story concludes with Yhwh dispersing the people over all the earth (Gen. 11:9). This conclusion brings the story into harmony with Genesis 10, a segmented genealogy of geographical dispersion—the dispersion of Noah's sons among the nations; in other words, the dispersion of everyone (10:1). And it prepares for the genealogy that follows the tower of Babel story, a genealogy that concludes with Abram and Sarai, and a conclusion that moves the focus away from universal humanity, the subject of Genesis 1–11, to one man and one woman: one family, who will become Israel.

God's defense of creation in response to the serial threats narrated in these early chapters of Genesis produce if not peace then an armistice in the lethal rivalry between humanity and God. Even so, the possibility of threats and of fractured peace remain part of the world that God has brought into being. The *tohu wabohu* of Genesis 1:2 may recur as a threat (Jer. 4:23), and God's acknowledgment of the human heart's constitutively evil inclination sounds a baleful note (Gen. 8:21). Finally, God's response to the Babel project, divinely disturbing the peace of a united humanity at Shinar—mixing up languages and scattering humanity—creates the possibility of rival nations and thus of wars, possibilities realized on a grand scale in Israel's and the world's history. The work of God the Creator—*as* the Creator—does not end at Shinar. Or in Genesis.

is a divine check on collective pride as much as the divinely ordained age limit in the antediluvian period was intended to arrest the growth of heroic power (Gen. 6:1–4)." *Ethos of the Cosmos*, 184.

4

"In Primeval Days"

CREATION TEXTS BEFORE THE BIBLE

Creation stories, ancient and modern, can be found around the world. One contemporary creation story goes by the name "the Big Bang." A book by a respected author on the subject, James F. Trefil, bears the title *The Moment of Creation: Big Bang Physics from before the First Millisecond to the Present Universe*. What I am able to understand of the creation story that Trefil and other scientists tell is fascinating, and it is dramatic: what became our unimaginably expansive and complex universe derived from energy concentrated in a point tinier than an atom. But this creation story lacks an existential connection. It may explain the origin of the present universe from before the first millisecond, but it leaves entirely out of account the origin and constitution of the world of our people and our *place*—of our people's origin and place. Scientific descriptions of "creation"—I put the word in quotation marks because scientific accounts do not typically involve a creator—have as their subject the universe. They are, by definition, universal in scope. Creation stories from earlier times—and from modern storytellers unconstrained by astrophysics and enriched by tradition—offer more particular accounts, accounts that join the origin of the world with the origin of a people.

The phrase "in primeval days" opens a Sumerian creation text called *Gilgamesh, Enkidu, and the Underworld* described in Clifford, *Creation Accounts*, 23.

Ancient or traditional creation stories may tell of the world's origin and the creation of people within it but not of people in general, formed or brought into being by forces or god(s) in general. Rather, they tell the story of people of a particular place and of the particular deities who brought them and their world into existence. And not just existence in general but a particular kind of existence, defined both by place and by the character or structure of the world that stories of creation or origin themselves help to define. In the first three chapters of this book, I described something of how the stories of God the Creator—Elohim and Yhwh Elohim and Yhwh (Gen. 1–11)—serve to define the character and structure of the world in which Israel will live its history. It is also the case that ancient Israel lives that history in the context of—perhaps in the light or shadow of—earlier stories of creation and its gods. Below I will comment on three ancient texts from Mesopotamia, but I begin with a creation story both ancient and contemporary.

Hopi Origins and Hurúing Wuhti

The Hopi origin or creation story, or one form of it in Hopi tradition, involves the deity Hurúing Wuhti: "the deity of hard substances."[1] The Hopi are an Indigenous or Native American people living primarily on the Hopi Reservation, surrounded by the vastly larger Navajo Reservation, in northeastern Arizona. Though the Hopi live far from any ocean or significant body of water, Hopi tradition teaches that in the distant past all was water and that there was an ocean in the east and an ocean in the west. Also, there was a Hurúing Wuhti of the east and one of the west. Besides these two female deities, only the sun existed. The Hurúing Wuhti of the east and the one of the west cause dry land to appear, with waters receding to the east and to the west. The sun, in completing its course, then notices no life on the dry land. East and West Hurúing Wuhti then meet and agree to form a bird from clay—a wren; after they sing a song over it, the wren comes to life and goes in a vain search for life on the dry land. The East and West Hurúing Wuhti form many more birds from clay and give them life, and in the same way they form animals, the first woman, and, finally, the first man.

The Hopi creation tradition also incorporates episodes within historical memory. The Hurúing Wuhti of the east and of the west grant the humans language. Subsequently, Spider Woman—a deity revered among the Navajo—then

1. Voth, *Traditions of the Hopi*. Find this online at http://www.sacred-texts.com/nam/hopi/toth/.

forms Spaniards from clay, women and men, and teaches them Spanish. Eventually, the Spaniards become angry and come with guns against Hurúing Wuhti. She persuades them to lay down their guns so they can lift a stone. With their hands glued to the stone, she grinds their guns to powder. When the Spaniards agree to an equitable exchange of goods, she releases their hands.

This Hopi story is one of divinely arranged—imposed—disarmament and then justice and peace. It reflects and incorporates Hopi historical experience with Don Pedro de Tobar, who, under the command of the legendary explorer Francisco de Vásquez de Coronado, led the Spaniards into a violent confrontation with the Hopi.[2] But the Hopi story transforms that violent historical memory into a vision of comity and peace. The Hopi tradition also bears comparison with Genesis 1, with water in the beginning ("the deep" in Gen. 1:2), dry land appearing, and then creatures—including humans. In Genesis 2 and in the Hopi tradition, humans are formed from clay. All three "texts"—Genesis 1, Genesis 2, and the Hopi tradition—conclude with a vision of peace.

My description of the Hopi story depends on H. R. Voth's *Traditions of the Hopi*. Heinrich Richert Voth was an 1874 Mennonite immigrant from Russia to Kansas. A few years later, he moved to Oklahoma territory as a missionary among the Cheyenne and Arapaho. Already fluent in High and Low German (*Plautdietsch*) and in Russian and English, he learned the Cheyenne and related Arapaho languages. In 1892, he and Martha, his wife, moved to Oraibi, in Arizona, where they established a mission among the Hopi. Quickly learning the Hopi language, Voth began working as an untrained but increasingly expert ethnographer, sending reports, translations, and artifacts to the Field Columbian Museum—the Field Museum—in Chicago, which published multiple volumes of Voth's descriptions of Hopi life and rituals, ones that have formed much of what may count as public knowledge of the Hopi.

For the Hopi, some of what Voth published he should never have seen, much less made public, and for more than a century—beginning in his own lifetime—he has been a controversial figure, charged with fomenting a division within the Hopi people and desecrating sacred sites and traditions to feed public knowledge.[3] He neither sought nor realized financial gain or renown; he retired as a Mennonite minister in the remote village of Goltry, Oklahoma. But in the interest of finding out, insistently observing, and precisely documenting

2. James, *Indian Blankets and Their Makers*.

3. Documentation of the controversy is thorough in Whitely, *Orayvi Split*. Online: http://digitallibrary.amnh.org/bitstream/handle/2246/5954/A087%20part%202.pdf?sequence=10.

what was going on in Hopi stories and rituals, Voth, to whom I am related by marriage, violated and exploited the Hopi.

While the Hopi Tribe,[4] with its origin in antiquity, continues as a people able to insist on the integrity of their sacred objects, rituals, and traditions, the literary and other "remains" of ancient nations and empires—of people—in the Mediterranean and Persian Gulf regions lie scattered abroad in museums and libraries and private collections around the world, and especially in Western European institutions. In some instances, evidence makes it clear that the ancient texts were expected to be copied and disseminated broadly, as indeed happened.[5] But while the Hopi stories of creation and the creators Hurúing Wuhti and Spider Woman continue a tradition from antiquity to the present, the following accounts from Mesopotamia remained unknown for centuries, even in the places in Iraq where the clay tablets recording them were discovered and taken.

The Epic of Gilgamesh, Enuma Elish, and *Atrahasis*

In its issue of October 7, 2019, the *New Yorker* published an article that recounted the story of George Smith, of London, "who had left school at the age of fourteen and was employed as an engraver of banknotes"[6] but who was intrigued by artifacts held by the British Museum, including ones discovered in Iraq and brought to England. Over lunch hours, Smith studied at the museum, which eventually hired him to help decipher clay tablets from Iraq. By 1872, after a decade of work, Smith had translated an ancient tablet describing a universal flood that only one family had survived. What Smith translated turned out to be part of Tablet XI of *The Epic of Gilgamesh*.[7] The clay tablet Smith worked to translate had been discovered in Nineveh (at contemporary Mosul) in the ruins of the palace of the Assyrian king Ashurbanipal. Naturally, Smith and others assumed that the story of a universal flood he had deciphered was an echo of the Genesis flood story. A few years later, in 1876, Smith published part of a Babylonian creation story. This, too, he understood to be echoing Genesis. As was common in Smith's time, the book's title amounted to a summary of its contents: *The Chaldean Account of Genesis, Containing the Description of the Creation, the Fall of Man, the Deluge, the Tower of Babel, the Times of the*

4. "The Hopi Tribe: The Official Website," https://www.hopi-nsn.gov/.

5. E.g., the fragments of *Enuma Elish* discovered in Ashurbanipal's library. See https://www.britishmuseum.org/collection/object/W_K-9511.

6. Acocella, "How to Read 'Gilgamesh.'"

7. Acocella, "How to Read 'Gilgamesh.'"

Patriarchs, and Nimrod; Babylonian Fables, and Legends of the Gods; From the Cuneiform Inscriptions.[8]

Subsequent discoveries and scholarship proved Smith mistaken about Genesis as a source of *The Epic of Gilgamesh* or of the Babylonian creation story now known, from its opening words, as *Enuma Elish*, but Smith's achievement remains remarkable and consequential. He was not the first to decipher the cuneiform of texts from Mesopotamia; that began early in the nineteenth century. And Henry Rawlinson, Smith's predecessor and sponsor—Smith dedicated his *Chaldean Account of Genesis* to Rawlinson—had made progress in translating the cuneiform of the Behistun Inscription in Iran. But Smith's publications created a public sensation and contributed significantly to the emergence of comparative studies of the biblical texts in relation to this new "light from the east": in this case, from Mesopotamia.[9] These comparative studies, relating the biblical accounts to those from Mesopotamia, quickly became controversial. They produced what came to be called the *Babel-Bibel Streit*—the conflict over the relation of Babylon (i.e., texts from antiquity, especially from Mesopotamia) to the Bible. In 1921 Rudolf Kittel, complaining that it seemed everything in the Old Testament was to be understood with reference to—and had its source in—these recent discoveries, exclaimed that it was as if "*extra babylonem nulla salus*" (outside of Babylon there is no salvation), Kittel's sardonic twist on an ancient Christian confession that outside the church there is no salvation.[10]

In a similar vein, in his presidential address to the Society of Biblical Literature forty years after Kittel's comments were published, the eminent New Testament scholar Rabbi Samuel Sandmel complained about "parallelomania" in biblical scholarship. He defined it as "that extravagance among scholars which first overdoes the supposed similarity in passages and then proceeds to describe source and derivation as if implying literary connection flowing in an inevitable or predetermined direction."[11] Given his expertise in both rabbinic and New Testament literature, Sandmel was most concerned with—and irritated by—the undisciplined manner in which supposed parallels between New Testament and rabbinic texts were identified and their significance assumed.

Parallels or resemblances, significant or not, between biblical texts and contemporary and/or more ancient ones have been adduced in abundance. The third edition of *Ancient Near Eastern Texts Relating to the Old Testament*

8. According to https://www.gutenberg.org/files/60559/60559-h/60559-h.htm.

9. C. J. Ball discusses the fragments Smith translated in *Light from the East*.

10. Kittel, "Die Zukunft der alttestamentlichen Theologie," 96, quoted in Ollenburger, *Old Testament Theology*, 10.

11. Sandmel, "Parallelomania," 1.

(*ANET*), long a standard anthology in English of ancient texts from Anatolia (Turkey) to Egypt and from Syria to Persia (Iran), includes several hundred texts "relating to" the Old Testament. That imprecise way of putting it leaves helpfully undefined the way or ways in which a particular ancient text—*Enuma Elish*, for example—may bear, or even if it bears or should bear, on the interpretation of a biblical text (Gen. 1, for example). Neither *ANET* nor any other anthology, and no particular text demonstrably more ancient than the Bible, could *determine* the interpretation or the meaning of a biblical text or of some larger swath of the Bible. Biblical texts were read responsibly and with profit by Jews and Christians before Henry Rawlinson or George Smith read a syllable of cuneiform and before Thomas Young or Jean François Champollion understood a single hieroglyph on the Rosetta Stone.

Christopher B. Hays in the "Prolegomena" to his own anthology—*Hidden Riches: A Sourcebook for the Comparative Study of the Hebrew Bible and Ancient Near East*—quotes William W. Hallo's remark that the point of comparative study "is not to find the key to every biblical phenomenon in some ancient Near Eastern precedent, but rather to silhouette the biblical text against its wider literary and cultural environment."[12] My focus in this book has been on the biblical text itself, and in previous chapters I made few references to other ancient texts. But some features of the biblical text may come more sharply into view when read "against its wider literary and cultural environment"—depending in part on the reading conventions and commitments of particular interpretive communities, religious or academic or both.[13] In any case, the wider environment of Genesis includes both of the texts Smith had translated in part: *The Epic of Gilgamesh* and *Enuma Elish*, a Babylonian creation story. It includes other texts as well, texts unknown to Smith.

The Epic of Gilgamesh

The story of the flood and its comparability with the Bible's account most excited George Smith about *The Epic of Gilgamesh*, and it remains perhaps its most widely known feature. But *The Epic of Gilgamesh* is a rich piece of ancient literature apart from the flood story; not without reason is it called an epic. Gilgamesh, a king "two-thirds god and one-third human" (I, 48),[14] experiences

12. Hays, *Hidden Riches*, 35.

13. I count, for example, the Society of Biblical Literature, of which I have been a member since 1972, as an interpretive community, one that includes diverse and contradictory reading conventions and convictions; in some instances, these convictions are religious in nature.

14. *Epic of Gilgamesh*, 2. References in the text refer to tablets and lines in the epic. The standard edition of the epic may be dated to 1250 BCE according to Sparks, *Ancient Texts for the Study of the Hebrew Bible*, 275–78.

the joys of deep friendship and profound loss, learns "the benefits of civilization over savagery,"[15] and fears death and gains wisdom but not immortality, a theme that also figures in Genesis. Gilgamesh learns wisdom from the immortal survivor of the flood, Uta-napishti, who tells him of a plant in the sea that will restore his youth (XI, 283–90). Having secured the plant, Gilgamesh bathes in the cool water of a pool; as he bathes, a snake steals the plant (XI, 300–307). This loss and the death of his beloved friend, Enkidu, aid Gilgamesh's journey from proud youth to mature ruler—mature but remaining, as he was at the beginning, proud.

The Epic of Gilgamesh offers several points of comparison with Genesis: both involve a snake, immortality is mentioned, and both describe a flood. In *Gilgamesh*, Uta-napishti releases a dove, then a swallow, and finally a raven when the boat rests on the ground (XI, 142–56), while in Genesis, Noah releases first a raven and then a dove, twice (Gen. 8:7–11). These and other points of comparison often prove illuminating—in the way the background of a silhouette can be—and may, in surprising ways, enrich a reading of Genesis.[16] The epic does not offer much about creation, or about the god or gods who made the world, but when, in his quest for extended life, Gilgamesh meets Shiduri, the tavern-keeper, and asks her how to find Uta-napishti, she reminds him, "When the gods created mankind, death they dispensed to mankind, life they kept for themselves" (SI, 3.2–5).[17] Yhwh Elohim makes a similar reservation in Genesis 3:22–23, reaffirmed in 6:1–3, as I discussed earlier in chapter 3. Themes, motifs, and idioms in more ancient texts—including *Gilgamesh*—form part of the literary inventory available to scribes composing later texts, including Genesis.

Gilgamesh the man was king of Uruk (south of current Baghdad) "between 2800 and 2500" BCE.[18] References to and legends about him grew in the centuries following, and their influence spread widely. Indeed, Hans Ulrich Steymans has argued for the existence of "an unbroken oral tradition of stories about Gilgamesh in Canaan, Phoenicia, and Israel."[19] This cannot be finally proved, of course, but Steymans makes the case that the Gilgamesh tradition did have currency among cultures along the Mediterranean coast. That some form of it was known among the first readers of Genesis seems likely.

15. *Epic of Gilgamesh*, xiii.
16. See, e.g., Hamori, "Echoes of Gilgamesh in the Jacob Story."
17. Regarding this tablet, see *Epic of Gilgamesh*, 122–23.
18. Dalley, *Myths from Mesopotamia*, 40.
19. Steymans, "Gilgamesh und Genesis 1–9," 201.

Enuma Elish

If *Gilgamesh* offers minimal comparison with, if it narrowly "silhouettes," biblical texts that depict God the Creator, then "The Babylonian Epic of Creation"[20]—commonly known from its first words as *Enuma Elish*—would seem to provide a broader comparison. Indeed, Alexander Heidel, in the mid-twentieth century, titled his work on the epic *The Babylonian Genesis*. The title, in addition to being slightly hyperbolic (the book itself is a work of serious scholarship), doesn't capture the overriding purpose of the complex epic, which includes creation but does so in service of Marduk's elevation as Babylon's high god. As Andrea Seri writes, "When considered in its entirety, it becomes apparent that *Enuma Elish* was composed to justify the installation of Marduk as the head of the Mesopotamian pantheon by displacing the god Enlil. Although there is a consensus about the ultimate goal of the composition, it is unquestionable that the theme of creation—or better the recurrence of multiple creations—occupies a fundamental place in the poem."[21]

The first of the multiple creations Seri alludes to opens the epic, with the salt-water ocean personified as Tiamat mingling with Apsu, the fresh underground water. From their union, gods were begotten, not made, as Wilfred G. Lambert translates:

> When the heavens above did not exist,
> And earth beneath had not come into being—
> There was Apsu, the first in order, their begetter,
> And demiurge Tiamat, who gave birth to them all;
> They had mingled their waters together
> Before meadow-land had coalesced and reed-bed was to be found—
> When not one of the gods had been formed
> Or had come into being, when no destinies had been decreed,
> The gods were formed within them.[22]

Enuma Elish opens, then, with a theogony—an account of the genesis, the birth, the begetting of the gods.[23] The younger of these deities prove to be rambunctious and noisy. Their noise disturbs Apsu; despite Tiamat's objections, he plots to kill them. The god of wisdom, Ea, learns of the plot, casts a spell on Apsu,

20. Lambert, *Babylonian Creation Myths*, 1.
21. Seri, "Role of Creation in *Enuma Elish*," 4.
22. Lambert, *Babylonian Creation Myths*, 51.
23. In Lambert's translation, the older deities are the "begetters" of the younger ones. See *Enuma Elish*, I, line 128, in Lambert, *Babylonian Creation Myths*, 57.

and kills him. Ea then rules the fresh waters, but his murder of Apsu infuriates Tiamat. In her rage, she produces monstrous, demonic, chaotic deities, "bearing weapons that spare not, fearless in battle."[24] After Apsu's demise, Tiamat makes Qingu her consort and appoints him over the chaotic forces. She then determines that she will wage war against the gods who are her offspring. Learning of it, Ea and his fellow deities decide to fight Tiamat and her chaotic deities. Champion of the younger gods is Marduk, regarded as Ea's son.

Marduk achieves victory over Tiamat—over the Sea—whom he slays. As creator, Marduk then divides Tiamat's body, forming the heavens from one part and the earth from the other.[25] He also places the sun, moon, and stars in the heavens, establishing the calendar year, its months and days. The night he entrusts to the moon. A final act of creation remains. Marduk has a plan to relieve the gods of their labor; humans will serve this purpose. Ea proposes humans be formed from one of the gods, a guilty one. Qingu serves this purpose; Ea blames him for inciting Tiamat to warfare. From Qingu's divine blood humans are formed to relieve the gods. In gratitude, the gods build the city of Babylon and, within it, Marduk's temple, the Esagila. There Marduk rules the cosmos, whose order and peace he has established.

Marduk's separating the waters, placing the sun and moon and stars in their places and establishing the calendar year, and finally forming humans . . . all of these call to mind Genesis 1. To be sure, Elohim's mode of creation in Genesis 1 differs dramatically from that of Marduk in *Enuma Elish*. Does Genesis 1 respond to *Enuma Elish*? I will have more to say about this below. But for now, it will suffice to point out that Marduk was known to Old Testament prophets; he appears under the name or title Bel (meaning "lord") in Isaiah 46:1, Jeremiah 50:2, 51:44, and also in Bel and the Dragon, among the additions to Daniel in the Deuterocanonical books.

Determining precisely when *Enuma Elish* was composed proves impossible, in part because its composition did not take place all at once. But on the authority of the leading scholar on the text, Lambert, it seems safe to conclude that a form of the epic resembling the one we can read was in place by 1000 BCE.[26] But *Enuma Elish*, while becoming the most familiar, was neither the only nor the first creation epic.

24. "Creation Epic," 62.

25. This division of Tiamat's body represents the severing of an original union of heaven and earth (Lambert, *Babylonian Creation Myths*, 170). This motif appears in other texts, including the Sumerian *Enki and Ninmah*. Clifford, *Creation Accounts*, 40.

26. Lambert surveys the evidence and the history of discussion in *Babylonian Creation Myths*, 439–44.

Atrahasis and the Great Flood

The name Atrahasis, meaning "surpassing wise," appears in *The Epic of Gilgamesh* as an epithet of the hero of the all-encompassing flood, Uta-napishti (XI, 197).[27] Atrahasis (or Atra-hasis) is the hero in the epic bearing his name, an epic whose earliest known tablets, themselves copies of earlier ones, are from the seventeenth century BCE.[28] The text first describes a crisis involving the older gods, the Anunnaki, and the younger ones, the Igigi, who are made to do all the work:

> When the gods instead of man
> Did the work, bore the loads,
> The gods' load was too great,
> The work too hard, the trouble too much,
> The great Anunnaki made the Igigi
> Carry the workload sevenfold.[29]

The Igigi, bent on war, threaten all-powerful Enlil/Ellil, leader among the higher gods, by surrounding his temple and announcing their complaints. Anu (sky god) and Ea/Enki (lord of the Apsu) prove sympathetic, and it is Ea who proposes a solution: since Belet-ili, the birth goddess, is present, she can create humans who will relieve the gods of their labor. Ea then proposes that a god be slaughtered, his blood mixed with clay:

> That god and man
> May be thoroughly mixed in the clay. (I.iv, 212–13)

An otherwise unknown deity, We-ila, is slaughtered. After Belet-ili completes her work of mixing divine blood with clay, she declares:

> I have removed your heavy work,
> I have imposed your toil on man. (I.v, 240–41)[30]

Thus was the first crisis resolved through an act of creation—the creation of humans.

27. *Epic of Gilgamesh*, 222.
28. Lambert and Millard, *Atra-Ḫasīs*, 23.
29. Dalley, *Myths from Mesopotamia*, 9. As Y. S. Chen says, "The entire story is largely presented in the form of crisis and resolution." *Primeval Flood Catastrophe*, 114.
30. Both quotations are from Lambert and Millard, *Atra-Ḫasīs*, 59. In this context the birth goddess is called, without irony, Mami.

In several respects, *Atrahasis* as here summarized resembles the later *Enuma Elish*, particularly regarding the purpose for which humans were created: to relieve the gods of their labor. In both stories, this creation requires the death of a god. But while in *Enuma Elish* Qingu is slain because of his guilt, in *Atrahasis*, We-ila, "who had personality,"[31] is slaughtered seemingly at random, without any suggestion of crime or guilt on his part. Also different from *Enuma Elish*, in *Atrahasis*, lethal combat between the ranks of gods is avoided. But the most significant difference between *Enuma Elish* and *Atrahasis* is the latter's continuation of the story. *Enuma Elish* finds its goal in the supreme elevation of Marduk and the gift of his city, Babylon. *Atrahasis* continues the human story, which presents a second crisis.

While humans do relieve the gods of their labor, they prove to be surprisingly fecund. Their reproduction and their semidivinity—humans were created of divine blood and clay—result in overpopulation. Moreover, while in *Enuma Elish* the younger gods are rambunctious and noisy, in *Atrahasis*, raucous people, and too many of them, disturb Enlil's rest: "The country was as noisy as a bellowing bull" (I.vii, 240).[32]

Enlil seeks to reduce human population by introducing disease, then drought, and then famine. In each instance, Ea finds a way to avoid the destruction of humans in response to the urgings of a very wise man, Atrahasis. In his final effort, Enlil decides to bring a flood, admonishing Ea not to warn Atrahasis of what is coming. Ea goes to Atrahasis's house but in obedience to Enlil does not speak to Atrahasis; instead, he addresses the wall and the reed hut, issuing instructions to build a roofed boat. Of course, Atrahasis hears Ea's instructions and builds a boat. He gathers his family on it, along with every species of animal, and then seals the door with bitumen. All others perish, but those aboard the boat survive.

At the flood's end, after seven days and nights, Atrahasis offers a sacrifice. The starving gods, who have been deprived of the nourishment people's sacrifices provide, gather around "like flies" (III.v, 35).[33] People, it turns out, prove necessary to the gods. As Yhwh does in Genesis 8:21, the gods concede that humanity has to be endured—but in the case of *Atrahasis*, with limitations. Enlil, recovered from his anger over Ea's trickery, asks Ea and Nintu to limit the human population. They do so by determining that a class of women, priests, will not bear children; permitting demons to snatch infants from their mothers' laps; and introducing mortality: humans will die.

31. Lambert and Millard, *Atra-Ḫasīs*, 59.
32. Dalley, *Myths from Mesopotamia*, 18.
33. Dalley, *Myths from Mesopotamia*, 26.

Peace among humans is not a concern in *Atrahasis*, despite the poignant and persistent efforts of Ea and the compassion of Nintu (= Belet-ili/Mami) on their behalf (III.iv, 4–13). But the gods enjoy peace among themselves, with human capacity to disturb that peace restrained. Order, cosmic and mundane, has been achieved.

Points of comparison between *Atrahasis* and Genesis are transparent: humans created from clay and divine blood in *Atrahasis* and one human formed from clay (dust) and enlivened by divine breath in Genesis (2:7); humans created in *Atrahasis* to relieve gods of their labor, and in Genesis to be a farmer and then a gardener (and then a farmer again); a flood in which animals and one family are saved in a boat; birds sent from the boat to seek dry ground (a dove, a swallow, and, finally, a raven in *Atrahasis*; a raven and then a dove, twice, in Genesis); after the flood, the gods gather like flies to the aroma of sacrifice in *Atrahasis*, whereas Yhwh smells the soothing aroma of Noah's sacrifice (8:21).[34] Beyond these details, however, lie broader points of comparison.

Like *Gilgamesh* and Genesis, *Atrahasis* reflects a concern with human mortality or immortality. While in *Gilgamesh* immortality stands as the object of a disappointed quest, in *Atrahasis*, mortality is imposed on humans. In Genesis, ambiguity attends the matter of immortality: whether the first couple enjoyed it originally and lost it or could have enjoyed it had they consumed fruit from the tree of life before eating from the tree of knowledge, or permutations of these possibilities. Intertwined with or supervening in the matter of (im)mortality is that of the relation—or the distinction—between divine and human. Above, I quoted Stephanie Dalley's translation of *Atrahasis*'s first line: "When the gods instead of man . . ." Lambert and Millard translate the line "When gods like men . . ."[35] But Helge S. Kvanvig disagrees, proposing that the line should be translated "When the gods were human . . ."[36] I am not competent to assess the competing translations. Regardless, Kvanvig's conclusion, that the story of *Atrahasis* involves "the interplay between gods and humankind . . . and the fusion of the divine and the human,"[37] has echoes in *Enuma Elish*, where either Marduk or Ea creates humankind from the blood of Qingu (VI, 33).[38] It has broader echoes as well, biblical ones.

34. Ellen van Wolde makes more sophisticated comparisons between *Atrahasis* (also *Gilgamesh*) and Genesis in *Words Become Worlds*, 190–99.

35. Lambert and Millard, *Atra-Ḫasīs*, 43.

36. Kvanvig, *Primeval History*, 39. Kvanvig's translation is not novel, as he demonstrates with a review of scholarship on the matter (39–43).

37. Kvanvig, *Primeval History*, 43.

38. Dalley says the text is ambiguous in line 33 about who created humankind, and the ambiguity may be intentional (*Myths from Mesopotamia*, 276). In *Enuma Elish*, at VI, 35, Ea is said to have been the creator of humankind.

As I showed in the two chapters preceding this one, the relation between God and humanity—and, crucially, their distinction—constitutes a major theme in Genesis 2–11. According to Genesis 1, Elohim created humankind—*'adam*, male and female—in the image and likeness of God to be God's royal representative within the (nonhuman) created order (vv. 26–28). This representative role, with humanity as the icon of God, distinguishes humans from other created things, including animals, but Genesis 1 envisions no possibility of confusion, competition, or rivalry between Creator and creature. Matters differ in Genesis 2 and 3. There Yhwh Elohim forms *'adam* from the dust of the soil and breathes the breath of life into his nostrils (cf. Ezek. 37:9). Bernard F. Batto comments, "Humankind had been animated with divine 'breath,' which is to say, humankind was similar to the deity in that it possessed divine spirit. The creator seemingly recognized the potential for confusion between divinity and humanity, which led to the deity forbidding the man and the woman access to the 'tree of knowledge' (wisdom)."[39]

Although claiming that humankind possessed divine spirit may overinterpret Genesis 2:7 (the breath of life also inspires animals in 7:22), Genesis 6:3 does say that Yhwh's spirit is somehow in *'adam*. And Batto is certainly right that the Creator recognizes the potential for—and then the reality of—"confusion between divinity and humanity." The narratives in Genesis 2–3 (the tree of knowledge and the tree of life); 6:1–4 (the sons of God and the daughters of mortals); and 11:1–9 (the tower of Babel) narrate this potential and then real confusion. In these narratives, divine-human confusion, or rivalry, occurs with respect to knowledge, (im)mortality, and power. God responds to these forms of confusion by imposing limits. In the end, after 11:1–9, the possibility of at least the latter two of those forms of divine-human, Creator-creature confusion is eliminated. The remainder of Genesis 11 traces the line of Noah, and thus of Adam (5:1), from his firstborn, Shem, to Abram, who marries Sarai and gives birth to Israel and its history. Kvanvig writes of *Atrahasis*, "The transition between the two ages"—antediluvian and postdiluvian—"does not come with the flood itself, but with the new order set for humankind after the flood. After the flood, humankind became mortal."[40] A reading of Genesis 2–11 could reach a similar conclusion. Humankind was obviously mortal prior to the flood in Genesis—Cain killed someone, as did Lamech. But beyond the flood, a new order was set for humankind after Genesis 11:1–9, an order that found its focus not in universal humanity but in one family. In 12:1–4, Yhwh says to Abram, "Go! . . . and Abram went"—to a far country.

39. Batto, *In the Beginning*, 47.
40. Kvanvig, *Primeval History*, 39.

Genesis versus Mesopotamia?

Scholars have sometimes interpreted the early chapters of Genesis as a polemic directed against Mesopotamian accounts and theologies, as Gerhard Hasel did many years ago, in considering "the cosmology" of Genesis 1.[41] Hasel and others have pointed to a linguistic connection between the Tiamat of *Enuma Elish* and *tehom*—the deep—of Genesis 1:2 and other places in the Bible.[42] Of course, the deep of Genesis 1, menacing as it may be, does not beget gods. In the previous chapter, I cited Andrew Giorgetti's interpretation of 11:1–9 as mocking grandiose Mesopotamian building accounts.[43] When 1:26 speaks of "the image [*tselem*] and likeness [*demut*] of God" to describe *'adam*—all humankind—it is difficult not to consider this a response to royal theologies in which these words—words meaning "image" and "likeness"—are used of the king, as in an Aramaic text from Tell el-Fakhariyeh. Similarly, *The Epic of Tukulti-Ninurta* declares the king to be "the eternal image of (*tsalam*) Enlil."[44] This is not to claim that any of the Bible's authors had read any of these texts. In the case of *Enuma Elish* and perhaps *Atrahasis*, however, the possibility cannot be ruled out that they knew some version or summary of both. Texts recounting these stories, or parts of them, were copied, edited, and transmitted over generations. Hesiod's *Theogony*, from the late eighth century BCE, may reflect influence from *Enuma Elish* (see *Theogony* 104–38). Berossus, a third-century BCE Babylonian priest, knew the material in *Enuma Elish* and *Atrahasis*, and Damascius, a sixth-century CE philosopher, summarized *Enuma Elish*.[45] The broad influence of these texts over centuries does not prove that the Bible's authors knew them, though Alan Lenzi has argued that Proverbs 8:22–31 responds directly, critically, to *Enuma Elish*.[46] It is safe to say, at least, that *Enuma Elish*, *Atrahasis*, and other texts from Mesopotamia—and from Egypt—contributed to the literary and intellectual milieu in which the Bible's language about creation and God the Creator took shape.[47]

41. Hasel, "Significance of the Cosmology in Genesis 1." Similarly, Kenton L. Sparks argues that some of the Pentateuch's narrative and ritual texts imitate Mesopotamian texts—specifically, *Enuma Elish*—for polemical purposes. "*Enūma Elish* and Priestly Mimesis."

42. E.g., Mark Smith, *Priestly Vision of Genesis 1*, 18.

43. Giorgetti, "'Mock Building Account.'"

44. The quotation is of Callender in *Adam in Myth and History*, 27, adapting the translation of Peter Machinist in "Literature as Politics." Callender, *Adam in Myth and History*, 27. The Tell el-Fakhariyeh inscription is from the ninth century BCE, *The Epic of Tukulti-Ninurta* from the thirteenth.

45. I rely here on Heidel, *Babylonian Genesis*, 75–81.

46. Lenzi, "Proverbs 8:22–31." See also Sparks, "*Enūma Elish* and Priestly Mimesis."

47. For Egypt, see Quirke, "Creation Stories in Ancient Egypt."

On one matter—the matter of violence—interpreters tend to draw a sharp contrast between "the glorification of violence" in *Enuma Elish* and its complete absence in Genesis 1.[48] After rehearsing the violence done to Tiamat in *Enuma Elish*, Catherine Keller claims, "The text of Genesis 1 does not even hint at violence."[49] Keller valorizes *tehom* and what she calls the chaos of Genesis 1:2 against "a brutal *order*" that its conquest would impose.[50] But the *tohu wabohu*—the emptiness and void—and the darkness over *tehom* do not describe some font of life or "the womb of the world."[51] They describe a situation of absence (what is darkness but the absence of light?) and the impossibility of life. The darkness, the deep, and the waters here pose no active opposition to the Creator. Rather, they stand inert, in the way of creation: a static nothingness. To employ the nouns *tohu* and *bohu*—the latter a rhyming affirmation of the former—in relation to some "thing" is to say that *absence* defines it.[52] Elohim interrupts and intervenes against this uncreated stasis in an act of sovereign power.

> Elohim's self-directed "Let there be light" marks and constitutes an imperious, imperial—a sovereign—and violent interruption in, and intervention against, the . . . static totality that Elohim proceeds to invade. Darkness is not annihilated, and neither the deep nor the waters. But the anti-creation stasis, the life-inhibiting silence, that they constituted, along with the earth's then being *tohu wabohu*—all of this is conquered by the violence of speech. As Rolf Rendtorff put it: "The 'weapon' God employs in Gen 1 is the word."[53]

The violence of God's verbal weapon in Genesis 1 brought about the initial possibility of a world that supports the whole range of life that the first chapter of Genesis goes on to describe—a whole world of life at peace. This was not the violence of Marduk killing Tiamat and rending her body in two "like a fish for drying" to form earth and sky (*Enuma Elish*, IV, 137).[54] This was Elohim's sovereign imposition of light into darkness and then their forced separation (*hibdil*) from and then relation to each other (Gen. 1:3–5). Genesis 1 differs from *Enuma Elish* in these and many other respects. Even so, J. Richard Middleton's

48. Middleton, *Liberating Image*, 163. See also his "Created in the Image of a Violent God?"
49. Keller, "'Be This Fish,'" 18.
50. Keller, "'Be This Fish,'" 18 (italics original).
51. Keller, "'Be This Fish,'" 18.
52. See my discussion of "out of nothing" at the beginning of chap. 2.
53. Ollenburger, "Creation and Violence," 33. The embedded quotation is from Rendtorff, *Theologie des Alten Testaments*, 2:8.
54. Dalley, *Myths from Mesopotamia*, 255.

characterization of *Enuma Elish* as glorifying violence seems wide of the mark.[55] What the epic celebrates, as Dalley writes, is that "the forces of evil and chaos are overcome, whereupon the present order of the universe can be established, with its religious centres, its divisions of time, its celestial bodies moving according to proper rules, and with mankind invented to serve the gods." The epic glorifies not violence but Marduk, whom it credits with overcoming "the forces of evil and chaos."[56] Genesis 1 glorifies Elohim, who speaks light into what is, for all practical purposes, nothing and creates life-sustaining order—creating the divisions of time, mandating roles for the celestial bodies, and establishing the premises for the institution of the Sabbath—at a time before time, when no life was possible.

While God made a place for darkness, the deep, and the waters in this creative ordering—in this intervention into *tohu* and *bohu*—both the deep (*tehom*) and the waters retain the capacity to stand in the way of God's creative (and redemptive) intentions, even if to do so would be in vain:

> The waters saw you, O God,
> the waters saw you and writhed.
> Even the deeps trembled. (Ps. 77:17[77:16])

Here the waters and the deeps (the plural of *tehom*) exercise a form of agency, even if it amounts only to their being terrified upon the approach of God. Other biblical texts portray a more active agency and opposition, together with God's aggressive response—a response in defense of creation sometimes depicted in violent imagery. We will examine some of those texts next.

The Hopi of Arizona told the story of a divinely imposed disarmament. Is it possible that, as the Hopi did with their historical memory, a biblical tradition portraying divine violence—on behalf of creation—can be appropriated to a vision of peace? Or that it can power such a vision? Those questions biblical scholarship itself lacks the capacity to answer.

55. Middleton, *Liberating Image*, 163.
56. Dalley, *Myths from Mesopotamia*, 228.

5

"Who Is the King of Glory?"

GOD THE CREATOR IN THE PSALMS

One summer afternoon in 1977, after several hours studying Aramaic grammar, I rewarded myself with a movie, which at that time meant going to a theater. I remember nothing about the motion picture I saw that day, not even its title. But I do remember the occasion, because the theater showed a lengthy preview (a "trailer," in today's parlance) of another movie to appear later that year. It was called *Star Wars*. I felt sorry for those involved with the movie, because I was certain that *Star Wars* would be a colossal flop. My prediction fell just wide of the mark.

Perhaps the massive and continuing appeal of *Star Wars* has something to do with the simplicity of its plot. It portrays a life-and-death struggle between good and evil, with characters lining up unambiguously on one side or the other—except, initially, for the romantic mercenary played by Harrison Ford, who is redeemed from his amoral adventurism by the self-sacrificing courage and commitment of his newfound friends. Of course, Hollywood has explored that plotline countless times, but in *Star Wars*, the drama is played out in the stars. The struggle is cosmic; it is a struggle for cosmic order between the totalitarian forces of tyranny and repression, on the one hand, and those of liberty, freedom, and humanity, on the other. The forces of evil have their embodiment in the ominous Darth Vader, while the monkish Obi-Wan "Ben" Kenobi serves as priest of the good. Evil has as its ultimate weapon of destruction the Death Star, while Ben Kenobi has "the Force." There are always alternatives to violence, Ben Kenobi says. But the struggle in *Star Wars* remains violent. It is also primeval. It took place, we are told, in a galaxy long ago and far away. We could imagine ourselves living here and now as the beneficiaries of that mythic, primeval, and cosmic struggle between the powers of good and evil, a struggle that produced the peace we could enjoy, should we preserve it.

Star Wars is a kind of creation myth, and biblically alert viewers may recognize in it echoes from the Bible.[1] I aim in this chapter to explore, in the Psalms, some "voices" that *Star Wars* may echo but without further reference to *Star Wars*. The focus here will be on God the Creator in the Psalms, some of which describe poetically God's action in primordial and sometimes historical struggle against hostile powers. Patrick D. Miller has written that "*poetry is the natural language of creation*."[2] It should not be surprising, then, that the Psalms speak so often and so richly, and lyrically, of God the Creator.

The (Hostile) Power of Water

The first three chapters of this book discussed Genesis 1–11, or passages within those chapters. In Genesis 1, of course, God's creation of the heavens and the earth proceeds in liturgical cadences through a progression of six days and does so without active opposition. In Genesis 2 and 3, and in 11:1–9, God acts in defense of creation against threats posed by godlike human knowledge, godlike human longevity, and godlike human power. Chapter 4 examined texts from Mesopotamia, including the Babylonian epic of creation, *Enuma Elish*. In that epic, Marduk's creation of the world and of people follows a lethal struggle among the gods in which Marduk slays Tiamat—the salt-water ocean and his mother—and from her body forms the sky and the earth. I mentioned that comparisons between Genesis 1 and *Enuma Elish* often draw absolute contrasts between the violence in the latter and its absence in the former. Differences between the Babylonian epic and Genesis 1 are plentiful and obvious. But I issued a caution against passing too lightly over 1:2–3.

1. While its title is sensational, Conrad Flynn's brief popular essay "What Star Wars Stole from the Bible" offers examples.

2. P. Miller, "Poetry of Creation," 95 (italics original).

In the second verse of Genesis 1, we have a hint, perhaps a vestige, of something more troubling, more menacing, more foreboding. Genesis 1:2 does not describe this "something more," merely naming it as *tohu wabohu*, a no-thing, featuring darkness, the deep, and the waters. Then the chapter moves on with its litany of creation. But if we pause over that verse, we may ask if the word God then spoke, in verse 3 and in the verses that follow, was perhaps spoken *against* something—against something that is named only in verse 2 and then left behind. Not only the second verse of Genesis 1 but other Old Testament texts as well provoke this question. In these other texts God's word is spoken—God takes action—against something. God speaks and acts against something hostile to creation: forces that threaten or destroy the arrangements of the world as God intends them, forces thus inimical to peace. Creation, in these texts, means the defeat or the disarmament—the pacification—of those forces. And those forces, in the Psalms and elsewhere in the Bible (reminiscent of Gen. 1:2), are the personifications of water, as in *Enuma Elish*, where Marduk fought against Tiamat, the Sea. In Psalm 74:13, God achieves victory over the Sea—that is, over *water*.

My family hails from western Oklahoma, in the Panhandle, where water is a scarce resource. My mother grew up near the Beaver River, which is a wide stretch of sand with a bridge across it; sometimes, after a rain, a stream cuts a bed through the sand. Janice, my wife, grew up in western Kansas, close by the Arkansas River. In the mountains of Colorado, the Arkansas River provides white-water recreation. By the time it reaches Garden City, Kansas, the river has gone underground; the riverbed amounts to another stretch of sand. Mark Twain (allegedly) said that he once fell into a California river and got all dusty; he could have written the same about some rivers in Oklahoma. The Cimarron River, near where I grew up, was a river with precious little water in it. But then came the summer of 1957. In Okeene, where I lived with my parents, it rained . . . and rained, days and nights on end. Muddy creeks that meandered through pastures became raging rivers, far outside their banks, carrying away buildings, fences, and farm animals. Families who may have forgotten that they lived near a stream were rescued by boat from the second stories of their farmhouses. And all of these streams emptied into the Cimarron River, which grew to be three miles wide. My father and I drove to Salt Creek, one of the Cimarron's tributaries. Salt Creek was normally discernible mainly by a trail of tall grass that wound its way from west to east between a set of chalky hills, and by a narrow wooden bridge that crossed it. Now the bridge was gone, swept away by a crashing, roiling torrent frightening in its noise and fury. I had never seen or heard such raw, unrestrained power.

I suppose people in the ancient world also experienced torrential rains and floods—saw meandering streams turn into raging rivers that destroyed homes and farms, witnessed the sea turn from a placid mirror into a raging monster that crushed ships like toys and wrecked harbors. It is possible, in other words, to experience water as a hostile power. In these terms, it is not so surprising that Psalm 74 describes creation as God's victory over water. But more than the experience of floods and rough seas lies behind this text. Here is my translation of verses 13–15:

> It was you who shattered by your might (the) Sea;
> you smashed the heads of the dragon on the waters.
> It was you who crushed the heads of Leviathan;
> you gave him as food to wild animals.
> It was you who split spring and stream.
> It was you who dried up perpetually flowing rivers.[3]

I will comment further on Psalm 74 below, explaining also the awkward English of my translation. But here notice the psalm's confession that God used the instrument of God's own power or might to shatter (*porarta*) Sea. Some translations and commentaries have God dividing the sea, as in Exodus 14:21, which reports that "the sea" was divided or split (*baqa*ʿ, the verb used in Ps. 74:15 before "spring and stream") and that dry ground provided the Hebrews' escape from Pharaoh's pursuing army.[4] An association of God's action against the sea with the exodus from Egypt—and even with a new exodus—will become explicit later in this chapter and in the next. But in Psalm 74, "Sea" does not refer simply to a body of water: it is paired with the dragon and with Leviathan. "Sea," in Psalm 74, unlike *tehom*—the deep—in Genesis 1:2, does not simply stand as an obstacle in the way; it represents, rather, along with the other aquatic forces named in Psalm 74:13–15, a hostile power to which God responds with head-crushing force. The Sea's personification in this psalm is intensified or concentrated in the sea monster Leviathan.

3. I am drawing from my essay "Creation and Violence," 28. With Joüon, #136b, I understand the plural *tanninim* in v. 13b as intensive: "dragon."

4. Frank-Lothar Hossfeld and Erich Zenger, in *Psalms 2*, draw Psalm 74 into the context of the exodus from Egypt (248–49), as did J. J. Stewart Perowne in 1878 (*Book of Psalms*, 2:29) and the Targum centuries before them (cf. my "Creation and Violence," 29–30). Robert Alter translates v. 13 "You shattered the sea-god with Your strength" (*Book of Psalms*, 259). Mitchell Dahood also argues for "shattered" instead of "divided" in *Psalms III*, 205. The LXX has *suntripsas*, meaning "shattered" or "crushed."

Leviathan appears also in Psalm 104, twice in Job, and once in Isaiah. But that sea creature has a history that precedes its appearance in the Bible. It appears in texts from Ugarit, written between 1400 and 1200 BCE in a Northwest Semitic language closely related to Hebrew and Aramaic but predating both—a language named, sensibly enough, Ugaritic.

The Goddess against "Sea"

For millennia before 1928, no one had seen a Ugaritic text. While Hittite and Egyptian texts mentioned Ugarit, no one since antiquity knew its location. Ugarit's discovery was accidental. A farmer near the Mediterranean coast, in what is now Syria, heard his plow strike something hard. He and some friends returned in the evening, removed several stones, and discovered both a tomb and much pottery. A report of this discovery made its way to the archaeologists René Dussaud and Charles Virolleaud—the region was at that time administered by France under a United Nations mandate—and excavations soon began, under the direction of Claude F.-A. Schaeffer, at the larger site of Tell Ras Shamra, a few hundred meters inland. Excavations at the site eventually produced a library of texts, in several languages, and uncovered a city of considerable size and, at one time, importance: Ugarit.[5]

The cuneiform tablets from Ugarit include a wide variety of genres, including ritual and mythological texts. One cycle of stories among the mythological texts involves a struggle among the gods, chief over whom is El, whose consort is Athirat, the mother goddess. In this cycle of stories, the storm god, Baal,[6] struggles against other, rival deities in order to establish his kingship in the divine assembly and take his royal seat in his palace. Baal's principal enemies are Yam (Sea—paired poetically with Nahar [River]) and Mot (Death); Yam and Mot are El's favorites.[7] Defending Baal are his allies, Anat and her twin or alter ego, Astarte; they form a matched pair of warrior deities. Yam attacks Baal first, but Anat comes to his rescue. Mot then battles Baal and defeats him, swallowing him down his gullet: Baal descends down the gaping maw of death. El finally intervenes, through the agency of another deity—Shapash, the sun goddess—who brings Baal back from the underworld.[8]

This story, too, is a creation story. It does not describe the origin of the world,

5. Bordreuil and Pardee, *Manual of Ugaritic*, 1; Yon, *City of Ugarit*, 8–9.

6. See Greenfield, "Hadad," 378.

7. In some instances, *Ba'al* (meaning "lord") is an epithet of the storm god Hadad. Greenfield, "Hadad," 378.

8. Robert D. Miller II discusses the Baal Cycle and issues of its interpretation in *Dragon, the Mountain, and the Nations*, 95–107.

of course. But the struggle among the Canaanite deities is at the same time a battle for cosmic order. The survival, or revival, and eventual triumph of Baal achieve or maintain the proper order of the world, including both its political order and the order of the natural world. Baal fights, or other deities fight on his and their behalf, against the forces of chaos (Yam) and death (Mot), which, should they prevail, would unhinge the world. As Robert D. Miller II writes, "When Baal is victorious, the result for the world . . . is bread in place of dust, peace (*shlm*), and tranquility or love (*arbdd*)."[9]

Psalm 74: Creation contra Leviathan

I rehearse the preceding story because the names of four of the Canaanite deities or personified powers I just mentioned appear as Hebrew terms in Psalm 74 (El, the common Semitic word for God, appears in v. 8). Moreover, in the Canaanite myth, Baal and Anat are said to have killed the Sea-Dragon and the sea monster, Leviathan. Anat says, for example:

> Did I not strike El's beloved, Yam [Sea]?
> Did I not finish off Nahar [River] the great god?
> Did I not muzzle the Dragon . . . ?
> I have struck the twisting serpent,
> The coiled one of seven heads. (*KTU* 1.3 iii.38–41; cf. 1.5 i.1–4 re: Baal)

These personifications of the hostile Sea also appear in Psalm 74. Indeed, all of these Canaanite deities and powers appear, one way or another, in the Old Testament, including the two warrior goddesses. One of Israel's judges was named Shamgar ben Anat—Shamgar the son of Anat (Judg. 3:31; 5:6)[10]—and the city of Anathoth, Jeremiah's home, bore her name (Jer. 1:1). King Solomon worshiped the goddess Astarte (1 Kings 11:5). He built her a shrine, which remained until King Josiah destroyed it some centuries later (2 Kings 23:12). The deities of Ugarit or their personified powers appear variously in the Bible, as the following table illustrates. Ugaritic names are followed by their transliterated Hebrew spellings and their English translations.[11]

9. R. Miller, *Dragon, the Mountain, and the Nations*, 98–99. The italicized words are unvocalized Ugaritic terms. *Shlm*, of course, is a cognate of Hebrew *shalom*.

10. Spronk, "Shamgar ben Anat."

11. At Ugaritic, Mot seems to be less than a full deity—the texts do not list him as receiving sacrifices, as is the case with Yam, who is included in the divine assembly and receives sacrifices (*KTU* 1.148.9); even so, Mot is called "divine Mot" (*ilm mt*; e.g., *KTU* 1.5 i.14).

Deities and Powers at Ugarit

Ugaritic Name	Hebrew (Biblical) Version	English Translation
'El	'El	God
Ba'lu	Ba'al	Lord
'Anat	'Anath	'Anat
'Athtarte	'Ashtoreth	'Astarte
Yammu	Yam	Sea
Naharu	Nahar	River
Mutu	Mot	Death
Shapash	Shemesh	Sun
Tunnan	Tannin	Sea monster / dragon
Litan/Lotan	Livyatan	Leviathan

Psalm 74 and other Old Testament texts reflect their historical and cultural contexts, of course, and are at the same time an integral part of that context, helping to shape and transmit it.[12] Certain themes and motifs, images and names, with their proximate origins in fifteenth- to thirteenth-century Ugarit, find expression in the Psalms but, among other biblical texts, also in Isaiah and Daniel, the Old Testament's latest book, composed—"published"—eleven centuries after Ugarit ceased to exist.[13] The author of no Old Testament book or text was reading a Ugaritic clay tablet inscribed with cuneiform. It remains the case even so that, in this instance, Psalm 74:13–15 exhibits striking similarities to Ugaritic texts. And it employs the language of violent battle against the Sea, the dragon, and Leviathan to describe the primordial work of God the Creator, appealing to God to act as Creator once again.

In its structure the psalm is a communal lament, responding to Babylon's destruction of the temple (Ps. 74:1–11).[14] The opening questions "Why, O God, have you rejected us forever? Why does your anger smoke against the flock of your pasture?" (v. 1) have their complement in the questions of verses 10 and 11: "How long, O God, will the adversary scoff, and the enemy revile your name forever? Why do you hold back your hand, even your right hand enclosed in your bosom?"[15] A confession of trust follows the complaint: "Yet God is my king from of old [*miqqedem*], / Working salvation in the midst of the earth" (v. 12).

12. James Anderson, *Monotheism and Yahweh's Appropriation of Baal*, 92–93.
13. Daniel will be one of the subjects of chap. 9.
14. Hossfeld and Zenger provide details of structure and dating in *Psalms 2*, 241–44.
15. Psalm 74:11b is difficult, as a glance at different translations will confirm. The LXX has "Why do you keep your hand in your bosom to the end [or completely]?" while the Targum has

The confession continues through verse 17 and includes the memory of God's primordial battle against the Sea and its attendant aquatic powers. That this confession of trust describes God the Creator, active primordially in bringing about the ordered world, verses 16 and 17 make explicit:

> Yours is the day and also the night;
> you established the luminary [moon] and the sun.
> You fixed the bounds of the earth.
> Summer and winter—you formed them.

The implication is clear that in defeating the watery forces of chaos, God was creating the world in which God reigned as King on Zion, the divine dwelling place (v. 2).

Some scholars have denied that texts like Psalm 74 speak of God creating, because (for example) these texts have something other than creation as their governing concern, and *something* already existed, even if it was Leviathan. Dennis J. McCarthy argued, decades ago, that what we have in these biblical texts "is scarcely creation in any technical sense since it does not touch at all on the absolute beginnings of our world."[16] On McCarthy's definition, and as he wrote, it would be improper to speak of Genesis 2–11 as having to do with creation.[17] In that case, the definition would require revision. McCarthy, an Old Testament scholar of sterling reputation and a Jesuit intimately familiar with and respectful of the church's teaching on creation, warned against the imposition of the doctrine of *creatio ex nihilo*—creation out of nothing—on the interpretation of biblical texts.[18] Yet his insistence on the "technical sense" of creation as "the absolute beginnings of our world" is a dogmatic definition. In what other realm of discourse do we use "creation" in that absolute sense, perhaps excepting the Big Bang? Artistic creation employs the materials at hand, even if they are ruins. No one would deny—certainly, no one *should* deny—that Pablo Picasso's *Bull's Head* (1942), which he formed by welding together a bicycle seat and handlebars, is an artistic creation and something Picasso created.[19] He

"Take your hand from within your bosom and destroy the trouble," which agrees more closely with the MT.

16. McCarthy, "'Creation' Motifs," 79.

17. McCarthy, "'Creation' Motifs," 76. Why McCarthy excluded Gen. 1 is unclear to me.

18. McCarthy, "'Creation' Motifs," 75. See also my comments at the beginning of chap. 2 in this book.

19. "*Bull's Head* is a found object artwork by Pablo Picasso, created in 1942 from seat and handlebars of a bicycle." "*Bull's Head*, 1942 by Pablo Picasso," Pablo Picasso, https://www.pablopicasso.org/bull-head.jsp.

created neither the seat nor the handlebars, nor the bicycle of which they were a part, but *Bull's Head* was his creation. While the psalmist in Psalm 74 may not deny the possibility that God created the Sea and Leviathan, he (the psalm is attributed to Asaph) affirms that God created a defined, bounded world of day and night, sun and moon, summer and winter—and that this world is God's.

My translation of Psalm 74:13–17 above emphasizes the psalm's repeated use of the pronoun "you," which reflects its emphatic use in the Hebrew text, as if to say, "You yourself, and no other, shattered or split the Sea. . . . You yourself, and no other, crushed the heads of Leviathan" (vv. 13–14). This work, which God and no other did primordially, the psalm urges God to perform once more. The forces of Babylon have proved to be forces of chaos, and they have left chaos in their wake. Babylon desecrated and destroyed the sanctuary on Zion, God's dwelling (vv. 2–3, 7). This calls into question the power of God—God as King (v. 12)—a question that Zion's apparent destruction put in sharp relief. Further, the destruction of Jerusalem raised the specter of God's faithlessness in failing to care for the poor and oppressed (vv. 19–21). In this context, the psalm, rather than urging God to act again as Creator, implores God to "attend to the covenant!" (v. 20). Psalm 74 does not elaborate on this covenant or specify its content. Psalm 89 does both.

Psalm 89: Creation and God's Anointed

Psalm 89 combines praise and lament. It rehearses God's acts of creation and God's promises regarding David and his dynasty, promises that historical experience has called into question and contradicted.[20] Following introductory references to God's enduring faithfulness, the psalm quotes God (without explicit attribution) as saying:

> I made a covenant with my chosen one;
> I have sworn to my servant David:
> Forever I will establish your progeny,
> and I will build your throne for all generations. (89:4–5[89:3–4])[21]

The psalm's use of *build* here is unusual. We would expect to read that God swore to *establish* David's throne, as with David's progeny, or to secure it forever. But the use of the term *build* (*banah*) in verse 5[4] ties the promise of David's forever dynasty to God's ever-enduring faithfulness in verse 3[2], which says

20. On the complicated question of Ps. 89's genre, see Hossfeld and Zenger, *Psalms 2*, 403–5.

21. Psalm 74 refers to God as Elohim, while Ps. 89 uses Yhwh. Nothing of importance or interest attaches to this difference for our purposes, so far as I can tell.

that God's faithfulness (*chesed*, NRSV: "steadfast love") is "built" forever. The ever-enduring security of David's throne, then, is grounded in the eternal assurance of God's faithfulness. Second, the same term, *build*, ties the beginning of Psalm 89 to the narrative in 2 Samuel 7 in which David's desire to build a house—a permanent shrine—for God is initially endorsed, then rescinded, and transformed into a promise that God would build a house, a royal dynasty, for David. Psalm 89 solemnizes that promise as a covenant grounded in and guaranteed by the faithfulness of God the Creator.

Before Psalm 89 returns to the subject of David in verses 21–39[20–38], it praises God's incomparability among "the holy ones" and "the sons of God" (vv. 7–10[6–9]), then celebrates God's rule over the sea (vv. 10–13[9–12]). "The assembly of the holy ones" (v. 7[6]) refers to the divine beings, the council that surrounds God, and the same holds true for "the sons of God" (v. 8[7]), who were mentioned in Genesis 6:2. Here in Psalm 89, as in 29:1 (cf. Job 1:6; 2:1), they are, as Hans-Joachim Kraus puts it, "ministering spirits in the heavenly world."[22] The demonstration of God's incomparability then takes the form of divine action reminiscent of Psalm 74.

> You [Yhwh] rule the surging of the sea;
> when its waves rise, you calm them.
> You smashed Rahab like a dead body.
> With your strong right arm you scattered your enemies.
> (89:11–12[89:10–11])

The sea here lacks the clear personification it had in Psalm 74:13–14, but it does receive embodiment in the mythic monster Rahab.[23] Frank-Lothar Hossfeld and Erich Zenger take Rahab here as "a metaphor for Egypt."[24] Rahab's association with Egypt is clear in Psalm 87:4, which pairs Rahab with Babylon, and in Isaiah 30:7, where it serves as part of an epithet for Egypt. Isaiah 51:9, like Psalm 74:13–15, implores God to act in the present as God had done in the past, "in ancient generations," hewing Rahab in pieces and piercing the dragon. This ancient, primordial divine act Isaiah 51 then links to the exodus from Egypt and the crossing of the sea: God "dried the sea, the waters of the great deep [*tehom*]," so that "the redeemed" had a way to cross (v. 10). Isaiah's linking Rahab with

22. Kraus, *Psalms 1–59*, 348.

23. On Ps. 89:10–13, see R. Miller, *Dragon, the Mountain, and the Nations*, 178–80. The name of the prostitute Rahab (*rachab*) in Jericho who hid Israelite spies is unrelated to *rahab*, the sea monster.

24. Hossfeld and Zenger, *Psalms 2*, 409.

Israel's crossing the sea in the exodus does not reduce Rahab to a metaphor for Egypt. To the contrary, Isaiah draws Israel's exodus from Egypt and crossing the sea into the realm of God's acts as Creator against personified aquatic powers. Rahab in Isaiah 51 and in Psalm 89 has the same profile as Leviathan in Psalm 74, a profile Job 26:12 expresses clearly: "By [God's] power he stilled the Sea; by his understanding he smashed Rahab."[25]

God's crushing the heads of Leviathan and smashing Rahab were acts of creation. They established God's claim of ownership of the world. In Psalm 89, echoing Psalm 74, God's primordial conquest of Rahab/Leviathan entails God's ownership of the heavens and the earth, *because* God "founded [*yasad*] them and all that is in them" (89:12[89:11]). Psalm 24 makes the same claim:

> The earth is Yhwh's and everything in it;
> the world [*tebel*] and all its inhabitants,
> because he founded [*yasad*] it on the seas
> and established it on the rivers. (vv. 1–2)

By virtue of God's *foundational* act of creation, achieved in Psalms 74 and 89 through conquest of hostile watery powers, the heavens and the earth—in other words, everything—exist within the sphere of what belongs to God. In Psalms 24:1–2, 74:16, and 89:12[89:11], God's creation of the world establishes God's ownership of the world. Psalm 95:5 expresses the same connection between creation and ownership: "His is the sea, for he made it; and the land, which his hands formed" (NJPS).[26] And in God's sovereign freedom as Creator of the world and all within it, God chose David and made a covenant with him (89:3–5[89:2–4]).[27]

God's covenant with David in Psalm 89 fits within a discussion of God the Creator because that covenant has its foundation and guarantee in God's acts of creation. In the structure of the psalm, God's covenant with David precedes both the affirmation of God's incomparability and God's calming the sea and smashing Rahab. And the instruments of those creating acts—God's hand(s) and right arm—will sustain and protect David (v. 22–24[21–23]). Finally, in a dramatic extension of the kind of royal theology Psalm 72 expresses, God will place the king's hand on the sea and his right arm on the rivers. Psalm

25. Further on Rahab, see Spronk, "Rahab."

26. Martin Metzger describes the relationship between God's creating something and its being God's possession in "Eigentumsdeklaration und Schöpfungsaussage," esp. 38–46.

27. Timo Veijola has argued that Ps. 89 refers not to an individual or to the Davidic dynasty but to the community. His seminal work is *Verheissung in der Krise*. Marcel Krusche provides a compelling counterargument in "Collective Anointed?"

89, through verse 38[37], thus declares David to be God's viceroy in the suppression of hostile powers and on behalf of the order God has brought about. What Gerlinde Baumann has written in relation to Psalm 74 applies to Psalm 89 as well: "It is an everlasting duty of the divine to care for world order. The *Chaoskampf* is the mythical means of speaking about this."[28]

I have not previously used the term *Chaoskampf*, or "Combat Myth"—the deity's battle against chaos; that is, powers hostile to the deity and the created order—although I described above such a battle among the deities in the Ugaritic Baal Cycle. Some scholars have denied that the Old Testament provides examples of a *Chaoskampf*, even in Psalms 74 and 89.[29] Neither the details nor any potential results of the scholarly debate need concern us here. It remains the case that both of these psalms describe God having brought about or sustained the habitable and beneficial order of the world by acting fiercely against aquatic powers hostile or inimical to it.

Both Psalm 74 and Psalm 89 describe God's creative acts as happening in the past (74:12; 89:10–13[89:9–12]). Psalm 74 recalls those acts in circumstances that call on God to exercise again the "duty of the divine to care for world order," since the world has become disastrously disordered. Psalm 89 opens with a celebration of God's covenant with David, celebrates God's rule over the sea and smashing of Rahab, praises God's faithfulness, then expansively—over many verses—rehearses God's enduring promises to David, solemnized in a covenant (v. 29[28]) guaranteeing that David's throne, and his successors on it, will endure forever—like the sun and the moon (vv. 37–38[36–37]). The remainder of Psalm 89 points out not only that no son of David sits on David's throne but that there remains neither throne nor kingdom. The psalm makes the complaint unmistakably clear to God:

> You have repudiated your covenant with your servant.
> You have defiled his crown on the ground. (v. 40[39])
>
> You have brought to an end his splendor,
> and his throne you have thrown to the ground. (v. 45[44])

Just as Psalm 89:11–12[89:10–11] emphatically credits God with establishing governance over the sea and smashing Rahab, so verses 39–46[38–45] emphatically accuse God of breaking covenant and being faithless to God's own

28. Baumann, "Psalm 74," 101.
29. Bernard F. Batto makes the case for the presence of a *Chaoskampf* in the Bible against arguments to the contrary in "*Kampf* and *Chaos*."

promises. The psalm has God the Creator in mind here, expressly so in a bit of Qoheleth-like wisdom: "Why did you create [*bara'*] all people for emptiness?" (v. 48[47]). With this existential question, the psalm broadens despair over God's apparent faithlessness—"How long, O Lord? Will you hide yourself forever?" (v. 47[46] NRSV)—to question why God bothered to create all of humankind (*kol-bene-'adam*).

Psalm 77 and a Way through the Sea

Psalm 89 asks God, "Will you hide yourself forever?" (v. 47[46] NRSV), while Psalm 77 asks, "Will the Lord reject forever?" (v. 8[7]). The voice in Psalm 77 is that of one deeply troubled ("my soul refuses to be comforted," v. 3[2] NRSV), troubled because God's *chesed*—God's faithfulness or steadfast love—seems to have ended (v. 9[8]). In these straits, the author of Psalm 77 turns to memories of God's acts in the distant past, as did the authors of Psalms 74 and 89. "I consider former days, years long past" (77:6[77:5]), "and I will call to mind the Lord's ancient acts" (v. 12[11]). Those ancient, recollected acts involved neither Leviathan nor Rahab, but they did involve the sea.

The final section of Psalm 77 consists of a hymn, comprising verses 14–21[13–20]. The hymn opens with praise of God's incomparable greatness (v. 14[13]) and power, which God demonstrated by redeeming "the sons of Jacob and Joseph" (v. 16[15]).[30] The hymn's conclusion, in verse 21[20], credits God with leading Israel "like a flock by the hand of Moses and Aaron" (NRSV). Verses 14–16[13–15] and 21[20] envelop verses 17–20[16–19], which make evident—crucially, in verse 20[19]: "Your way was in the sea, and your path in the mighty waters"—that God's redeeming and leading Israel was through the sea, in the exodus. The imagery of Psalm 77:17–20[77:16–19] draws from the same ancient inventory as Psalms 74 and 89. So while Psalm 77 certainly employs verses 17–20[16–19] to evoke the exodus and the passage of liberated Israel through the sea, verse 20[19] depicts God—not the people—passing through the sea and its mighty waters. The memory of God's primordial battle against hostile powers plays a part in Psalm 77, but absent here is God's crushing or smashing or otherwise destroying or forcibly disempowering the sea and the mighty waters and the deeps. Simply—or powerfully—the perception of God's presence puts those powers to flight (v. 17[16]).[31]

Psalm 77, like Psalms 74 and 89, *remembers* God's primordial acts against hostile powers, and remembers them by way of appealing to God to act once

30. On the unique pairing of Jacob and Joseph, see Hossfeld and Zenger, *Psalms 2*, 279.
31. B. Weber, "'They Saw You, the Waters,'" 115–17.

more in disastrous circumstances whose repair would require God acting again as if against the Sea and River and the dragon, Leviathan, or Rahab. Psalm 77 joins this memory of God's primordial acts with the historical memory of the exodus. As Beat Weber concludes, regarding Psalm 77, "One can discern a differentiation between . . . the ordering of the cosmos and the salvation of Israel—but there is no attempt to separate the two."[32] In other words, God the Creator acted primordially, acted historically, and will act—so the psalms pray—in the calamitous present. None of these psalms offers or contains an account of the absolute beginning of all that is. But they do indeed invoke the memory of God acting as Creator—thus in creation—and they express the hope that God will act as Creator once more.

While Psalms 74 and 89 portray God's conquest of Sea, Leviathan, the dragon, and Rahab—hostile aquatic powers—a number of other psalms either depict or assume God's acts of creation but without the imagery of conquest. For example, Psalm 24 declares,

> The earth is Yhwh's and all that is in it,
> the world and its inhabitants,
> for he founded it upon the seas,
> and on the rivers he established it. (vv. 1–2)

The Sea and Rivers appear in Psalm 74:13 and 15, but in Psalm 24:1–2 God wages no battle against them. Clearly, these verses speak of God's creating the world—founding it and establishing it,[33] and thus owning it. It may be that a divine conquest of the Sea and River lie somewhere in the background of the psalm—it does sing of "the King of glory, Yhwh, strong and mighty; Yhwh, mighty in battle" (v. 8). But it describes no battle. Similarly, Psalm 29 celebrates the awesome power of God, whose "voice is over the waters; the glorious God thunders over the mighty waters" (v. 3). And "Yhwh sits enthroned over the flood; Yhwh sits enthroned as king" (v. 10). Some scholars found this psalm so reminiscent of Ugaritic poetry that they considered it to be of "Canaanite" origin.[34] But again, while God's sitting enthroned over the flood (*mabul*) as King may have a forcible suppression of that flood as its background, the psalm describes no conflict or conquest.[35] Even in

32. B. Weber, "'They Saw You, the Waters,'" 123. Similarly, R. Miller, *Dragon, the Mountain, and the Nations*, 176–77.

33. On the verb *kun* with reference to God's acts of creation, see Jeremias, *Das Königtum Gottes in den Psalmen Israels*, 23.

34. Baruch Marglit addresses the matter critically in "Canaanite Origin of Psalm 29 Reconsidered."

35. The word *mabul* in Ps. 29:10 occurs in the Bible only here and in the Genesis flood narrative. In Ps. 29, it refers to the occasionally unruly subterranean waters.

Psalm 77, discussed above, God does not battle the sea and the mighty waters, even though they are hostile forces; they flee upon perceiving God's presence. This motif has echoes in the psalms that celebrate God's reign on Zion.

Songs of Zion

The power of God's presence as King and Creator comes to expression in Psalms 46, 48, and 76—Zion psalms that celebrate God's defensive presence on Zion as King and Creator.[36] Psalm 48 describes kings assembled in assault against Zion retreating in panic at the sight of it (v. 6[5]).[37] The psalm describes no battle against hostile powers or their personifications, but it does describe "the city of our God, God's holy mountain . . . Zion" as "at the heights of Zaphon" (v. 2). The word *tsaphon* means "north," so the NRSV and other translations translate as if Zion were "in the far north," which makes little sense. Zaphon is Baal's mountain,[38] and Psalm 48 announces Baal's dethronement and God's—Yhwh's—reign from and in defense of Zion. Psalm 46 also stresses God's dwelling on Zion—"the city of God" (v. 5[4])—which is the source of its security (v. 6[5]): while the nations may rage, the power of God's voice is sufficient to melt the very earth. God's voice becomes a roar in Psalm 76. In Psalm 46:10[46:9], God makes wars cease (*shabat*) and disarms enemies by shattering the instruments of war: the bow, the spear, and the shield. In Psalm 76, similarly, the God who dwells on Zion (v. 3[2]) shatters the arrows, the shield, the sword, and war (v. 4[3]).[39] And—"at your *ge'arah*, O God of Jacob, both chariot(eer) and horse lay stunned" (v. 7[6]). The Hebrew noun I left untranslated most English translations render as "rebuke." But God was not merely expressing strong disapproval of the military powers threatening Zion, or scolding them, any more than "the foundations of the world were uncovered" by God's strongly worded disapproval of their behavior (18:16[18:15]; similarly, Nah. 1:4). Rather, it was God's blast (NJPS), God's roaring, that left the horses and their chariot drivers as if asleep. God's powerful voice felled cedars and made mountains skip in Psalm 29, and God's voice can melt the earth in Psalm 46.[40]

36. See Ollenburger, *Zion, the City of the Great King*, 140–44.

37. The Assyrian king Esarhaddon testified that "the terror (-inspiring sight) of the great gods"—Ishtar of Nineveh and Ishtar of Arbela—overwhelmed his enemies and "they became madmen." Oppenheim, "Babylonian and Assyrian Historical Texts," 289.

38. God-lists at Ugarit include Zaphon, who receives offerings (e.g., *KTU* 1.27.11; *DDD*, 928).

39. Translators typically add "weapons of" before "war" at the end of v. 4[3]. But the Hebrew (MT), Greek (LXX: *kai polemon*), and Latin (Vulg.: *et bellum*) simply have "and war."

40. On God's roaring, see below on Ps. 104.

In the three Zion psalms—46, 48, and 76—the God who reigns on Zion as King and Creator retains the capacity to disarm the chaotic, hostile powers that threaten creation but also extends it to defend against hostile human powers that threaten Zion. In these different ways, against cosmic and mundane threats, God creates peace, which is to say that God orders and sustains a world.

Psalm 33: God's Character as Creator

After enjoining praise of God in its opening verses, Psalm 33 describes God as Creator:

> By the word of Yhwh the heavens were made,
> and by the breath [*ruach*] of his mouth all their host.
> He gathered the waters of the sea as a heap,[41]
> putting the deeps into storehouses.
> Let all the earth fear Yhwh,
> all the world's inhabitants be in awe of him.
> For he spoke and it came to be,
> he commanded, and it stood firm. (vv. 6–9)

Reminiscent of Genesis 1:3—"And God said, let there be light"—God's creation of the heavens and their host is by Yhwh's speaking . . . God's speech-acts.[42] While Psalm 33:7 mentions the sea and the deeps, reminiscent of Psalms 74 and 77, these are not personified in Psalm 33. They do not represent powers; they are but water. But while God's creating in verses 6–9 does not confront hostile watery powers, God does exercise royal power in Psalm 33 as well.

The text quoted above falls between Psalm 33:4–5, describing God's character, and verses 10–12, in which God counteracts threats of disorder. First, then, the psalm establishes God's character by employing a series of nouns: *uprightness*, *faithfulness*, *righteousness*, *justice*, and *steadfast love* (NRSV), the latter of which fills the earth. Following the description of creation in verses 6–9, the next unit contrasts the counsel and plans of the nations with God's counsel and plans. While God cancels and frustrates those of the nations and peoples, God's counsel and plans "stand firm" (v. 11). Just as God's creation "stood firm" (v. 9b), so stand God's plans (the verb *'amad* in both instances). The nations and peoples constitute a potential threat, not to cosmic order directly but to "the nation whose God is Yhwh, the people he chose as his heritage" (v. 12). Jean Marcel

41. The LXX has "bottle" or "wineskin," which the NRSV follows.
42. Alter, *Book of Psalms*, 114.

Vincent, commenting on the structure of Psalm 33 and the close connection between God's character and creation, describes creation as the "realization of the love (*chesed*) of God."[43]

The realization of God's *chesed* also covers all of the verses that follow in Psalm 33. Verses 13–15 again refer to God as Creator, the one who alone "formed" (*yatsar*) the human heart, just as God "formed" (*yatsar*) the first human (Gen. 2:7). As elsewhere in the Psalms, God the Creator is also sovereign. Here God observes "from his dwelling place" all earth's inhabitants and their deeds (Ps. 33:13–15). And in this light—in light of God the Creator and Sovereign—kings and their warriors and armaments of war have no hope of prevailing (vv. 16–17).[44] Regarding Psalm 33, Hans-Joachim Kraus comments, "Since the realm of creation is at the same time the realm of [Yhwh's] sovereignty (v. 10; cf. Ps. 24:1–2), the plans of the nations that strive for dominance in history cannot come to fruition (cf. Isa. 8:10). The creator of the world is the sovereign Lord of history in every moment. His plan alone prevails (Ps. 33:11)."[45]

That is the testimony of Psalm 33.

Psalm 104: Water and Leviathan Pacified

Psalm 104 presents the most extensive depiction of God the Creator in the Psalms. Psalm 33 opens with an imperative—"Rejoice in Yhwh, O righteous ones" (v. 1)—as does Psalm 104. But Psalm 104:1 enjoins the poet's own *nephesh*—soul or self—to "bless Yhwh." The injunction introduces an affirmation of God's greatness:

> Yhwh my God, you are exceedingly great.
> You clothe yourself with majesty and splendor. (v. 1)

The remainder of the psalm, like its opening verse, consists of praise, and it turns immediately to praise of God as Creator.[46] Indeed, verse 2 continues the description of God in verse 1 with participles, the first of which extends the image of God's clothing: "wrapping yourself in light like a garment." In other words, the psalm describes God as being clothed in majesty and splendor, terms redolent of royalty, and as being wrapped in light. *Light* was the first of God's creations in Genesis 1. Other psalms associate God with light—the light of God's face, for

43. Vincent, "Recherches exégétiques sur le Psaume XXXIII," 449.
44. See my book *Zion, the City of the Great King*, 93–99.
45. Kraus, *Psalms 1–59*, 264.
46. See P. Miller, "Poetry of Creation."

example (Ps. 80:4[80:3])—and Isaiah draws strong connections between God and light (Isa. 60:1, 19–20). But given what follows immediately in Psalm 104, an allusion in verse 2 to Genesis 1 seems plausible.[47] The second half of Psalm 104:2 makes abundantly clear that God the Creator is the subject of praise: "the one who stretches out the heavens like a tent" (cf. Isa. 40:22; 51:13).

God's creation—both God's acts of creating and what God created—remains the subject in Psalm 104 through verse 30. Verse 3 reflects ancient cosmology, with God laying the beams of his upper chambers in the waters. In Genesis 1:6–7, God made a dome, a vault, "in the midst of the water(s)," to separate the waters under the dome from those above it.[48] Then, in the flood, God opened the windows of the heavens to flood the earth (Gen. 7:11). Consistent with the picture of God's abode being above the vault—an image that Psalm 104:13 repeats—with its beams in the waters, the rest of verse 3 describes God making the clouds his chariot, moving about (*hamhallek*) on the wings of the wind. God comes on the wings of the wind in Psalm 118:11 and rides on the clouds in Psalm 68:5[68:4]. In Daniel 7:13, one in human form (*kebar 'enosh*) comes on the clouds of heaven.[49]

The following verses, Psalm 104:5–9, employ language recalling psalms considered earlier in this chapter:

> [Yhwh] set the earth on its foundations,
> so that it will never totter.
> The deep [*tehom*] covered it like a garment,[50]
> the waters stood above the mountains.
> At your roar, they fled,
> at the sound of your thunder, they ran away.
> The mountains rose up, they descended to the clefts,
> to the place you founded for them.
> You set a boundary for them that they may not cross,
> so that they will not return to cover the earth.

As did previous psalms, Psalm 104 depicts God acting against water—against the waters and the deep (*tehom*, v. 6). The earth exists, according to verse 5, but the waters and the deep leave it submerged. Hossfeld and Zenger write, "The primal flood covers the earth, even the tops of the mountains (cf. Gen. 1:2; 7:10

47. P. Miller, "Poetry of Creation," 89.
48. Levenson, *Creation and the Persistence of Evil*, 55.
49. This imagery is ancient: "Rider on the clouds" was an epithet of Baal (e.g., *KTU* 1.2 iv.8, 29).
50. In verse 6 I follow the translation John Day proposes in *God's Conflict*, 29.

[the flood]; Ps. 46:3)."[51] And Patrick D. Miller acknowledges, "The focus on water in creation does . . . point to God's ordering and control over what might potentially be chaos."[52] But here in Psalm 104, neither struggle nor violence ensues. Similar to Psalm 76 (discussed above), here God's "roar" and thunder bring order.[53] The waters hurry to their appointed place and remain within the boundary God set for them (Job 38:4–11; Ps. 33:7; Prov. 8:29; Jer. 5:22). God's action eliminating the waters as a potential threat underwrites the assurance in Psalm 104:9 of the earth's enduring stability.

Psalm 104 makes a remarkable shift with verse 10. After describing God's elimination of the waters as a threat, the psalm continues, without pausing, to praise God's use of water to nourish animals—undomesticated ones—and birds, who sing among the branches. But God also makes grass grow for cattle and plants as food for humans, even wine (v. 15). The psalm's effusive praise of God the Creator for ordering such a magnificent world extends to God's creation of the moon and the sun—the moon for marking seasons and the sun for marking the day for work and its ending. Its ending is marked by darkness, which God also makes—"makes," not "made." Psalm 104:20 does not contradict Genesis 1:2, which assumes darkness before God's creation of light (cf. Isa. 45:7). God's creating darkness in Psalm 104 is a daily affair. The psalm celebrates not a deistic God who set the world running like a clock and then ceased activity but a God whose active preservation of the world and life within it is constant and gracious (vv. 27–30).

Psalm 74 describes the Sea and Leviathan, chaotic powers, and God's conquest of them. Psalm 89 portrays God crushing Rahab, Leviathan's counterpart. Psalm 104:24–26 marks its distance from this violence by celebrating the marvels of the sea, one of God's wondrous works, filled with innumerable living things and ships. And Leviathan! Leviathan, far from appearing as a threat to be vanquished in defense of a divinely ordered world, appears here as a creature God "formed," as God formed *'adam* in Genesis 2:7. In Genesis, God formed the man for a purpose, a function. In Psalm 104, God apparently forms Leviathan in order to enjoy watching the creature sport in the sea. The psalm hopes that God will take pleasure in the natural world of God's creation: "May Yhwh rejoice in his works" (v. 31). But it also affirms that God created the "natural" world for the pleasure and benefit of its creatures, both human (v. 15) and nonhuman (vv. 16–18).

51. Hossfeld and Zenger, *Psalms 3*, 49.
52. P. Miller, "Poetry of Creation," 90.
53. For the argument that the verb *ga'ar*, often translated "rebuke" in these contexts, means something closer to "roar," see Kennedy, "Root *G'R*."

Psalm 104 regards the world and its structure, its order; the waters and its sea monsters; the fantastic variety of animals and birds and the grasses and seeds—and yes, in the case of lions, other animals—that feed them; people and the wine they enjoy . . . all of the world as God's good creation, and all of its parts dependent on God, not just themselves, for their continuing existence.

Conclusion

The world of God's creation in Psalm 104 is a world at peace and, perhaps with the exception of God's roaring at the waters and the deep (v. 7), a world of peace—the world as it should be, corresponding to God's intentions for it. At the conclusion of the previous chapter, I asked, "Is it possible that, as the Hopi did with their historical memory, a violent biblical tradition can be transformed into a vision of peace? Or that it can power such a vision?"

It may be tempting to pit Psalm 104 against Psalms 74 and 89, for example, as an implicit critique of them. God does act against the waters and the deep in Psalm 104 with roaring and thunder, but the sea—the object of God's violent action in Psalm 74—amounts to nothing more than a great body of water, supporting life and transportation, in Psalm 104. Perhaps, then, it represents an advance—a moral or theological advance?—beyond the picture of God crushing and smashing the personifications of the Sea. Perhaps.

The two psalms—74 and 89—that I have contrasted with Psalm 104 reflect and address circumstances of desperation and despair. Psalm 74 reflects the destruction and desecration of Jerusalem and the temple—the violation of Zion—by historical (Babylonian) forces of chaos that the people themselves have no means of contesting. The psalm thus appeals to the ancient memory of God's solitary conquest of chaotic forces. Psalm 89 recites God's promises to David, promises regarding his throne, and grounds them in God's calming the sea and smashing Rahab, securing an ordered world—giving those promises the guarantee of God the Creator. And it complains that, by all empirical evidence, those promises have been violated and the world cast into disorder. If Psalm 104 contemplates the wonder of God the Creator from a cruise between Santa Barbara, California, and the Channel Islands, Psalms 74 and 89 appeal to God—and precisely to God the Creator—from the ruins of life and hope. Psalm 104 presents not a vision of peace but a peaceful vision. Psalms 74 and 89, neither of which envisions any sort of human violence or any human action at all, recognize that only the action of God the Creator can repair what human power and violence on a transcendent scale have destroyed. The people whose voices both psalms represent—along with Psalms 33, 46, 48, 76, and 77—remember God the Creator, and they hope to enjoy the creation Psalm 104 celebrates.

There could be no better summary of God the Creator in the Psalms than Psalm 146:6–7, which identifies Yhwh, the "God of Jacob" (v. 5), as the one

> who made heaven and earth
> and all that is in them;
> who keeps faith forever;
> who does justice for the oppressed,
> giving food to the hungry.
> Yhwh releases prisoners.

The title of this chapter asks, quoting Psalm 24, "Who is the King of glory?" The answer, of course, is "Yhwh, strong and mighty; Yhwh, mighty in battle" (v. 8). The divine victory in that battle means peace.

6

"The LORD by Wisdom Founded the Earth"

GOD THE CREATOR IN WISDOM LITERATURE

Cultures from antiquity to modernity have compressed traditional wisdom into aphorisms or proverbs. Often, these affirm or confirm something characteristic of the way the world works—the way the world *truly is*, even if that reality may not be obvious. Sometimes these proverbs offer encouragement, as did my childhood neighbor's proverb: *Kann man über den Hund, kann man auch über den Schwanz*—"If you can make it over the dog, you can make it over the tail." In other words, if you have prevailed over the biggest obstacles, you will be able to prevail over the final one. Other proverbs have a critical bite, as did my grandmother's Low Saxon (*Plautdietsch*) proverb: *Je jeleada, je vetjeada*—"The more highly educated a person, the more lacking in good sense." She spoke this proverb regarding an educated man and professor, her employer, who lacked the common sense she—a nineteen-year-old immigrant from (what was then *the*) Ukraine—supplied in a critical situation. Another of her proverbs, whose variations remain familiar in different languages, also counsels humility, but in light of God: *Der Mensch denkt, aber Gott lenkt*—"Humankind proposes, but God disposes." This counts as an interpretation of a biblical proverb:

> The human mind may entertain many thoughts,
> but the counsel of Yhwh—*it* will prevail. (Prov. 19:21)

That proverb calls to mind Psalm 33 (discussed in chap. 5 above), with its contrast of the plans and counsel of the nations with those of God the Creator. The Old Testament's Wisdom literature—here considered to include Proverbs, Job, and Ecclesiastes[1]—does not consist only, or even primarily, of aphorisms. But the aphorisms in Proverbs do reflect and presuppose convictions about a world of which God is the Creator. Walther Zimmerli rather famously—famously among the cadre of biblical scholars who may remember Zimmerli—wrote that "wisdom theology is creation theology."[2] If Zimmerli's observation, or his claim, remains true, it does so over an expanse of diverse, even contradictory, texts. Whether to answer fools in their folly receives both a positive and a negative answer (Prov. 26:4–5).[3] Contemporary experience itself seems to contradict the confidence of Proverbs that those "who conceal their offenses will not prosper" (28:13).

Wisdom literature has often been described as "empirical" in nature because it appeals to observation, for example, rather than to a divine word. But that description proves to be inadequate, should it be taken to mean that the Proverbs consisted simply of collected observations over time.[4] Israel's sages—those who produced the Old Testament's Wisdom literature—were not blind to the reality that, despite "no harm happens to the righteous person" (Prov. 12:21), harm does indeed come to the righteous. Rather than simply reporting observations, or repeating early ones, *reflecting* the way the world works, the sages were also *imposing* an order on the world—bringing it under a conception of the world conformed to the conviction that God was its Creator. In this they were aided by a rich store of international wisdom. William McKane introduces his commentary on Proverbs with more than 150 pages of discussion and examples of wisdom instruction and proverbs from Egypt and Mesopotamia.[5] Some of this international wisdom rings either sadly true or profoundly so:

> The great man who behaves arrogantly is highly respected.
>
> A man who has no village—his (own) personality is his family.[6]

1. Debates about Wisdom literature, its reality or definition, do not bear significantly on the discussion here. For the debate, see Kynes, *Obituary for "Wisdom Literature."* The book's dramatic title notwithstanding, nothing but a scholarly consensus has died. Strictly speaking, "Wisdom literature" can be found in other places in the Old Testament—in Ps. 90, for example.

2. As quoted in Murphy, *Tree of Life*, 118. See also Zimmerli, *Old Testament Theology in Outline*, 39: "Wisdom ideology is controlled by the perspective of creation."

3. Murphy, *Tree of Life*, 21.

4. M. Fox, "Epistemology of the Book of Proverbs."

5. McKane, *Proverbs*, 51–208.

6. McKane, *Proverbs*, 124, 128.

The sages were aware of counterexamples. Sometimes even if one makes it over the dog, the tail becomes insurmountable. Sometimes God's disposing—God's acting in disregard of or contrary to human proposals—seems altogether unfortunate. Thus Job accuses God of malfeasance in the office of Creator. The book of Ecclesiastes portrays the teacher, Qoheleth, conducting comprehensive *empirical* research into the world and life within it and concluding that the way the world works and the way God does remain inscrutable to wisdom. Wisdom literature in the Bible may lack a seamless profile, but all of it shares one characteristic: poetry. Job and Ecclesiastes include prose narratives, of course, but poetry remains a significant feature of both books, and for Job a defining one. Gerhard von Rad expresses the importance of poetry in Wisdom literature: "One peculiarity must strike us at once, a peculiarity which unites them above and beyond their great differences in form and content; they are all composed in poetic form, they are poetry. And in no circumstances can that be considered to be an insignificant, external feature. Indeed, this peculiarity cannot be separated from the intellectual process as if it were something added later; rather, perception takes place precisely in and with the poetic conception."[7] "The world is not dumb," Roland E. Murphy wrote.[8] And it comes to expression through the intellectual work and artistry of poetry.

The previous five chapters of this book made only occasional mention of the natural world—to *creation*, as it is commonly understood[9]—or to historical, human life within the world. In the preceding chapter, discussing the Psalms, I might have pointed to Psalm 65 as joining both dimensions—the natural world and human life within it—with a focus on God the Creator. The psalm's first six verses (five verses in ET) celebrate God's forgiveness and deliverance of the nation. The psalm then turns to praise of God the Creator:

> Who establishes the mountains in his strength,
> girded in might;
> silencing the roaring of the waters,
> the roaring of their waves,
> the tumult of the peoples. (vv. 7–8[6–7])

In its concluding verses, the psalm praises God for watering the earth, providing bounteous grain, and making verdant the hills and valleys.

7. Von Rad, *Wisdom in Israel*, 24. Perdue's *Wisdom and Creation* remains an essential resource on the subject.

8. Murphy, *Tree of Life*, 120.

9. As, for example, in discussions of creation care. See Moo and Moo, *Creation Care*.

Israel's Wisdom literature, the focus of this chapter, makes extensive reference to the natural world, understanding it as God's creation, and to human life within that world. But it makes no reference to concrete historical experience; "Israel" is mentioned only at the beginning of Proverbs (1:1) and Ecclesiastes (1:12). Because of this absence of concreteness and historical particularity—because of the book's "universality"—Gerhard Lorenz Bauer declares Proverbs to be the most purely theological of the Old Testament's books.[10] To Proverbs we turn next, before discussing Job and Ecclesiastes.

Proverbs

Proverbs does not mention the acts of God in Israel's history, but it does depend on, and embed itself in, Israel's traditions in at least two significant ways. To Bauer's stated chagrin, Proverbs retains what he calls "the name of the national deity"[11]—Yhwh. In speaking of God the Creator, Proverbs also recalls the kinds of traditional material we have seen in the Psalms. It does so in Proverbs 3 and 8.

Proverbs 3:19–20

At the beginning of Proverbs 3, a parent speaks to a child on behalf of wisdom, promising success for obeying the parent's wise commandments. This includes religious counsel in verses 5–12: "Trust in Yhwh with all your heart; do not rely on your own understanding" (v. 5). Abruptly, verse 13 turns to praise of wisdom as what is most to be valued: "Happy is the person who finds wisdom, the one who obtains understanding."[12] Here wisdom is personified as a woman; she is "more precious than pearls" (v. 15). On the face of it, counsel to place trust in God alone and to "fear Yhwh" (v. 7) would seem to contradict the extraordinary value Proverbs 3 places on finding wisdom and obtaining understanding. The sages behind Proverbs hold these things together because they affirm that wisdom and the world are very closely connected and—more precisely—because the connection between them is established in God's creation of the world. They make this point in 3:19–20:

> By wisdom Yhwh founded the earth,
> establishing the heavens by understanding.

10. Bauer, *Beylagen zur Theologie des alten Testaments*, 135. I describe Bauer's work in *Old Testament Theology*, 5.

11. Bauer, *Beylagen zur Theologie des alten Testaments*, 135.

12. See M. Fox, *Proverbs 1–9*, 154–55.

By his knowledge the deeps were split open,
and the clouds drip down dew.

Some of the language here will be familiar from psalms we have considered. For example, in Psalm 24:2, God *founded* the earth and *established* it (cf. Pss. 89:12[89:11]; 104:5). "The deeps" are mentioned in Psalm 33:7 and 77:18[77:17], and the singular—"the deep" (*tehom*)—occurs first in Genesis 1:2 but also in Psalm 104:6. Psalm 74:13 says that God "*split* spring and stream," while in Proverbs 3:20 God "*split open*" the deeps (the same verb, *baqa'*, in both verses). In other words, Proverbs 3 employs traditional, poetic language and imagery to portray God's creating the earth and the heavens. But verses 19–20 stress that it was by wisdom, by understanding (cf. Ps. 136:5), and by God's own knowledge that Yhwh founded and established the world. That is to say, the world itself—including the earth, the heavens, and the deeps—is the product of the Creator's wisdom as the instrument or medium of God's creating. Wisdom, understanding, and knowledge are to be nurtured—grasped and clung to (Prov. 3:18)—as virtues necessary to living well in the world that God formed "by" them.[13] Trusting in God the Creator can take the form of valuing wisdom above all else.

Proverbs elsewhere attests the close relationship between Wisdom and God. In Proverbs 1:23–24, Wisdom speaks:

See, I will pour out my spirit upon you,
I will make known to you my words.
Because I called, but you refused.

Had the speaker not been identified as Wisdom, we would likely assume that it was God speaking through a prophetic voice. In Joel 2:28, Yhwh promises, "I will pour out my spirit."[14] Several Old Testament passages report God calling and the people not responding (Isa. 65:1; Zech. 7:11, 13; 2 Chron. 33:10). In Proverbs 1, Wisdom speaks with the authority of God and in the prophetic voice of God. The near identification of Wisdom with God—and specifically, God the Creator—is not limited to examples of prophetic forms of speech.[15] For example, just as by wisdom God founded the earth, so it is by wisdom that "kings

13. On "the cosmogony" in Prov. 3:19–20 in relation to the recommendations of wisdom, see Clifford, *Proverbs*, 55. Psalm 33:4–9 associates justice and righteousness with God's creating (see chap. 5 above). For Hans Heinrich Schmid, justice, righteousness, and wisdom form part of the same matrix within creation theology. "Creation, Righteousness, and Salvation."

14. The verb for "pour out" in Prov. 1:23 is *naba'* and in Joel 2:28 *shaphak*.

15. On the close relation between Wisdom and God, see O'Connor, "Wisdom Literature."

reign and rulers issue just decrees" (Prov. 8:15). This particular coordination recalls Psalm 89, in which God the Creator's rule over the sea (vv. 10–11[9–10]) extends to and empowers the king's rule (v. 26[25]).[16] In Proverbs 8 it is wisdom that extends to kings, empowering them to reign and to rule justly. But Wisdom here is not merely the instrument or medium of God's empowerment. Wisdom speaks for herself: "*By me* kings reign" (v. 15 NRSV). And further in the divine voice: "I [Wisdom] love those who love me" (v. 17 NRSV). The close association between Wisdom and God the Creator comes to expression also and especially in Proverbs 8.

Proverbs 8:22–31

Wisdom continues speaking in Proverbs 8, and she speaks of God the Creator in verses 22–31. These verses expand on 3:19–20, but here Wisdom becomes more than the instrument or medium of God's creating.

The translation of Proverbs 8:22 is contested. The NRSV translates the verse "The LORD created me at the beginning of his work, the first of his acts of long ago." The controversy concerns the word *qanani*, which the NRSV and many other translations (and the LXX and the Vulg.) render in this context as "he created [or made] me." Some scholars, however, insist that the better translation would be "acquired me"[17] or "begot me."[18] The difference between "acquired" and "created" may be negligible.[19] Commenting on Psalm 24 earlier, in chapter 5, for example, I pointed to the relation between creating something and owning it: the earth is the Lord's; the Lord made it. But in the history of its interpretation, Proverbs 8:22 and the translation of the verb *qanah* became entangled in Christian theological debates that resulted in the creedal confession that Jesus Christ was "begotten, not made" (in Greek, *gennēthenta ou poiēthenta*; in Latin, *natum, non factum*).[20]

While philological and contextual considerations point to "created me" as the preferred translation in Proverbs 8:22,[21] in subsequent verses—verses 23–25—

16. See the discussion of Ps. 89 in chap. 5.

17. O'Connor, "Wisdom Literature," 192; Lenzi, "Proverbs 8:22–31," 692.

18. Yee, "Theology of Creation," 88–90. Richard J. Clifford offers "begot" as the translation of v. 22 but then argues that the meaning of the root *qanah* here is "to create" (*Proverbs*, 91, 96).

19. Michael V. Fox insists that "acquire" is the lexical meaning of *qanah* but observes that "something can be acquired . . . by creation" (*Proverbs 1–9*, 279). Gerhard von Rad had made the same observation. *Wisdom in Israel*, 151.

20. Michael Fox rehearses some of this development in his commentary (*Proverbs 1–9*, 279), as does Clifford in his (*Proverbs*, 98–99). Greek, English, and Latin texts of the Nicene-Constantinopolitan Creed of 381 can be found at https://earlychurchtexts.com/public/nicene_creed.htm.

21. Clifford cites Ugaritic and Phoenician evidence. *Proverbs*, 96.

Wisdom says that she was "established" or "formed" (v. 23) and "brought forth" or "born" (vv. 24–25). The text here does not reflect a concern to articulate a doctrine about the manner of Wisdom's origin. Rather, it employs terms and imagery from a range of domains to stress both Wisdom's intimate relation to God the Creator and Wisdom's temporal priority over any of God's (other) works of creation. God created Wisdom "at [or as] the beginning" (v. 22): in ancient or primordial time, at or preceding the world's origin (v. 23).

Following these extraordinary and unprecedented claims about Wisdom, the poem then turns to cosmogony, God's creation of the world. "The deeps," through which God made a way (cf. Ps. 77:17[77:16]), did not yet exist when Wisdom was born, and neither did the springs of Psalm 74:15. Neither mountains nor hills, or even the earth itself—or the very heavens—preceded Wisdom (Prov. 8:27). Indeed, Wisdom attended God's creation of them or their appointment to their places and roles and limits (v. 29). When God circumscribed "the face of the deep [*tehom*]" (v. 27)—"the face of the deep" that darkness covered in Genesis 1:2—Wisdom was there. Wisdom's liveliness in Proverbs 8, her celebration of her presence with God—her "being there" with God at creation—expands dramatically on but does not contradict the earlier cosmological poem in Proverbs 3:19–20, which affirms that by wisdom and understanding God created the earth and the heavens. Alan Lenzi argues that 8:22–31 is in fact an interpretation of the passage in Proverbs 3.[22] Here in chapter 8, Wisdom is given greater personality; indeed, she comes to voice as a person. While in chapter 3 she was instrumental in God's creating, here she attends that creating, and she speaks in the first person.

The personal vitality of Wisdom comes to expression in Proverbs 8:30–31. Unfortunately, verse 30 is beset with translation difficulties. Here are some representative translations of the verse, in which Wisdom is speaking:

> Then I was beside him, like a master worker,
> and I was daily his delight,
> rejoicing before him always. (NRSV)

> I was alongside him as a master. I was delight daily, playing before him all the time.[23]

> I was beside him, a darling child. I was his delight day after day, playing before him continually.[24]

22. Lenzi, "Proverbs 8:22–31," 694–98.
23. Lenzi, "Proverbs 8:22–31," 693.
24. Yee, "Theology of Creation," 88.

> I was at his side, a sage. I was daily taking delight, rejoicing before him at all times.[25]

> And I was near him, growing up, and was his delight day by day, frolicking before him at all times.[26]

> I was with Him as a confidant, a source of delight every day, rejoicing before Him at all times. (NJPS)

The irreconcilable variety of these translations, all of them by eminent scholars, illustrates the difficulty in arriving at a proper understanding of the verse. Evidently, Wisdom and delight are associated, even though scholars disagree whether God was delighting in Wisdom or whether Wisdom was doing the delighting. About Wisdom's self-description, disagreement is wide: "master," "master worker," "darling child," "sage," "confidant." The issue in this case is how to understand the Hebrew word *'amon*, the word that generates all those discordant translations.

The differences matter, because the various translations sponsor different interpretations of the place and role of Wisdom in relation to God the Creator. If the text were to be read as if Wisdom declares herself to be a master worker, this could suggest her active role—perhaps as architect—in the cosmogony. Other translations suggest a child at play, perhaps watching in wonder as God forms the world and then receiving God's delight and rejoicing with God. These issues of translation and interpretation remain unresolved. The final verse in Proverbs 8, verse 31, presents no serious translation issues: Wisdom speaks of her rejoicing or playing in God's inhabitable world, or perhaps sporting in it—the verb is the same used to describe God's forming the sea for Leviathan to sport in (Ps. 104:26). And regardless of whose delight is the subject in Proverbs 8:30, here Wisdom declares unambiguously her delight in being with people (*'et-bene 'adam*), with us.

Kathleen M. O'Connor comments that, regardless of any ambiguities in the text and its translation, the poem of Proverbs 8:22–31 "asserts . . . Wisdom's status as companion to the Creator."[27] The precise form that companionship takes may remain unresolved, but its origin lies at the very beginning, and it includes playful delight.[28] O'Connor's further claim about these verses—that "ultimately they subordinate God to her" (i.e., to Wisdom)—cannot be sustained.[29]

25. Clifford, *Proverbs*, 92.
26. M. Fox, *Proverbs 1–9*, 264.
27. O'Connor, "Wisdom Literature," 193.
28. See Lenzi, "Proverbs 8:22–31," 705–11.
29. O'Connor, "Wisdom Literature," 194.

Wisdom's identity and God's come close together, as I noted above in commenting on Proverbs 1. Analogously, perhaps, in some Old Testament texts, the identities of "the Lord" and "the angel of the Lord" become fluid, as in the first chapter of Zechariah. Proverbs brings any such analogy to its breaking point by describing Wisdom as *a person in relation to* God the Creator, but it remains God who brings about the world, and it is, finally, in *God's* world that Wisdom plays (8:31)—Wisdom who is prior to all that is not God.

Beyond the cosmogony of these verses, Wisdom continues to beckon and give counsel, promising that whoever finds her "obtains favor from Yhwh" (Prov. 8:35).

Ecclesiastes

Qoheleth—"the teacher" who speaks in Ecclesiastes—expresses no interest in obtaining God's favor (*ratson*), a term often having to do with God accepting sacrifices (e.g., Lev. 1:3; 19:5). Her interest, or is it his . . . ? The Hebrew *qoheleth* is grammatically feminine, as is *chokmah*—wisdom. But the misogynistic comments about women in Ecclesiastes 7:26–29 do not immediately suggest a woman's voice. The book itself proposes that Qoheleth is Solomon, "son of David, king in Jerusalem" (1:1) and "king over Israel in Jerusalem" (1:12). But some of the observations Qoheleth makes about kings and nobility (e.g., 4:1) and bits of wisdom s/he offers—for example, "Better to be a living dog than a dead lion" (9:4)—hardly seem "Solomonic."[30] And Qoheleth's counsel to "enjoy life with the woman you love" (9:9) ill fits the monarch with seven hundred wives and three hundred concubines (1 Kings 11:3).[31] Regardless of the gender of *qoheleth*, Ecclesiastes casts "the teacher" as male and wise, though doubting the benefits of his wisdom: "Then I said to myself, 'What happens to the fool will happen to me also; why then have I been so very wise?' And I said to myself that this also is vanity" (Eccles. 2:15 NRSV).

Qoheleth's interest lies in using his wisdom to examine everything and describe what he observes: "I set my mind to seek out and, through wisdom, to discover all that happens under heaven" (Eccles. 1:13). He discovers that much of human life is characterized by *hebel*, a term the NRSV and other translations render as "vanity." *Vanity*, given its meaning in contemporary American English—as in the lyrics "You're so vain, you probably think this song is about

30. Murphy, *Ecclesiastes*, xx–xxi. My references to Qoheleth will be to the character in the book and not to the book itself, which is often called Qoheleth (or Qohelet); e.g., Sharp, "Ironic Representation."

31. Jennifer L. Koosed offers a densely theoretical treatment of issues of gender and the body of Qoheleth in *(Per)mutations of Qohelet*.

you"[32]—hardly suits as a translation of the Hebrew *hebel*, which has nothing to do with vanity in that sense. *Hebel* serves as the name of Abel in Genesis 4. Abel and his name suggest transience, as in Proverbs 31:30: "Charm is deceptive and beauty is fleeting [*hebel*]." The transience, the impermanence, of perceptible *human* reality and experience and its inscrutability to divine purpose or justice are components of the *hebel*—the "vanity"—Qoheleth observes.[33]

Qoheleth observes not only impermanence but also, to the contrary, constancy, sometimes of a lamentable kind. The book opens with a lament about human transience and futility:

> What benefit to people is all the toil
> at which they toil under the sun?
> A generation goes, and a generation comes. (Eccles. 1:3–4a)

But it continues by contrasting this human transience with the earth's constancy:

> The earth stands forever.
> The sun rises and the sun sets
> and rushes to the place where it rises.
> The wind blows to the south
> and then around to the north;
> round and round goes the wind,
> and on its rounds the wind returns.
> All rivers run to the sea,
> but the sea is not full;
> to the place where the streams flow,
> there they continue to flow. (1:4b–7)

The earth that God created *stands* forever, according to verse 4, echoing the affirmation of Psalm 33:8–9 that God spoke and commanded and the earth *stood*—"stood firm" (v. 9 NRSV). Qoheleth does not question but assumes that God the Creator made the world, an assumption perhaps formed on the basis of Qoheleth's reading of Genesis. As many others have noted, Ecclesiastes reflects knowledge of Genesis, as in Ecclesiastes 3:20 and 12:7, where dust is humanity's origin and destiny.[34] And as in Genesis, God made the world—including humanity—good: "God made humankind (up)right" (Eccles. 7:29).

32. Carly Simon, "You're So Vain," 1972, track 3 on *No Secrets*, produced by Quackenbush Music Ltd., ASCAP.

33. Kimmo Huovila and Dan Lioy have surveyed the many interpretations of *hebel* that scholars have proposed. "Meaning of *Hebel*."

34. Matthew Seufert has surveyed the literature in "Presence of Genesis."

To a surprising degree, for Qoheleth creation has to do with time.[35] God made the world with everything appropriate to its time—fitting its time (Eccles. 3:11). Indeed, if any part of Ecclesiastes has become familiar in popular culture, it is likely to be "to every thing there is a season," the KJV translation of 3:1. The folk singer Pete Seeger, in 1959, made these the opening words of a song that the rock band The Byrds made popular in a 1965 recording. Seeger based his lyrics on Ecclesiastes 3:1–8, a litany of contrasting things for which there is a time (love/hate, war/peace; v. 8). For Seeger, the litany conveyed a positive message, as his song's concluding line makes clear: "A time for peace, I swear it's not too late."[36] Qoheleth is less sanguine.

Qoheleth's litany of opposites, of God fitting everything to its season, points to the futility of expecting or striving for change: "What do workers gain from their work?" (Eccles. 3:9). God has determined the time, and human effort cannot affect it. Qoheleth expresses his resignation to the determination of time early in the book in a verse that concludes with a statement that became a cliché:

> What has happened, that is what will happen again,
> and what has been done, that is what will be done again.
> There is nothing new under the sun. (1:9)

Von Rad expresses the point well. Qoheleth, he writes, "is aware of something which mysteriously rules and orders every event; he usually refers to this phenomenon by the neutral word 'time' and thereby touches on the fact that every activity and every event is subject to a certain determinism. . . . There is, however, no comfort in this determination of every phenomenon, for often enough, as a result of it, what [humankind] has learned by hard toil is rendered useless."[37]

But while Qoheleth may despair over the futility of his own labor "under the sun" (Eccles. 2:20), his resignation does not leave him joyless:

> Enjoy life with a woman you love,
> all the days of your fleeting [*hebel*] life that [God] has granted you under
> the sun—
> all your fleeting days,

35. Van Leeuwen, "Creation and Contingency in Qoheleth."

36. Pete Seeger, "Turn! Turn! Turn!," 1962, track 6 on *The Bitter and the Sweet*, produced by John Hammond, https://genius.com/Pete-seeger-turn-turn-turn-lyrics.

37. Von Rad, *Wisdom in Israel*, 228–29. He then quotes Eccles. 9:11–12.

because that is your lot in life,
and in the work you do under the sun. (9:9)

Even though righteous people may be treated as though they were wicked, and wicked people as if they were righteous—"this also is *hebel*" (8:14)—Qoheleth commends enjoyment: people should eat, drink, and be merry "for the days of their lives that God grants them under the sun" (8:15). Even in his resignation, Qoheleth acknowledges that to eat, drink, and find pleasure in work comes "from the hand of God" (2:24): God the Creator.

"Remember your creator while you are young" (Eccles. 12:1), Qoheleth counsels in the final chapter of Ecclesiastes—a chapter portending, in its first eight verses, the "end of the world," according to C. L. Seow.[38] Before the end, and before its portents inflict misery and loss, remember your Creator. Those are Qoheleth's final words. And they are the conclusion to his project of employing his mind and the instrument of wisdom to seek out and discover all that happens (1:13). The project, Qoheleth concludes, amounts to "wind chasing."[39] Qoheleth mentions God (Elohim) relentlessly, and he knows that God is the Creator and cause of everything, but God's purposes remain inscrutable to his comprehensive observation of the world (11:5).

The book's final verses (Eccles. 12:9–14) do not erase the words of Qoheleth, "son of David, king in Jerusalem." The concluding verses of Ecclesiastes "canonize" Qoheleth's words, certifying them as wisdom while also closing Wisdom's canon: "The end of the matter; all has been heard"—and concluding with counsel that cannot be derived from even the most thorough observation and employment of wisdom: "Fear God and keep his commandments, for that is the whole duty of everyone" (12:13 NRSV).[40] In this, we may suppose, one can find peace—relief from anxious concern over God's inscrutability, over the passage of time without change, and over the transience of life itself.

Job

Job "the righteous sufferer" seeks peace, peace with and from God, whom he confronts with his charge of malfeasance in the office of Creator. The book itself does mention peace, *shalom*, and includes the claim that God—God the

38. Seow, "Qohelet's Eschatological Poem," 234.
39. Brown, "When Wisdom Fails," 221.
40. On the textual and interpretive issues in this verse, see Murphy, *Ecclesiastes*, 124–26. I highly recommend Sharp's brilliant essay, "Ironic Representation," 67–68.

Creator—makes peace (Job 25:2). But this claim comes from Bildad, one of Job's friends who urge Job to acknowledge his offenses, which must be the source of his suffering, since God—as Bildad has said earlier—does not bend or suppress justice (8:3). Job wants to argue the point in court, with God the Creator as the defendant.

While the divine speeches in Job 38–41 are the best-known and most extensive passages relating to creation, texts earlier in the book also refer to or contain echoes of creation. Norman C. Habel, for example, writes of the "cosmogonic connections" between Job 3:1–9 and Genesis 1:1–15.[41] In the Joban text, Job curses the day of his birth: "Perish the day on which I was born" (Job 3:3). He then calls for what amounts to the reversal of creation: God's "let there be light" in Genesis 1:3 becomes "let there be darkness" on Job's lips (Job 3:4). Later in chapter 3, Job calls on those who curse the night to curse the day (or perhaps the sea), those who are prepared to rouse or awaken Leviathan (3:7–8).[42] Leviathan we met in the Ugaritic texts (above in chap. 4) and in Psalms 74 and 104. According to Psalm 74:13–14, God conquered the Sea and the dragons and the chaos monster, Leviathan, in bringing about or preserving an ordered world. In Psalm 104:26, God made Leviathan to sport in the sea; there it is neither a monster nor associated with chaos—powers hostile to God. Job offers a lengthy description of Leviathan later in the book (Job 40:25–41:26[41:1–34]), a description that seems unrelated to the Leviathan named in Job 3:8. Commentators offer contradictory interpretations of the rousing of Leviathan.[43] I offer none of my own here (but see below), content to notice early references in Job to creation, references whose mention of God in 3:4 and 3:23 hardly laud God the Creator.

As it happens, "God" in Job 3, and in many other places in Job, is the translation of *'eloah*, a word for God that appears in some other Old Testament texts but most frequently by far in Job. It may be that the author of Job chose this name to accord with the non-Israelite character of Job and the friends who engage him in dialogue—all of them from east of Israel[44]—but the Job who comes powerfully and eloquently to speak in the dialogues knows the tradition, as his speeches, his laments, in chapter 7 demonstrate.

41. Habel, *Job*, 104. Habel's comparison of the Job and Genesis passages depends on Fishbane, "Jeremiah 4:23–26 and Job 3:3–13."

42. On the Hebrew text and its translation, see Seow, *Job 1–21*, 351–52.

43. E.g., C. L. Seow, who refers to ancient beliefs about a "celestial dragon" swallowing the sun or the moon (*Job 1–21*, 352), and Robert D. Miller II, who concludes that "[one] rouses the dragon in order to slay it." *Dragon, the Mountain, and the Nations*, 221.

44. Seow, *Job 1–21*, 341.

In chapter 3, Job refers to Leviathan, and in chapter 7—as if drawing again on Psalm 74—he refers to Sea (*yam*), the chaotic force that Leviathan embodies: "Am I Sea or Dragon that you place a watch over me?" (7:12). Job complains that God regards him as if he were a force, hostile to the created order, that God needs to restrain. Job recognizes and laments "the ephemeral nature of human life,"[45] which emboldens him to speak to God without restraint in his anguish and bitterness (7:11). After asking for silence so that he may speak, Job embraces the risk:

> Let come upon me what may.
> I will take up my flesh in my teeth
> and put my life in my hands. (13:13–14)

In chapter 7, Job makes bold to charge God with acting in the full power of Creator against a suffering mortal, and an innocent one. And in complaining of God's "watch over" him (7:12), Job takes up Psalm 8 and turns it around, as he did with Genesis 1 in Job 3.

The psalmist marvels that the Creator of the heavens above would devote attention to mere mortals:

> When I see the heavens, the work of your fingers,
> the moon and the stars you established,
> what are mortals [*'enosh*] that you keep them in mind,
> or people [*ben-'adam*] that you attend to them? (Ps. 8:4–5[8:3–4])

Indeed, God made them only a little less than divine and assigned them extensive dominion (8:6–7[8:5–6])—as in Genesis 1:26–28.[46] Job's question in Job 7:17 begins with the same words: "What are mortals [*'enosh*] . . . ?" (also 15:14). The rest of the verse proceeds in vocabulary different from that of Psalm 8 while asking the same question: Why do you make so much of mortals or pay such attention to them? Job asks his question not out of wonder and awe but in complaint. God the Creator pays unrelenting, oppressive attention not only to humankind but also to *him* (Job 7:18–19): "Leave me alone!" to live out my transient life (vv. 16, 19).[47]

Job does not intend to leave God alone, however; he wants to argue his case before El Shaddai (Job 13:3). He states his case extensively in chapters 29–31. At the same time, he recognizes the futility of trying to prove his case against God

45. Seow, *Job 1–21*, 495.
46. The verb for (exercising) dominion here is *mashal*, which Gen. 1:18 uses of the heavenly luminaries.
47. Seow, *Job 1–21*, 500.

the Creator. Even before God's speeches that begin in chapter 38, Job acknowledges the majesty and power of God in creation (9:5–12). He recalls again that God calmed the sea and shattered the dragon Rahab (26:12). Job's rehearsals of God's continuing power as Creator (9:6–7; 26:7–9) reveal the insurmountable problem he faces. As Job acknowledges, he and God do not share a common mortality, and there is no arbiter—no one who can adjudicate, no being who can supply common ground—between them (9:32–33).

> For [God] is not a man [*lo'-'ish*] as I am, that I should answer him,
> that we should come together for justice.
> There is no arbiter between us
> who could place his hand on us both. (9:32–33)[48]

The constitutive difference between the mortal Job and God the Creator receives the sharpest possible emphasis in God's two speeches in Job 38–39 and 40–41, in which God becomes the interrogator.[49] At the beginning of the first speech, God reiterates Job's identification of himself as a man (similar to 9:32 above). God now instructs Job, "Gird your loins as a man [*geber*]" (38:3). And in the interrogation that follows, God reminds Job of how unimaginably vast the distinction is between Job and the Creator of the world (38:4–38) and between Job and the world's wildly diverse creatures, including the scary creatures Behemoth (40:15) and Leviathan (40:25[41:1]).[50] Of Behemoth, God says to Job, you and he alike are creatures I have made (40:15). Both of God's speeches remove Job and the rest of humanity from the center of concern—Job shares his mortality with the other creatures—and do not address directly Job's protest and his complaint, his appeal for justice. The divine speeches do not concede or acknowledge that Job is in the right in his case against God. But God's speeches do express, at great length and with poetic power, what Carol Newsom calls "the alterity of the divine and the human,"[51] or what I have described in this book as the constitutive difference between God and humans. This is a theme of Genesis 1–11, as I argued in chapter 2.

In the divine speeches, God confirms Job's complaint that he and God share no common mortality or divinity—and no third thing, including a common

48. Job's confession that God is "not a man [*lo'-'ish*]" echoes God's declaration, explaining divine mercy, "I am not a man [*lo'-'ish*]" in Hosea 11:9. My use of masculine language in this instance is intentional.

49. Kathryn Schifferdecker describes the diverse scholarly interpretations of God's speeches in Job 38–41 (*Out of the Whirlwind*, 7–10) and summarizes their "non-anthropocentricity" (123).

50. See O'Connor, "Wild, Raging Creativity."

51. Newsom, *Book of Job*, 240.

morality—that would make conceivable a divine *apologia* or "any kind of self-interpretation" on the part of God the Creator.[52] But this confirmation hardly exhausts the content of God's answer to Job in the divine speeches. The two divine speeches address Job's charge of divine malfeasance in the office of Creator. The first speech points to God's "counsel" (*'etsah*, Job 38:2) or design in creating the cosmos (vv. 4–38) and then to the marvels of—and God's provision for—the sometimes violent creatures that populate God's creation (38:39–39:30). God created a habitable world of complex and inscrutable design in which wildly diverse creatures can thrive. The second speech points to God's power to restrain the proud and the wicked (40:12); Job's own right arm, by contrast, cannot save him (v. 14). Yes, the chaos monsters—Behemoth and Leviathan—are terrifying, but these, too, are God's creatures in which God takes pleasure.[53] And as Michael V. Fox has noted, in this divine speech, "neither beast actually does anything evil or aggressive."[54] By God's design, these chaos monsters—which even the God who created them observes with admiring awe—while dangerous, of course, pose no mortal threat . . . if left alone. O'Connor concludes, "God is not a bully in these speeches. Job is not humiliated. Instead he is presented with the beauty and wild freedom of creation and Creator."[55]

Job discovers, as Qoheleth observed,[56] that the world of God's creation is not a mechanical one in which the moral quality of a life has predictable consequences. Thus as Newsom describes Job's extended self-defense (Job 29:1–31:4), he "attempts to claim affirmation for a moral life lived in a moral community and situated within a moral universe."[57] But the world's workings, Job has learned, are marked by the mystery of their Creator's sovereign freedom. Job confesses God the Creator's sovereign freedom immediately upon the conclusion of the Creator's speeches. He does so in terms familiar from Genesis 11, which describes the building project of a united humanity on the plains of Shinar. Upon observing the progress of the project, God said of the united people that, from then on, "they will not be prevented [*lo'-yibbatser*] from doing anything they may propose to do" (Gen. 11:6). Job's first words—his "answer" (Job 42:1)—after God's speeches conclude: "I know that you [God] can do anything. No purpose

52. The quoted phrase is from von Rad, *Wisdom in Israel*, 225.

53. O'Connor, "Wild, Raging Creativity," 52–53. I have benefited from Mettinger, "God of Job."

54. M. Fox, "Meaning of the Book of Job," 14. For instructive comments on animals in Israel's Wisdom literature, see Walsh and the literature he surveys in "Beasts of Wisdom."

55. O'Connor, "Wild, Raging Creativity," 52.

56. Whether Ecclesiastes precedes Job historically, I do not know; it comes earlier in my treatment of the two in this chapter.

57. Newsom, *Book of Job*, 239.

[or project] of yours will be thwarted [*lo'-yibbatser*]" (v. 2).[58] Job confesses that the design of God's creation does not constrain God's freedom, a freedom that God extends to creatures whose own freedom is constrained only by God's beneficent design for creation's flourishing and God's enjoyment. Job comes to this confession having been *shown* the astonishing magnificence of God's created world. God's speeches were verbal, of course, and imaginably oral. But their sublime power still provokes the vivid imaginations—the awe—of contemporary readers. The power of God's speeches and the world they conveyed confronted Job with *God*: "Now my eyes have seen you" (Job 42:5).

Conclusion to Job

His eyes having seen God, Job repents in dust and ashes (Job 42:6), or so the NRSV renders the last part of the verse. Some interpreters have been dissatisfied with this interpretation, since it seems to have Job recanting the protest he courageously mounted in the book's dialogue. In response, in 1976, Dale Patrick proposed this translation of Job 42:6: "Therefore I repudiate and repent of dust and ashes."[59] His translation, Patrick claimed, "expresses Job's intention of abandoning the posture of mourning."[60] More recently, Pieter van der Lugt has argued that God is the speaker in verse 6, whose final clause should be translated "and I have compassion with dust and ashes."[61] "Dust and ashes" would then be metonymic for humanity, Job's and ours. Van der Lugt's case has biblical examples on its side: in each of the other three examples of "repent" as a first-person singular verb preceded by a conjunction, all of them from Jeremiah, God is the speaker. Two of them have the same Hebrew construction as Job 42:6: *wenichamti 'al*, meaning, in Jeremiah, "then I will repent concerning the disaster" (Jer. 18:8, 10).[62] Certainly, God is capable of repentance—or of changing the divine mind—as Exodus 32:14 and its echo in Jonah 3:10 illustrate (cf. 1 Sam. 15:11, 29, 35). Even so, in Job 42:6, it is Job who relents and repents "on dust and ashes."

Having seen God—that is, God having confronted Job with a vision of the Creator vastly beyond Job's imagination—Job repents on dust and ashes. The

58. On Gen. 11, see chap. 3 in this book.

59. Patrick, "Translation of Job 42:6," 369. Patrick remarks that "something like 'forswear'" would be preferable to "repent" (369).

60. Patrick, "Translation of Job 42:6," 371. Patrick's interpretation of the verse became widely accepted, including in Habel, *Book of Job*, 575–83.

61. Van der Lugt, "Who Changes His Mind?," 625.

62. Jeremiah 26:3 differs only in using a different preposition: *'el* rather than *'al*. Modern English versions translate the verb *nacham* in these contexts as describing a change of mind rather than the KJV's "repent."

collocation "dust and ashes" does not refer to Job's humanity.[63] It occurs elsewhere only in Job 30:19. Job there complains that God has cast him into the mud so that "I have become like dust and ashes." Job refers here not to his humanity or to ours but to his own misery: the misery to which—as he complains—God's inaction, God's unresponsiveness, has condemned him (vv. 1–20). Job's repentance on dust and ashes in 42:6 retrieves his complaint in 30:19. Job repents, following God's creation speeches in chapters 38–41, because he hadn't known what he was talking about or whom he had presumed to be addressing: both God the Creator and the world of God's creation are more complex, wilder, more dangerous, and more beautiful than Job could have imagined.

Neither God in the divine speeches nor the book of Job as a whole resolves the question of divinely permitted innocent suffering. Job does not insult innocent sufferers by offering them a justification for their suffering. The prologue to the book—its first two chapters—casts Job's suffering as a divinely sanctioned test of his disinterested faithfulness, a test proposed by the satan (*hassatan*), God's investigator and prosecutor among "the sons of God" (*bene ha'elohim*; Job 1:6). Throughout the book, Job remains ignorant of his being the subject of such a test. In the epilogue (42:7–17), God announces that, contrary to the arguments of Job's friends, Job alone has spoken what is true or correct (*nekonah*) about God (42:7). Yet as God says and Job acknowledges, Job has spoken "words without knowledge" (38:2; 42:3). These words he spoke vainly, hoping while also fearing that God would hear and respond. Job spoke these words in anguished, persistent, and fierce—if also fracturing—belief in God the Creator, even before God's theophanic appearance and revelation "out of the whirlwind" (38:1), a whirlwind (*se'arah*) that had swept Elijah into heaven (2 Kings 2:11). God's theophany and the magnificent poem it comprises do not answer Job's complaint, a complaint that admits of no answer. They locate Job within the vast space of God's lively and good created world—even, with perhaps some qualification, the "very good" world of Genesis 1:31.

Conclusion

All three of the Old Testament's Wisdom books—Proverbs, Ecclesiastes, Job—do not just assume that God created the world but say so expressly in passages discussed above. Proverbs 8:22–31 associates personified Wisdom intimately with God the Creator, who created the earth *by* Wisdom (3:19). Qoheleth affirms that God made humankind (Eccles. 7:29), and Ecclesiastes counsels the

63. M. Fox, "God's Answer and Job's Response," 20.

reader to "remember your creator" (12:1).[64] The book of Job, of course, makes repeated reference and allusion to God as the Creator. But uniquely within this Wisdom literature, in Job, God appears and God speaks, and God speaks of God's creation at unprecedented length. Part of Job's response to God's speech was to acknowledge that, as I characterized it above, he hadn't known what he was talking about. He had relied on what he had heard. Qoheleth relied on his own experience and background knowledge. All three sources proved inadequate.

In the eighteenth century, the Italian philosopher Giambattista Vico articulated what came to be called the maker's knowledge principle. He argued that "really to know the nature of something it was necessary to have made it."[65] God and nature, Vico said, fall outside the scope of what humans have made, while history and religion, both "made" by humans, fall within it. In Ecclesiastes, Qoheleth, in his comprehensive observation and experience of the world, cannot grasp "the nature" of the world beyond its persistent and oppressive imperviousness to anything new, its utter inscrutability to any divine purpose or presence. Job, however, in the dialogues with his friends, assumes knowledge of "the nature of" the world that includes God within what Newsom describes as Job's "moral universe."[66] Job's presumed knowledge of the world is shattered by the address *to him* by the God who made it and who alone truly knows creation's nature. Job repents. Ecclesiastes counsels, "Fear God and keep his commandments" (12:13). These examples of Old Testament Wisdom literature—Ecclesiastes and Job—testify that understanding the world finally depends on, and derives from, the God who made it.

Proverbs does not contradict the point; it provides an analogy. God's instruments in "building" the cosmos were wisdom, understanding, and knowledge, according to Proverbs 3:19–20. As Raymond C. Van Leeuwen observes, a homebuilder employs the same faculties, endowments, or instruments in designing, building, and furnishing a house, as described in Proverbs 24:3–4.[67] Commenting on these two texts, Van Leeuwen draws this conclusion: "The divine building of the cosmic house by wisdom is the model for human house building; human culture is a form of the *imitatio dei*, especially with reference to God's creation

64. As in the discussion of Ecclesiastes above, I distinguish Qoheleth, the figure who seeks to experience and understand everything, from the book of Ecclesiastes that reports his quest and provides concluding comments in chap. 12.

65. The quotation is from Patrick Gardiner's introduction to Vico in *Theories of History*, 10. Danilo Marcondes de Souza Filho traces the roots of the maker's knowledge principle to Philo in "Maker's Knowledge Principle."

66. Newsom, *Book of Job*, 57.

67. Van Leeuwen draws this analogy in "Creation and Contingency in Qoheleth," 412–13.

of the cosmos as the house in which all houses are contained."[68] Considering the various and sometimes malevolent constructions of human culture to be, altogether, an imitation of God—and thus universally to be the products of wisdom, understanding, and knowledge—requires some qualification. Andrew Errington is right, even so, in discussing "God's practical knowledge of creation": "There is indeed an analogy, the book of Proverbs strongly implies, between God's work of creation and human works, such as 'house-building,' done 'by wisdom.' 'Wisdom,' Proverbs 9:1 declares, 'has built her house.'"[69] God's "practical knowledge" of creation, knowledge as a component of God's action of "building" the cosmos, does have its analogy in human artisanry. At the least, the analogy may sustain Vico's claim that only the maker of something truly understands its nature. Understanding the nature of God and of God's creation by the wisdom of mortals thus lies beyond human apprehension, as does wisdom itself (Job 28). But the fear of the Lord is the beginning of wisdom. And Job learns the fear of the Lord, who challenges him to prepare for a mighty struggle—"gird your loins!"—and to learn something of the nature of what God has made.

Job repents of his claim to know how the world works—how cosmic order and God *should* work together to ensure justice for someone as righteous as Job. God the Creator confronts Job with a wider vision of cosmic order and of God's creation, one that sustains a beautiful and habitable world in which Job's suffering remained unrelieved. Job's suffering, while worthy of comfort, did not reorient the order of creation to its relief.

"The end of the matter; everything has been heard." So concludes Ecclesiastes 12:13 at the end of Wisdom. But God has not finished speaking. Also in the Prophets, God speaks as Creator, including in ways that portend reorienting the order of creation. We turn next to Isaiah.

68. Van Leeuwen, "Creation and Contingency in Qoheleth," 413.
69. Errington, "God's Practical Knowledge of Creation," 230.

7

Royal Theology

GOD THE CREATOR IN ISAIAH

In 1996, the Society of Biblical Literature held its international meeting in Dublin, Ireland. While in Dublin, I visited St. Patrick's Cathedral, which is a short walk from Dublin Castle. The castle was for centuries the site and symbol of England's rule in and over Ireland. From within its walls, agents of the English sovereigns governed the Irish people and protected themselves from Irish ire. A moat had once surrounded the castle, but the Dubliners took to dumping their garbage in it, tossing in dead animals, and depositing other kinds of filth, until the English occupants couldn't stand the stench; they filled in the moat. St. Patrick's Cathedral, though named for the Irish saint, was made part of the Church of England. In an overwhelmingly Catholic republic and city, it is an Anglican church. Within it, I saw the tomb of Jonathan Swift, an organ that Handel played, and other artifacts. In the choir, behind the pulpit, are two rows of chairs, thrones, each of them surrounded by armor and military emblems: the banners and the stalls of the Knights of St. Patrick, guardians of church and crown. And on the walls in the transepts are the old Irish regimental banners and monuments—monuments to military heroes, to fallen warriors, to regiments who fought in South Africa, in India, and in various parts of the once vast British Empire. They fought *for* the empire and for its kings and queens.

I learned my earliest theology lessons in the Ebenfeld Mennonite Brethren Church of Okeene, Oklahoma. That tiny sanctuary didn't have monuments commemorating heroic regiments or armor or military emblems. The only decorations in view were a framed certificate from the state of Oklahoma certifying that we were indeed a church (it hung in the nursery) and a picture of Jesus with his arms around children. But every sermon my father preached in that church he preached standing between two flags: the flag of the United States of America and a Christian Crusader flag. And every summer, on a Sunday night at the conclusion of Vacation Bible School, we preteen children marched to the front of the sanctuary behind those two flags. Before we gave testimony, in verse and in song, to what we had learned about Jesus in the preceding two weeks, we first pledged our allegiance to the flag and to the American republic for which it stands, one nation under God. In our severely low-church way, our Mennonite church resembled St. Patrick's Cathedral in reflecting at some distance what we may call *royal theology*.

Introductory Notes on Royal Theology

By *royal theology* I mean the view that God's purposes are identified with those of the nation and are mediated through the nation's sovereign—typically the king—who is God's representative agent on earth and, especially, the instrument of God's rule. In this book's first chapter I pointed out that in Genesis 1:26–28, *ha'adam* (humankind), created in or as the image of God, is collectively God's royal representative on earth. In royal theology, however, God's image is concentrated in one person—the person of the sovereign, who serves uniquely as God's royal representative. In chapter 4, in discussing literature from antiquity beyond Israel, I gave the example of the Assyrian king Tukulti-Ninurta. He claimed to be born of the gods and to be "alone the eternal image of Enlil," a supreme Mesopotamian deity.[1] While Tukulti-Ninurta may serve as an exemplary instance of royal theology, he is by no means unique. Royal theology or ideology formed part of the "common theology" of ancient Israel and its environment.[2] Indeed, the Old Testament itself includes an especially clear example of royal theology in Psalm 72. Psalm 72 expresses hope that the king's reign will bring peace—*shalom*. The meanings of *shalom* have been the subject of much discussion.[3] Here I propose understanding *shalom* as "things as they should

1. For the text, see Callender, *Adam in Myth and History*, 27.
2. Walter Brueggemann describes the components of this "common theology" in "Shape for Old Testament Theology," 32. He draws on Morton Smith, "Common Theology."
3. The most accessible treatment of *shalom* in the Bible remains Yoder, *Shalom*.

be, as God intended" in a well-ordered world or cosmos. *Shalom*, or peace, in this sense embraces at least three spheres or dimensions: natural, moral, and political. Each of those dimensions appears in Psalm 72.[4] In the psalm's third verse, *shalom* takes the form of agricultural produce that will contribute to the people's well-being. Verse 6 resumes this thought, now comparing the king himself to rain that falls on the fields:

> May he be like rain that falls on mown grass,
> like showers that drench the earth.

The king mediates nature's benefits because he is the mediator of God's blessings. But he serves also as the agent of peace and justice, responsible especially to extend justice to the poor (vv. 2, 13). He must also rescue the poor and oppressed who appeal to him, because they have no other recourse (see v. 12). In other words, *shalom*—peace—in Psalm 72 means prosperity that derives from nature, but it also means justice within the king's realm. On the king, then, and on his just rule depends the community's welfare in every dimension of life.

Psalms 2 and 89 (discussed earlier in chap. 5) offer other examples of royal theology. The hymn of creation early in Psalm 89 serves to connect God's creating an ordered world with the appointment of David as king and the establishment of his ever-enduring royal house (89:30[89:29]). Reinforcing this connection, creation also includes God placing the king's hands on the Sea and Rivers and thus over the unruly forces whose cosmic counterparts—personified by Rahab—God subdued and made part of God's creation (vv. 11[10], 26[25]). Some Mesopotamian royal theology held that kingship itself was a gift of the gods: "when kingship was lowered from heaven."[5] Nowhere does the Old Testament make that claim, but Psalm 89 does portray the king as being closely identified with God and God's purposes:

> I will crush his foes before him
> and strike down those who hate him.
> My faithfulness and my *chesed* will be with him. (vv. 24–25[23–24])
>
> He shall say to me, "You are my father,
> my God and the Rock of my salvation."
> And I will make him my firstborn. (vv. 27–28[26–27])

4. J. J. M. Roberts argues on behalf of royal theology and comments on Ps. 72 in "Enthronement of Yhwh and David."

5. "Sumerian King List," 265.

Royal Theology in Psalm 2 and Isaiah 9

The king's filial relationship with God also comes to expression in Psalm 2 and in Isaiah, our focus here. In Psalm 2:7 the king, God's "anointed" (v. 2), reports that God said to him, "You are my son; today I have begotten you" (NRSV) or "today I have become your father" (CEB).[6] Our concern here is with the book of Isaiah, and it, too, attests a bit of royal theology in the celebration of a royal birth: "A child has been born to us, a son given to us" (Isa. 9:5a[6a]). The continuation of verse 5[6] and the following verse make clear that the people are here celebrating the birth of a king. He is assigned throne names, titles, that associate him closely with God: "Wonderful Counselor, Mighty God, Everlasting Father, Prince of Peace" (9:5b[6b] NRSV). Peace follows in the next verse, and it is promised to "the throne of David and his kingdom" (9:6[9:7] NRSV).

Both Psalm 2 and Isaiah 9, then, refer to the "begetting" of a royal figure. Of course, when God says to the king, "Today I have begotten you" in Psalm 2:7, we are not meant to understand this as the literal birth of an infant on that day. Rather, Psalm 2 announces or affirms the king's accession—the elevation of God's anointed son to the royal throne on Zion—in the face of international rebellion (v. 2). Similarly, when the people celebrate the "birth" and gift of a son in Isaiah 9, we can understand this as referring to the enthronement—the accession to the throne—of a crown prince. It makes sense to think of Psalm 2 and Isaiah 9 as components of a royal accession ritual in which God first declares, "You are my *son*; today I have *begotten* you" (Ps. 2:7 NRSV), and the people respond, "A child has been *born* to us, a *son* given to us" (Isa. 9:5[9:6]).[7]

A distant example may provide a conceptual analogy. Catherine L. McDowell treats in detail the ritual dimensions of the creation and installation of divine images in Mesopotamia. She concludes that, while the image's construction from physical materials was acknowledged and described, "[the] image was *born* through ritual means."[8] I propose that, in these witnesses to royal theology in the Psalms and Isaiah, we have elements of a liturgy affirming that, born

6. The Hebrew verb is from *yalad* and typically means "to father" a child (as also in Isa. 9:5[9:6]). Gard Granerød discusses and provides background to the king's filial relationship with God in Ps. 2 in "Forgotten Reference to Divine Procreation?" I comment on the relationship between Pss. 2 and 72 in *Zion, the City of the Great King*, 64–65.

7. The italicized words mark terms shared between Ps. 2:7 and Isa. 9:5[9:6]. Gerhard von Rad drew this connection decades ago in "Royal Ritual in Judah," 230. His essay was originally published in German in 1947.

8. McDowell, *Image of God in the Garden of Eden*, 85 (italics mine). McDowell analyzes the relevant texts and discussions of them on pp. 43–85.

physically in mundane fashion, the ascendant to the throne was declared and acknowledged to be God's son—birthed as such—"through ritual means."[9]

Isaiah's example of royal theology in 9:5–6[9:6–7], within its context, requires further comment. Above, I pointed to Psalm 72 as an example of royal theology in Israel, or perhaps more precisely, in Judah. While the psalm's superscription associates it with Solomon, it could have served on any number of occasions as part of Judah's liturgical tradition and its rituals. Second Samuel 7:14 and Psalm 89 (quoted above) picture the relationship between God and the (Davidic) king as one of father and son, but only Psalm 2 and Isaiah 9 employ the imagery of birthing or begetting. In Isaiah 9:5[9:6], the royal child is "born *to us* . . . given *to us*." This celebration of a great gift, the gift of a son—of a new king—"to us" comes in the midst of a larger celebration of Judah's liberation from violent military aggressors and the destruction of their uniforms (9:3–4[9:4–5]). The people of Judah are celebrating, then, the restoration of peace without end and a kingship upheld by and in justice and righteousness (9:6[9:7]). This is remarkable on two counts. First, in the context of Isaiah 7:1–9:6[9:7], Judah already has a reigning king: Ahaz (7:1–14). Isaiah 9 portrays the people of Judah celebrating God's gift of a new king while the current monarch remains on the throne. Second, Isaiah 7 and the wider *literary* context (Isa. 5–10) set 9:1–6[9:2–7] in the *historical* context of a political and military crisis that pinches Judah between the imperial might of Assyria and an immediate military threat from Israel and Syria—allies in duress.[10] Those two nations—Israel and Assyria—facing imminent conquest and absorption into the Assyrian Empire, laid siege against Jerusalem hoping to place on its Judean throne a puppet who would join their coalition of anti-Assyrian resistance (Isa. 7:1; 2 Kings 16:5). Ahaz, for his part, solicited the aid of Tiglath-pileser, Assyria's king, in resisting the Syria-Israel coalition. Ahaz thus made himself the Assyrian monarch's vassal, subjecting Judah to the "yoke" of Assyria's oppressive rule. In the midst of this dire circumstance—not merely the threat posed by Syria's and Israel's ephemeral kings but also the imposition of Assyrian oppression—Isaiah 9:3–4[9:4–5] celebrates great victory and liberation from Judah's oppressor, a celebration that could take place only in the future.

Isaiah 9 celebrates a royal accession while there remains a king on the throne, and it celebrates a glorious liberation in a circumstance of vassalage

9. Typically, Ps. 2:7 has been understood in terms of adoption: God adopting the new king. This was von Rad's view in "Royal Ritual in Judah," 223–24. For more on Ps. 2 and royal ritual, see Granerød, "Forgotten Reference to Divine Procreation?"

10. I distinguish between *literary* and *historical* contexts because I have little confidence in the dating of any parts of the book of Isaiah. And it is in Isaiah's—the book's—presentation of God the Creator that I am interested here.

and oppression. The celebration, then, can only be prospective, expressing a hope and a promise.[11] And the celebration of a newly "born" king must be understood as criticism of—an implicit rejection and replacement of—the one in power: Ahaz, whose appeal to Assyria for "salvation" he cast in terms redolent of royal theology, saying to Tiglath-pileser: "Your servant and your son am I. Come up and save me" (2 Kings 16:7).

As in other samples of royal theology in the Old Testament, Ahaz here acknowledges that he, as Judah's king, is the servant of a superior, to whom he is related as a son to a father. The language is the same as that in 2 Samuel 7, where David acknowledges that, as king, he is the servant of a superior, to whom he is related as a son to a father. But David refers to himself as *God's* servant (2 Sam. 7:19 and nine other instances in that chapter), and it is to *God* that David's progeny are related as son to father (7:14), a filial relationship announced and promised and celebrated in the texts cited above. Ahaz's filial fealty to the Assyrian king elicits what R. A. Carlson calls "the oracle" in Isaiah 9:1–6[9:2–7]: "The oracle must be seen against the background of the OT royal ideological tradition, and as an actualization of certain aspects of it in a particular situation. That situation is, according to the prophet, the disastrous alliance with Assyria."[12] In the theological logic of Isaiah, the alliance with Assyria is disastrous, not (only) for possible strategic reasons but because it constitutes a faithless repudiation of God's exclusive prerogative as King and Creator, and the founder (14:32; 28:16) and defender of Zion.[13] In Isaiah 9, read together with its wider literary context, royal theology's human king is displaced in favor of God the King and Creator who dwells on and reigns from Zion (8:18). Royal theology did not disappear from the Bible—it continues in the New Testament—but it was subject to transformation, even in Isaiah. In the remainder of Isaiah, royal theology has as its subject God alone.

The book of Isaiah throughout presents God as King and Creator, but it does so in different ways in relation to different contexts and crises that can be gathered from the text of Isaiah itself. My discussion of the texts will divide between Isaiah 1–39 and 40–55 on the basis of the different contexts and the current, past, and impending crises those texts inscribe, all of them testifying to God the Creator. Isaiah 65:17–18 testifies most dramatically, in its announcement of God's new creation; chapter 9 below will include consideration of it and (other) *apocalyptic* Old Testament texts.

11. See Blenkinsopp, *Isaiah 1–39*, 50.

12. Carlson, "Anti-Assyrian Character," 132.

13. This I argued in *Zion, the City of the Great King*. See also Brueggemann, "Creation in First Isaiah."

God the Creator in Isaiah 1–39

Discussion of creation in Isaiah typically focuses on Isaiah 40–45, 65, which depict God as Creator (e.g., Isa. 40:26–28) or as creating something entirely new (65:17–18). Those texts situate themselves in the context of imperial powers Babylon and Persia. But texts earlier in Isaiah also describe God acting as Creator, texts that refer to Assyria and the crisis its imperial power and designs posed to Judah. As I suggested above, in Isaiah's terms, the crisis was in the first place a crisis of faith.

Faith is demanded of Ahaz, in Isaiah 7, as he faces the threat against Judah from Syria's coalition with Israel in the context of Assyria's imperial expansion. God issues this demand, which Isaiah reports to Ahaz, who is to "observe carefully [*hishamer*], be quiet, don't be afraid, and don't be fainthearted" (7:4). The threat from these minor kings was ephemeral—this was God's word to Ahaz through Isaiah—and so would their kingdoms prove to be (7:5–8). This Ahaz was required to believe: "If you do not believe, you will not endure," which amounts to a pun in Hebrew: *'im lo' ta'aminu, ki lo' te'amenu* (7:9b). This is a demand for faith, for belief, for trust, of the sort demanded of and exercised by the Hebrew people at the sea, who saw God's great work in delivering them from the Egyptians and believed (*ya'aminu*) in God and in Moses (Exod. 14:31). While Isaiah 7:1–9 embeds God's demand for faith within a narrative that has Isaiah confronting Ahaz, that demand—that requirement (7:9b)—is expressed with plural verbs (as also in Exod. 14:31), as if this demand extends beyond Ahaz and his court and even beyond the confines of the book to its readers.[14]

In Isaiah, this demand for faith in God has its grounds in God's assurances, as for example in Isaiah 8:9–10:

> Look with despair and be dismayed, O peoples;
> give ear, all the far reaches of the earth.
> Gird yourselves and be dismayed.
> Gird yourselves and be dismayed.
> Take counsel together that it may be annulled,
> discuss the matter, but it will not stand,
> because God is with us.

The divine assurances in this poem capture in brief the depictions in Psalms 46, 48, and 76—the Zion psalms—of God's defense of Zion against futile international

14. See Oswald, "Textwelt," 207–8.

threats.[15] The last clause of Isaiah 8:10—"God is with us"—is also the definitive assurance of God's commitment to Zion, the site of God's royal dwelling. In this regard, Psalm 46:6[46:5] declares that God's presence in Zion secures its "immovability" (see also below), while verse 8[7] promises that "Yhwh of hosts is with us." This is the same promise with which Isaiah 8:9–10 concludes: "God is with us"—in Hebrew, *'immanu 'el*, transliterated in 7:14 as "Immanuel" (also in 8:8).

God's assurance regarding Zion in Isaiah 8:9–10 assumes a mocking tone, as if daring the nations to form plans contrary to God's—plans such as those of Rezin of Syria and Pekah of Israel. Their plans (and those kings) "will not stand," God insists to Ahaz through Isaiah (7:7), and neither will the conspiratorial plans of the nations "stand" (8:10)—the verb is *qum* in both instances.

Isaiah 17:12–14, like 8:9–10, provides grounds for God's assurances and demand for faith.[16] Perhaps oddly placed within the oracles against the nations (Isa. 13–23), and specifically within an oracle concerning Damascus (17:1–18:7),[17] the text evokes the language of creation in expressing confidence in God's determination and ability to thwart the efforts of nations that would plunder "us."

> Ah! The thunder of many peoples;
> they thunder like the thunder of the seas,
> and the roaring [*sha'on*] of the peoples—
> they roar [*yisha'un*] like the roaring of mighty waters.
> The nations roar like the roaring of many waters.
> But [God] roars [*ga'ar*] at them and they flee away,
> pursued like chaff on the mountain before the wind,
> or tumbleweeds before the storm.
> At evening, terror;
> before morning, it is no more.
> This is the fate of those who rob us,
> the lot of those who plunder us. (17:12–14)[18]

While this text does not name God—Yhwh—it obviously reflects the Jerusalem cult tradition and God's defense of Zion, and it does so in language that

15. I discussed the Zion psalms in chap. 5.

16. In discussing God's call for faith in Isa. 28:16, Jaap Dekker associates that text with Isa. 8:9–10 and 17:12–14 in *Zion's Rock-Solid Foundations*, 335.

17. Sweeney, *Isaiah 1–39*, 212–17, 252–62.

18. On the translation of these verses, see Blenkinsopp, *Isaiah 1–39*, 306–7; Roberts, *First Isaiah*, 240–44.

echoes the creation language we have seen in the Psalms.[19] Psalm 104 describes God founding the earth, with the waters fleeing at God's roaring and the thunder of God's voice (v. 7). Here in Isaiah 17, God roars, and the threatening, thundering, roaring nations flee. Earlier, in chapter 5 on the Psalms, I suggested that the Hebrew verb *ga'ar*, typically translated "rebuke" in contexts like those of Psalm 104 and Isaiah 17, is better translated onomatopoetically as "roar." In Psalm 104, of course, the waters offer no resistance; they simply respond to God's (loud) voice. Similarly, in Psalm 106:9, God roars at the Reed Sea, and immediately it becomes dry. In Isaiah 17:12–14, however, there are competing voices—competing powers, competing roarings. The text compares the nations to the unruly, chaotic waters that God's voice sent scurrying to their places—nations that themselves roar and thunder and, thus, threaten. It is the same action of God the Creator that, primordially, scattered the waters to their place on behalf of the earth and now promises to defend Zion by scattering hostile, threatening mundane powers. And this promise, this reality—that God remains the Creator and the Defender of Zion—constitutes the foundation of the faith that God demands and Isaiah articulates.

The two Isaiah texts I have discussed here, 8:9–10 and 17:12–14, extend God's action as Creator beyond that of world formation or cosmic ordering into the political sphere. God's sovereignty as Creator thus extends internationally—it includes the nations "who take counsel together" and who roar like the chaotic sea. As Zion's Creator and Defender, God does not limit his sovereign *reach* to the city walls of Jerusalem or the borders of Judah. At the same time, God's assurances regarding the security of Zion do take Judean domestic affairs into account, as Isaiah 1–10 and 14:32 make explicit. In Isaiah's logic, Zion, the city of God, is not reducible to Jerusalem the city of David, despite their mundane geographic overlap. Zion, the site of God's dwelling (Isa. 8:18; Pss. 9:12[9:11]; 76:3[76:2]), will endure: "God is in [Zion's] midst; it is immovable [*bal-timmot*]" (Ps. 46:6[46:5]). Jerusalem, by contrast, is subject to destruction, a fate that the city eventually suffers—not merely by fate, though, but as God's judgment, according to the testimony of Jeremiah and Ezekiel (cf. Isa. 64).[20] With respect to the moral order of creation—God's created order in its cosmic, natural, and social-political dimensions—God assumes an impartial stance toward the nations. Assyria may be the roaring power, the threat against which God roars in defense of Zion—and Jerusalem—but Assyria may also be

19. Marvin A. Sweeney speaks of the "Jerusalem cult tradition" in *Isaiah 1–39*, 258–59. Cf. Ollenburger, *Zion, the City of the Great King*, 120–24; Ollenburger, "Isaiah's Creation Theology," 57–58.

20. Ollenburger, *Zion, the City of the Great King*, 119, with reference to Schreiner, *Sion-Jerusalem*, 256.

"the rod of my anger" (10:5): God's anger against Judah's faithless leadership and pervasive injustice.[21]

The psalms that were the focus of discussion in chapter 5 portray God in creative action, sometimes violent action, against hostile watery forces—the Sea, River(s), Leviathan, Rahab. These forces were historically embodied in military powers as forces of chaos, forces opposed to the kind of order conformed to God's intention. Chaos in its cosmic dimension and primordial time takes concrete temporal form in the "chaotic" arrogance of Assyria, ordained as the rod of God's anger but arrogating to itself the Creator's prerogative (Isa. 10:15). But Jerusalem's leadership as well—the royal court and the nobility—proved itself to be an agent of chaos through its pervasive practices of injustice and oppression, which Isaiah describes in chapter 1 and in 3:14–15, 5:1–24, and 9:7[9:8]–10:4. Those suffering injustice are typically the poor (*'ani*)—the poor who were to find refuge in Zion: "Yhwh founded Zion, and in it the poor of God's people will find refuge" (14:32). God the Creator founded (*yasad*) Zion as a refuge for the poor just as God had founded (*yasad*) the earth (Ps. 104:5). The exploitation and oppression of the poor by Jerusalem's nobility thus constituted action hostile to the creation and to the Creator. As Walter Brueggemann writes, "Refusing to do justice toward the poor, widows, and orphans not only violates covenant, but contradicts the nonnegotiable reality of creation as ordered by the creator, a contradiction that can only bring disaster."[22] Injustice and domestic violence (Isa. 1:21), reliance on foreign alliances and armaments for security, and turning to actual idols constitute forms of idolatry in Isaiah (see 2:6–8)—a refusal of the faith God demanded—and a contradiction of the reality of creation.

Disaster for Jerusalem did not follow immediately. Instead, in a moment of extreme crisis—Assyria's war against Judah and siege of Jerusalem under Sennacherib—Isaiah 37 offers the most explicit expression of God the Creator's defense against a hostile historical force. After reading a letter from Sennacherib mocking the Judeans' confidence in God to defend them, Hezekiah prays: "Yhwh of hosts, God of Israel, enthroned on the cherubim, you alone are God over all the kingdoms of the earth; you made the heavens and the earth" (37:16). The epithet "Lord [Yhwh] of hosts" is characteristic of Isaiah, occurring more than fifty times from 1:9 to 54:5. The martial imagery—God as commander of the heavenly armies—here combines with the picture of God enthroned on the cherubim, the winged creatures surmounting the ark (1 Sam. 4:4; 2 Sam. 6:2; 1 Kings 8:6–7), to portray God as King and Defender. Finally, the explicit

21. Brueggemann, "Creation in First Isaiah," 40–45.
22. Brueggemann, "Creation in First Isaiah," 40.

confession that God created the world grounds the claim of God's sovereignty over the earthly kingdoms, including that of Sennacherib, whose threats and conquests (Isa. 37:10–13) have driven Hezekiah to prayer. God's action as Creator extends into the political realm, as we see here once more.

God's action as Creator extends not only into the realm of history but also to history itself. While Sennacherib may have supposed that it was on his own initiative that he brought his imperial army against Judah and Jerusalem, the prophet Isaiah reports to Hezekiah a different word from God, one that refers again to the "roaring" of a hostile force: Assyria. As if addressing Sennacherib, God says through Isaiah: "Have you not heard? From long ago I made it; from days of old I have formed it. Now, I have brought it to pass. . . . Because you have raged against me, and your roaring has come to my ears, I will put my hook in your nose, my bit in your lips, and will turn you back on the way by which you came" (Isa. 37:26, 29).[23]

God's creative work here, the work of making (*'asah*) and forming (*yatsar*), does not have as its object primordial creation, as when God "made" the luminaries in Genesis 1:16 and "formed" the first mortal in 2:7. The text here employs the language of creation to make a claim about God's inclusion of even Sennacherib's western campaign within the sphere of God's sovereign action as Creator. The events of that campaign, including the Assyrian king's reducing cities to rubble (Isa. 37:11–13, 26b–27), are part of what God the Creator takes credit for making and forming. The text does not deny Sennacherib's agency, as expressed in his own (quoted) boasts of conquest (vv. 24–25), but God's making and forming supervene on Sennacherib's plans and actions, with the penultimate result of his ignoble abandonment of the field and hasty return home.[24] The arrogant raging and roaring of Sennacherib (v. 23) are silenced. Ultimately, Sennacherib's abandonment means the defense of Jerusalem and Zion and the preservation of their future (v. 32).

Isaiah 37:32 provides a coda to the entire episode: "The zeal of Yhwh of hosts will do this," an affirmation that previously concluded the announcement regarding the royal child born and the son given in Isaiah 9:5[9:6]. This late echo of royal theology in Isaiah 37 is extended at the chapter's end, where

23. For discussion of the text and translation, see my "Isaiah's Creation Theology," 56–57.

24. Historical reconstructions of the details of Sennacherib's campaign and siege of Jerusalem, not taken into account here, are available in brief (Ussishkin, "Sennacherib's Campaign to Judah") and in detail (Matty, *Sennacherib's Campaign*). Sennacherib had his own boasts inscribed on prisms, one of which is in the University of Chicago's Oriental Institute Museum; K. C. Hanson provides a translation of it at "Sennacherib Prism," October 19, 2020, http://www.kchanson.com/ANCDOCS/meso/sennprism1.html. Sennacherib's boast of confining Hezekiah in Jerusalem "like a caged bird" appears in column 3.

God promises to defend and save Jerusalem "for my own sake and for the sake of my servant David" (v. 35 NRSV). Here is royal theology, to be sure, but without a *royal*—with no earthly king—in view. Hezekiah's prayer availed much (37:15–21), but his entertainment of Babylon's king provokes Isaiah's pronouncement of an end to any expectations of dynastic succession beyond Hezekiah himself. In Judah's history following Hezekiah's reign, as 2 Kings and 2 Chronicles narrate it, the Davidic house continues for a season. But in Isaiah, Hezekiah is the final Judean king, whose concerns extend no further than himself (Isa. 39:5–8).

In Isaiah 37–39, royal theology recedes and God the Creator advances. Near the beginning of this chapter, I defined royal theology as the view that God's purposes are identified with those of the nation and are mediated through the nation's sovereign—typically the king—who is God's representative agent on earth and, especially, the instrument of God's rule. In the defense of Zion/Jerusalem against an Assyrian imperial army, the Judean king's only positive action is to pray, a prayer he directs to God the Creator (37:16). The only agent active in the defense of the city is God, or—which is to say the same thing—the angel of Yhwh (37:36–37). When Hezekiah does act, it is to offer generous—and in Isaiah's view, treasonous—welcome to emissaries from Babylon, whose own imperial armies would lay waste to Jerusalem.

God the Creator in Isaiah 40–55

Judean royal theology receives its most decisive modification in Isaiah 40–50, which assumes Babylon's conquest of Judah, the destruction of Jerusalem, and the forced migration to Babylon of Judah's civil, religious, and economic elite. Despite what would appear to be the decisive repudiation of the creation-grounded promises God made in Psalm 89 regarding the eternality of David and his throne, Isaiah 40:12–55:13 opens with an extended argument on behalf of God the Creator, acclaims God as King (41:21; 43:15; 44:6), and identifies a Persian emperor, not a scion of David's house, as God's anointed (44:28; 45:1). God's promises to David regarding his house are not denied, but they are distributed: God's eternal covenant with David remains in effect, but it is now a royal covenant made with *you* (plural, 55:3).[25] And the people addressed are

25. Isaiah's use of the terms *servant* and *chosen* to describe the community—Jacob/Israel—may also suggest its identity as a royal community, something for which Edgar W. Conrad argues in *Fear Not Warrior*, 79–107. On the theme of creation in these chapters of Isaiah, see Tull, "'Who Has Measured the Waters?'"

the very ones who suffer the consequences of what would seem to be not only Jerusalem's defeat but also God's defeat or abandonment. Isaiah addresses those complaining with what appears to be good evidence that they lie beyond the reach of God's concern and live in terror of what lies on the horizon (41:10). Isaiah's pastoral word to these people in exile is the declaration that they know better. His pastoral declaration takes the form of an argument. And he argues on the basis of what seems most in doubt: that God is the world's Creator. Because this is so—because God is the Creator—the people's complaints are groundless. Isaiah's pastoral and rhetorical strategy in 40:12–45:13 does not lack for boldness.

The argument, beginning with Isaiah 40:12, is directed to Jacob/Israel (v. 27), which I understand to be the Judean community exiled in Babylon, whom Isaiah addresses from Jerusalem.[26] The argument concludes with encouragement to wait for—to trust and place hope in—God (40:31). In between, the argument proceeds in three stages.[27]

The argument's first stage, in Isaiah 40:12–17, opens with rhetorical questions (vv. 12–14) from which Jacob/Israel should infer that God alone establishes the order of the world. In comparison with Yhwh, the nations—including the nations claiming to (re)order the world in their interests—amount to dust on the scales (v. 15). Before Yhwh, they are less than nothing; indeed, Yhwh considers them *tohu*, which the NRSV translates as "emptiness" (v. 17). *Tohu* first appeared in Genesis 1:2 in a rhyming combination—*tohu wabohu*—describing "the earth" before God's work of creating a "very good" world (1:31). Here in Isaiah 40:17, *tohu* describes the nations as emptiness, as unformed, as "formlessness" itself.[28] This first stage of Isaiah's argument reduces to absurdity the idea that the nations finally determine the world's order or could resist Yhwh's creation of it. The nations themselves are subject to the ordering power of the Creator.

Stages two and three of the argument (Isa. 40:18–24, 25–31) stress—again by way of rhetorical questions—Yhwh's incomparability, which verses 15–17 strongly imply. "To whom will you compare God [*'ēl*]?" Yhwh asks in verse 18, and in verse 25: "To whom will you compare me, and who is my equal?" The second stage (vv. 18–24) parodies the creation of idols. This kind of "creation" puts things upside down, as Patricia K. Tull writes: "Idolaters turn the order in creation upside down by worshiping objects that they have made rather than the

26. Agreeing with Goulder, "Deutero-Isaiah of Jerusalem."

27. I draw here from my "Isaiah's Creation Theology," 63–66. See also the compatible study J. Cook, "Everyone Called by My Name."

28. For the semantic range of *tohu*, see *DCH*, 8:592–93.

God who made them."[29] God then poses a series of rhetorical questions to Jacob/Israel: "Do you not know? Have you not heard?" (v. 21). The second of these questions echoes the one Yhwh posed to Sennacherib: "Have you not heard? From long ago I made it; from days of old I have formed it" (37:26). While these questions might have puzzled Sennacherib (would he have recognized them as rhetorical?), these questions Yhwh poses in Isaiah 40 assume acknowledgment, an assumption reinforced by a second pair of rhetorical questions: "Was it not declared to you [Jacob/Israel] from the beginning? Have you not understood from the foundations of the earth?" (v. 21). The content of what was declared to Jacob/Israel from the beginning and what they should now understand follows, spelled out in a series of participles describing God the Creator (vv. 22–23). The series concludes by describing God as the one who reduces dignitaries to nothing. And Yhwh "makes" the rulers of the earth *tohu*. Once more in Isaiah 40, those presumed to be—and who presume themselves to be—the powers governing the world are dismissed as *tohu* in (futile) comparison with God the Creator.

The reduction of nations, kings, and princes—of international powers—to *tohu* or nothingness is not for the purpose of divine exaltation in the abstract. Rather, as the third stage of the argument in Isaiah 40 makes explicit (vv. 25–31), the goal of the entire argument is to persuade Jacob/Israel that their complaint is unfounded. They are not beyond the reach of God's attention or beyond God's capacity to act on their behalf (v. 27). The solar and lunar and astral bodies to which God directs the people's attention (v. 26) are not divine patrons of the nations and kings and princes who compete for governance of the world and determine the fate of Jacob/Israel. Rather, they are creations of the Creator who calls them by name and summons their appearing. The identity of this Creator is no mystery: Jacob/Israel has known and has heard that the "God of *'olam*"—of past and future—"is Yhwh, creator of the earth from end to end" (v. 28).

Isaiah's argument in chapter 40 proceeds, then, in three stages:

Stage 1

- God alone planned and executed the creation of the world.
- Before God, the nations are as nothing and *tohu*.

29. Tull, "'Who Has Measured the Waters?,'" 61. Tull cites a number of Isaiah texts in which Hebrew verbs describing God's creating are used also of idol construction. Klaus Baltzer notes the use of *'el* ("God") in contexts contrasting God with humans (e.g., Num. 23:19; Hosea 11:9) in *Deutero-Isaiah*, 73.

Stage 2

- The incomparable God is the Creator.
- God reduces the world's princes and rulers to nothing, as if they are *tohu*.

Stage 3

- The incomparable God created and commands the heavenly host.
- This God the Creator is Yhwh, declared to and known by Jacob/Israel.

Isaiah 40's artfully constructed argument, in its characterizations of the Creator, elicits the assent of its readers at each stage. But only after Jacob/Israel names Yhwh as the subject of their complaint (v. 27) does Isaiah name *yhwh* as the Creator (v. 28)—and not only as mighty in power but also as unwearied and granting power to the powerless, the weary, the fainting.

Isaiah 40 takes the form of an argument because the claims it makes through chapter 45 would seem absurd on their face. In the historical context in which this part of Isaiah sets itself, Babylon has exercised imperial power. Images or artifacts representing conquered deities and their vassal regions—including Judah—reside literally under the feet of Marduk, Babylon's chief deity, in his temple in Babylon, the Esagila.

In this circumstance, when Jacob/Israel could reasonably conclude that Yhwh had abandoned them or had been defeated by Marduk, Isaiah urges them to believe what they had been told long ago: Yhwh—a deity apparently forced into exile with Judah's royalty and nobility while his temple lies in desecrated ruins—is the Creator of the heavens and the earth and thus the Lord of history and Israel's Redeemer (Isa. 41:14). The "thus" is not a matter of logic, of course. That a deity is identified as a creator or as *the* Creator does not entail that deity's entanglement with mundane historical affairs or with the governance of a nation's particular circumstances. These divine responsibilities and others may be apportioned among different deities. In Isaiah, they are all apportioned to one.

Debates about monotheism in Israel and in the Old Testament, including in Isaiah, continue.[30] We need not engage those debates here. But we have already seen, in the Psalms and in earlier chapters of Isaiah, that God acts as Creator not only *of* but also *in* the natural world. God acts as Creator with moral purpose in the realms of (inter)national political and domestic social arrangements. In Isaiah 45, Yhwh repeatedly insists on an exclusive claim to divinity: Yhwh alone is God, "and there is no other [*we'en 'od*]" (vv. 5, 6, 14, 18,

30. See Gordon, *God of Israel*; Mark Smith, "Monotheism and the Redefinition of Divinity."

21, 22). Whatever spheres of divine responsibility there may be, Isaiah claims, these Yhwh occupies.

Once again, then, the assertions of incomparability are not claims to (exclusive) divinity in the abstract. The three-stage argument in Isaiah 40:12–31, whose premises and whose conclusions are that Yhwh is God the Creator, is directed toward the promise that God is "creating a new future for Israel."[31] That argument prepares the way for the extended descriptions of God the Creator in Isaiah 44 and 45. For example, Yhwh is the God who formed Jacob/Israel and who claims that "I alone stretched out the heavens and [I] spread out the earth by myself" (44:24). Further, "I made the earth and created humankind upon it. My own hands stretched out the heavens and commanded their host" (45:12). Between these two statements comes the implausible announcement that God's appointed agent of Jerusalem's restoration and the temple's reconstruction is Cyrus the Persian, Yhwh's "shepherd" and "anointed" (44:28; 45:1).

This announcement was not only implausible; it was objectionable. That an alien military leader with imperial designs, who was terrifying and unsettling the Babylonian world (Isa. 41), was ascribed the properly Davidic titles of *shepherd* and *anointed* could be expected to elicit strong objections. Isaiah expected them. Isaiah prepared for the announcement about Cyrus with an extensive self-description of God the Creator in Isaiah 44:24–27. Its series of nine participles describes Yhwh as Creator—"the one who made everything" (v. 24)—a series that continues and culminates in verse 28 with the presentation of Cyrus as Yhwh's shepherd. Similarly, Isaiah responds to actual or anticipated objections with, again, reference to God the Creator: arguing with one's maker—Yhwh—would be analogous to the clay contending with its potter or criticizing the potter for making a pot without handles (45:9).[32] The Creator's prerogative, Isaiah insists, includes enlisting the agent of international terror and imperial conquest in the service of Jerusalem's—of Israel's—restoration, its redemption. It is as Israel's Redeemer that Yhwh is identified in the opening words of the extended description of Yhwh as Creator in Isaiah 44:24–28—the Redeemer "who formed you from the womb" (v. 24).

Above, I wrote that regardless of how broad the range of divine responsibilities may be, according to Isaiah, Yhwh exercises all of them. Isaiah 45 offers the most explicit support for this claim in the context of Yhwh's own claim to exhaust the category of divinity: "I am Yhwh [LXX: "the Lord God"] and there

31. Tull, "'Who Has Measured the Waters?,'" 56.
32. On this verse and its context, see Goldingay, *Message of Isaiah 40–55*, 278–80.

is no other; besides me there are no gods" (v. 5).[33] In verse 7, Yhwh expands on this claim as the one who

> forms light and creates darkness
> and who makes well-being [*shalom*] and creates calamity [*ra'*].
> I, Yhwh, do all these things.

The creation language in this verse echoes that of Genesis 1 and 2. In 1:3, God speaks light into existence, and here God forms it, as Yhwh forms (*yatsar*) the man in 2:7. Before God's "let there be light," darkness covered the earth (1:2). Here in Isaiah 45:7, God creates (*bara'*) darkness, as God created the heavens and the earth in Genesis 1:1. Here God makes (*'asah*) well-being—*shalom*, peace—as God made the dome that separates the waters above it from those below it (1:7). Most strikingly, in Isaiah 45:7, Yhwh claims to create (*bara'*) woe—or calamity, disaster, or evil (*ra'*).

This verse has provoked significant discussion and consternation, especially with its claim that Yhwh creates evil.[34] But the claim does not respond to, and neither is it intended to provoke, a philosophical question about divine responsibility for evil in the universe. The claim is situated within and at the conclusion of Yhwh's address to Cyrus that begins in Isaiah 45:1 and continues through verse 7. As Israel's Creator and Redeemer, and for the purpose of Israel's redemption, Yhwh has elected and anointed the Persian Cyrus and promises to bring about before him calamity, disaster, and evil to kings and nations, wreaking purposed and revelatory havoc. Then Cyrus himself will know, and so also Israel will know, that Yhwh, the God of Israel, has called Cyrus by name for Israel's sake and for God's purposes (vv. 1–4). The latter verses of Isaiah 44 and the first half of chapter 45 enfold the imperial ambition of Cyrus and his military conquests within God the Creator's purposes for Israel and the world.

The final sentence of Isaiah 45:7 summarizes both the entire verse and the address to Cyrus beginning in 45:1, even as it brings to a point the three-stage argument of Isaiah 40: "I, Yhwh, do all these things"—that is, the forming of light and the creating of darkness, the making of *shalom* and the creating

33. Following Blenkinsopp, *Isaiah 40–55*, 249–50. The noun is *'elohim*, which could be translated as "God" or "gods."

34. John Goldingay provides an extensive and historically informed discussion in *Message of Isaiah 40–55*, 268–72. See also Nilson, "Creation of Darkness and Evil." She also discusses Benjamin Sommer's proposal that Isa. 45:7, with its statement that Yhwh creates darkness, responds in disagreement to Gen. 1:2. Sommer, *Prophet Reads Scripture*, 142–44.

of disaster. These opposites serve here as "good and bad" did in Genesis 2. They serve as a merism for totality, which I explained at length in chapter 2 of this book. Michael DeRoche recognizes this in Isaiah 45:7, concluding that the final line in verse 7—"I, Yhwh, do all these things"—"summarizes in a more succinct manner the point of the first two: Yahweh is the creator of everything!"[35] However many divine responsibilities there may be—including the salvation (v. 17) and redemption (ten times in chapters 40–55) of Israel—Isaiah insists that they are apportioned to no one but Yhwh. Saving and redeeming—rescuing, delivering—were typically royal functions and responsibilities.[36] These, in every part of Isaiah, are claimed as Yhwh's exclusive prerogative.

Conclusion

Royal theology was the subject at the beginning of this chapter. It remains the subject at its conclusion—royal theology without a mortal king. Isaiah devotes divinely inspired poetic brilliance and rhetorical power to arguing in favor of—persuading Israel of—God the Creator and the legally heretical claim that the terrorizing Persian Cyrus is God's anointed agent of Jerusalem's and the temple's restoration. But Cyrus is not the subject of royal theology in Isaiah's latter chapters. Yhwh exhausts the category—exclusively occupies the office—of king, since Yhwh alone is the Creator: "I am Yhwh, your Holy One, Creator of Israel, your King" (Isa. 43:15). Cyrus's agency is genuine. But it is appropriated and delegated agency. God appropriated Cyrus's agency as a military commander and delegated it to the restoration of Jerusalem and the temple—on analogy with the delegated agency of the ruling luminaries, the sun and the moon, in Genesis 1:14–17. In Genesis 1, of course, the luminaries enact their agencies in exact correspondence to God's intention for them. God does grasp Cyrus's right hand and promise to go before him in conquest (Isa. 45:1–4) to carry out God's purposes (44:28), but those purposes do not determine, for example, whether Cyrus should attack Croesus, king of Lydia. Cyrus, who calls himself "King of the Universe,"[37] is free to make that determination and myriad others. Finally, the focus of Isaiah's royal theology is not on Cyrus but on Yhwh, inscribed for

35. DeRoche, "Isaiah XLV 7 and the Creation of Chaos?"

36. The king saves, rescues, and delivers, e.g., in 2 Sam. 19:10[19:9] and in Ps. 72:4, 12–13. Cf. Ollenburger, *Zion, the City of the Great King*, 94–95, 211.

37. This is recorded in the Cyrus Cylinder, now in the British Museum. The museum's website provides a translation: https://www.britishmuseum.org/collection/object/W_1880-0617-1941.

Yhwh's royal community, "my servant Jacob and Israel my chosen," for the sake of whom the God of Israel called Cyrus (45:4).[38]

In Isaiah, God the Creator designates agents, allies, and witnesses, all of them appointed for or enlisted in the return of Jacob/Israel to a restored Zion/Jerusalem. This return follows Yhwh's own return on a highway through hills and valleys prepared and made level by a divine assembly Yhwh addresses in Isaiah 40:1–11. Yhwh's announced return has its echo in the call for Israel's return in Isaiah 55. In between these framing texts, God anoints the warrior Cyrus, promises to transform the dry and barren wilderness on behalf of the oppressed and needy (41:17), and expects even jackals to offer praise in response to God's unexpectedly well-watered wilderness. The natural world—the heavens and the earth, its depths and its mountains, and the trees of the forest—joins in song at God's redemption of Israel (44:23). As Tull writes, Isaiah places not just human existence "but political geography and history within the circle of creation," thus underscoring "the unity within God's creative power." Nature, too, Isaiah places within this circle and this unity. Tull continues, remarking that, "like the humans, the nonhuman players belong to the story itself. This is illustrated in the many instances in Second Isaiah of the natural world's working in support of God's program for Israel."[39]

That program, God's program as Isaiah announces it, focuses on Israel, of course. But the nations, too, lie within the circumference of that focus. And in addition to placing "political geography and history" within the circle of creation, Isaiah includes topography. In Isaiah 2:2, echoed in Micah 4:1, Yhwh announces that "the mountain of Yhwh's house"—Zion—will be the highest of mountains, to which the nations will stream. They will come in procession to receive instruction (*torah*) and the word of the Lord, and the Lord will adjudicate disputes among them, turning obsolete weapons into farm implements and ending the need for instruction in war (Isa. 2:2–4). Isaiah envisions God the Creator's victory over war.

In remarks at the annual meeting of the American Academy of Religion and the Society of Biblical Literature in 1998, New Testament scholar N. T. Wright, then dean of Lichfield Cathedral in England, spoke of his anxiety having to preach the sermon on Remembrance Sunday. In the United Kingdom, Remembrance Day commemorates those who have served and those who have fallen in the nation's armed forces. The service is held on the Sunday closest to

38. Millard C. Lind's essay on Cyrus and the servant in Isa. 40–55 continues to be instructive ("Monotheism, Power, and Justice"). The original was published in *CBQ* in 1984. See also J. Gerald Janzen's response to Lind, "On the Moral Nature of God's Power."

39. Tull, "'Who Has Measured the Waters?,'" 60.

November 11, at 11:00 a.m., the date and time of the armistice ending World War I. What, Wright wondered, would he preach on this day that celebrated victory in war? The Lichfield Cathedral, he said, was full. "And faced with a church, a cathedral, full of politicians, local counselors, war veterans, and cadets in military uniform, I preached a sermon that the real victory is not victory in war but victory over war."[40] As prophet of God the Creator, this is the victory Isaiah envisions.

40. Wright's remarks were published in "Meaning of Jesus," from which I have quoted.

8

"Who Treads on the Heights of the Earth"

GOD THE CREATOR IN THE PROPHETS AFTER ISAIAH

If the Society of Biblical Literature were to commission a poll asking a random selection of people in churches and synagogues to name the book in the Bible that, more than any other, depicts or refers to God as Creator, the most common answer would almost certainly be "Genesis." That answer would not be entirely wrong, since only Genesis tells the story of God creating the heavens and the earth and their constituents. But "Isaiah" would count as the right answer, because of the book's extensive descriptions of and references to God the Creator, some of which the previous chapter examined. Isaiah was a prophet (Isa. 37:2; 38:1; 39:3).[1] As a prophet in particular circumstances, Isaiah was not concerned to narrate the origin of the habitable earth and its population. Genesis, too, was composed in particular circumstances—whatever those may have been—but in its stories of creation, and despite its allusion to Babylon in Genesis 11, it does not directly name or address those circumstances; Isaiah does. The book of Isaiah situates itself particularly and historically, through chapter 55, with

1. Earlier chapters of Isaiah describe him as a seer—one who saw a vision (1:1), saw a word (2:1), or saw an oracle (13:1).

reference to named Syrian, Israelite, Assyrian, and Babylonian kings and to Babylon itself as the destroyer of something so particular as Jerusalem—not to mention Cyrus the Persian, the terror of Babylon and the anointed of Yhwh, whose appointment and qualified endorsement Isaiah certifies on the authority of the freedom and sovereign promises of God the Creator.[2]

Introduction

An ancient editor of Aristotle's works gathered pieces of his writing on various topics and placed them after Aristotle's *Physics* so that they acquired the name *ta meta ta physika*—"the things after the *Physics*," or *Metaphysics*, as we know it.[3] This chapter discusses God the Creator in some of the prophetic books that come *after Isaiah* in canonical order.[4] The focus will be on three of those books (Amos, Jeremiah, and Ezekiel) and on particular passages within them. None of these books offer accounts of the world's origin, of course. But they do depict God speaking and acting as Creator.[5] So do the last chapters of Isaiah, and explicitly Isaiah 65, which I will discuss along with Zechariah and Daniel in the next chapter. Here, though, the focus will be on three prophets *after Isaiah* who announce judgment and promise restoration.

Acts of creation, divine or human, often involve de(con)struction as their initial moments. When our family first moved to our home, years ago, the space appeared to be well ordered: a symmetrical front lawn and a symmetrical backyard, both of them entirely in grass. But all of the symmetry and the grassy lawn seemed unnatural; they presented an aesthetically and ethically numbing *dis*order to Janice, my artist wife. Over time, most of the grass and all of the symmetry were destroyed. The limited grassy areas that now remain follow the contours of gardens planted with serviceberry bushes, hydrangeas, hostas, and a variety of other native bushes, trees, shrubs, and plants whose

2. Cyrus's divine endorsement was limited, in Isaiah, to rebuilding Jerusalem, establishing the foundations of the temple, and setting free the exiles (Isa. 44:28; 45:13). God's endorsement of Cyrus was further qualified, and superseded, by Yhwh's designation of the servant as the instrument of Israel's future. Lind, "Monotheism, Power, and Justice."

3. Cohen and Reeve, "Aristotle's Metaphysics."

4. Isaiah does not come first in all traditions. Greg Goswell notes, referring to ancient Greek manuscripts, "In Vaticanus (B), Alexandrinus (A), and Greek orders generally," the Book of the Twelve (Minor Prophets) precedes Isaiah, Jeremiah, and Ezekiel. "Order of the Books," 459.

5. Scholars have considered prophetic books besides these three in relation to creation, including Hosea (Paas, *Creation and Judgment*, 331–53); Jonah (Joel Anderson, "Jonah's Peculiar Re-creation"); and Zephaniah (Nogalski, "Zephaniah's Use of Genesis 1–11"). I will return to Zephaniah in chap. 10. Amos, Jeremiah, and Ezekiel will provide adequate range and illustrative variety for this chapter.

varieties I cannot name but that birds and bees visit with appreciation. Janice supervised and intervened in the destruction of an ordered but, as she saw it, perversely ordered—and so *dis*ordered—place. In its place, over time, she created something new. She did not create any of the plants or species that replaced the grass, of course, or the soil in which they were planted. But she did create a new environment, a new space that was also constituted by the social interaction it invited.

Without pressing the analogy, the prophets under discussion here and several in the larger prophetic canon also proceed from the announcement or the experience of judgment and destruction—God's judgment and the destruction of Israel and Judah[6]—but in anticipation of God's creation of a new space: the creation of Israel/Judah as a renewed space, a reconstituted space. This reconstitution may include topographical transformation—in Ezekiel 47, a river will flow from the temple; in Micah 4, Zion will be established as the highest mountain. But the definitive transformations will be social and political, spiritual and constitutional—constitutional not merely in a political sense but in the way God (re)constitutes or reconfigures the *nature* of the people God claims as Israel. The diverse collection of prophetic books *after Isaiah* offers persistent testimony to God the Creator.

Amos

The book of Amos may be best known in popular culture even today from Martin Luther King Jr.'s quotation of Amos 5:24. In Washington, DC, in 1968, King declared that African Americans were not satisfied with the achievements of the civil rights movement and would not be satisfied "until justice rolls down like water and righteousness like a mighty stream."[7] King quoted those words from Amos after listing just a few of the injustices Black people suffered in the United States. Likewise, Amos 5 condemns Israel's—the Northern Kingdom's—gross injustices, oppressing the poor and needy, subverting justice with bribes (vv. 11–12).[8] Indeed, condemnation of injustice pervades Amos; it joins seamlessly with—it is constituent within and constitutive of—Israel's infidelity to Yhwh (e.g., 3:13–4:5). Martin Luther King Jr. echoed Amos in seeing the prevailing social and political order as *dis*ordered, as perversely

6. Louis Stulman and Hyun Chul Paul Kim survey the prophetic literature with respect to the trauma of destruction and concern for survival in *You Are My People*.

7. The text of King's "I Have a Dream" speech is available at https://www.mtholyoke.edu/acad/intrel/speech/dream.htm.

8. Translation of parts of these verses is complicated. See Paul, *Amos*, 157, 171–75.

ordered and—expressly in the case of Amos—under divine judgment. Amos gives explicit testimony to God the Creator in a series of hymn fragments (4:13; 5:8–9; 9:5–6), which I will mention again below. These serve to punctuate and confirm the sovereignty God exercises as Creator, not only as the God of Israel but as what James Luther Mays describes correctly, if infelicitously, as "world God."[9]

God the Creator as Judge

Amos begins not with indictments of Israel and Judah for their injustices but with announcements of God's judgment against nations surrounding Israel and Judah: from Damascus (Syria) to Gaza, from Tyre to Edom, and from Ammon to Moab. These nations do not come under indictment for idolatry—for making offerings to "other gods" and worshiping "the works of their own hands" (Jer. 1:16)—because, unlike Judah and Israel, they have no covenantal relation or obligations to Yhwh that would demand the veneration, let alone the exclusive veneration, of Yhwh. The violations these neighboring nations committed, as Amos 1:3–2:3 describes them, include treaty violations, human trafficking, and crimes against humanity. All of them could be considered violations of natural law—a shared (if not quite universal) sense of what must not be done. Relations among these nations call to mind the rivalries in Genesis, beginning in Genesis 3 with the serpent (see chap. 3 in this book). Amos does not speak of rivalry here but calls the nations' violations "transgressions," using the noun *pesha'*, a term that is at home in the realm of law or of politics.[10] It falls within the same semantic range as "sin," as in Amos 5:12, where "transgressions" and "sins" (*chatta't*) are parallel. The nations indicted and sanctioned for their violations of "what must not be done" were not subject to charges of idolatry and faithlessness—of sin—as was Israel. Even so, Amos regards their actions as transgressions, not in some general sense but as transgressions precisely against Yhwh.[11]

Amos 2:4 continues seamlessly the series of national indictments that began in 1:3 but turns arrestingly to one of God's covenant peoples, Judah. Amos describes Judah's transgressions as amounting specifically and exclusively to violations of Judah's relationship to Yhwh. In 2:6, attention shifts to Israel, whose transgressions include acts of injustice and oppression—"selling the innocent

9. Mays, *Amos*, 8–9. Paas, *Creation and Judgment*, provides a thorough discussion of Amos as well as of Isaiah and Hosea.

10. Mays, *Amos*, 28; Paul, *Amos*, 45–46.

11. Paul, *Amos*, 46.

[*tsaddiq*] for silver and the poor for sandals"—and profaning Yhwh's holy name (v. 7). The chapter continues, through verse 11, narrating God's particular acts of deliverance and beneficence on behalf of Israel, including bringing them up from Egypt (v. 10), thus stressing the unique claim Yhwh has on Israel's fidelity. Israel's *in*fidelity, especially the form it takes in pervasive injustice, and then God's announcements of judgment against it dominate the book of Amos. But in the rhetorical structure of Amos's first two chapters, Israel and Judah are joined with the nations. All of them stand guilty of transgressions against Yhwh. In this way, Amos makes a claim about God the Creator: even the nations beyond Judah and Israel are brought within the circumference of God the Creator's universal domain. Terence E. Fretheim writes in this regard of a "creational claim" as "probably the most fundamental theological grounding of these oracles."[12]

Going further, Fretheim describes "creation theology as key to understanding Amos," the title he gives a section in his commentary on the Book of the Twelve. Fretheim notes Amos's pervasive concern with (in)justice, of course. But he suggests that the "justice perspective" of Amos's first two chapters—along with that of other prophetic texts—is rooted "in a creation theology" that includes "a created moral order" perceptible to all the nations and to which they are thus accountable.[13] Fretheim also refers to "the natural order" and "the cosmic order," both of which are disturbed by the nations' and Israel's unjust practices, which violate the created moral order.[14] Israel's oppression and violence, and their other acts of faithlessness to Yhwh (Amos 3:9–4:11), are met with natural calamity: famine (4:6), drought (v. 7), and plague (vv. 9–10), God "mediating from sins to their effects," as Fretheim says.[15]

That the prophets could associate injustice, corruption, and the collapse of social order with natural calamity Hosea 4:1–3 makes explicit: lying, killing, theft, adultery, and an epidemic of lethal violence in Israel had devastating effects on the land, on the people, and on the animals, including birds and fish. It is not difficult to imagine, especially with contemporary examples at hand, that the kind of corruption and social decay Hosea describes can lead to ecological disaster. But in Amos 4, natural and social calamities do not follow as natural consequences of Israel's faithlessness—its refusal to "return" to Yhwh. Rather, these calamities arrive, again and again, as God's judgment on Israel's refusal. And contrary to Fretheim's characterization, God does not simply *mediate* "the

12. Fretheim, *God and the World*, 167.
13. Fretheim, *Reading Hosea–Micah*, 117.
14. Fretheim, *Reading Hosea–Micah*, 117–20.
15. Fretheim, *Reading Hosea–Micah*, 119.

movement from sins to their effects."[16] As Fretheim acknowledges, in multiple instances God claims, in effect, "I did this":

> I gave you cleanness of teeth . . . (v. 6)
> I withheld the rain . . . (v. 7)
> I struck you with blight and mildew . . . (v. 9)
> I sent pestilence against you . . . (v. 10)
> I killed your young men with the sword . . . (v. 10)
> I overthrew some of you as when God overthrew Sodom . . . (v. 11)[17]

In Amos 4, that is, God claims complete credit for bringing about the natural and social-political calamities for which Israel is to blame. All these calamities could be understood as coming about naturally, of course: drought and famine, plague, disease, causalities of war—all of them disasters familiar in antiquity and also today. Amos, eschewing a picture of God that might be more palatable to us, understands each of the calamities as judgments of God and as acts of God. Rather than mediating between sins and their effects—the effects being those described in the list above—God, according to Amos, brings about those effects. The effects, God's judgments, are in several instances natural phenomena. These, as well as historical forces (e.g., 6:14), are subject to summons from God the Creator to be employed as instruments of judgment.

My difference from Fretheim here may be negligible. And the difference may have to do with Fretheim's emphasis on "creation theology," while my focus is more narrowly on the text's presentation of God the Creator. Some contours of that presentation can be inferred from the way in which Amos assumes and declares God's inclusion of nations beyond those expected to venerate Yhwh—nations beyond Judah and Israel—within the domain of Yhwh's judicial superintendence, what Fretheim describes as "God tending to the created moral order."[18]

But Amos does not leave us to infer whether the text actually has to do with God the Creator. Hymns proclaim the fact.

16. Fretheim, *Reading Hosea–Micah*, 119.

17. Or perhaps, "I destroyed some of you as when God destroyed Sodom" (NJPS). The verb here (*haphak*)—NJPS takes it as a noun, but see Joüon, #49e—means to turn something or to overturn it, sometimes, as with reference to Sodom, with the sense of "destroy" (cf. Jon. 3:4). The phrase "as when God destroyed Sodom" occurs also in Isa. 13:19 and Jer. 50:40. Genesis 19:21 uses the verb in the account of Sodom's destruction.

18. Fretheim, *Reading Hosea–Micah*, 119. For Amos, of course, God's superintendence is not merely judicial (9:7).

The Doxologies of Amos

In three places, the text of Amos erupts in hymnic praise: 4:13, 5:8–9, and 9:5–6. Scholars have considered these differently: as a single hymn subsequently distributed within the prophetic text; as hymnic fragments or doxologies unrelated to each other; as late, postexilic insertions; and as part of the book's original composition, among other possibilities.[19] Whether these three texts were originally part of a single hymn is impossible to determine with certainty, as are other questions about their date and composition. Regardless, the book of Amos presents itself to us with them—these doxologies—as a part of it, and as part of the book's testimony to God the Creator.[20]

Amos 4:13 identifies Yhwh as the one who forms, creates, and makes, employing verbs familiar from Genesis 1 and 2 and from passages in Isaiah. In this instance, Amos describes God as the one who "forms [*yatsar*] the mountains," "creates [*bara'*] the wind," "discloses [*galah*] his intentions to humankind" (cf. Amos 3:7), "makes [*'asah*] the morning darkness," and "treads on [*darak*] the heights of the earth" (4:13). Amos here includes among Yhwh's actions as Creator disclosing his thoughts or intentions to humankind and treading on the earth's heights.[21] The latter phrase will be repeated in Micah 1:3, which announces God's proceeding from his (dwelling) place, coming down (*yarad*), and treading on the earth's high places. Micah goes on to make a wordplay on "high places." While it means something like the highest points of the earth, for example, mountaintops in Micah 1:3 (cf. Deut. 32:13; Job 9:8; Ps. 18:33; Isa. 14:14), "high places" becomes, in Micah 1:5, the illicit shrines—the high places—that Yhwh comes to "tread on" and to tread down.[22] Shrines—those of Gilgal and Bethel—also figure prominently in Amos 4:4–13, with verses 4–5 issuing a mock call to worship: a call to come sin at these shrines. While the shrine at Bethel was a royal sanctuary (1 Kings 12:28–29), the location of these shrines does not matter to Amos; that they are sites of and serve to sanctify injustice and infidelity does matter profoundly. As in Micah so in Amos: Yhwh treading the earth portends

19. Shalom M. Paul surveys the proposals and the literature in *Amos*, 152–53. Stefan Paas's discussion is comprehensive. *Creation and Judgment*, 209–326.

20. Gavin Cox, along with several other scholars whom he cites, reads Amos against the background of Sumerian City Laments, and he considers Amos 4:13, 5:8–9, and 9:5–6 (plus 7:4) in relation to flood accounts, including the Genesis account, in "'Hymn' of Amos." For comparison with Amos's hymns, see especially Lament for Sumer and Ur on p. 85.

21. Amos 4:13 presents some challenges to interpreters. For example, the noun *seach* (plus possessive suffix), rendered as "his thoughts" by the NRSV, occurs only here in the MT. To his translation of the term ("his [God's] intention"), Paul adds the note "Hebrew obscure." *Amos*, 137–38.

22. The CEB, anticipating what follows, (mis)translates the latter part of Mic. 1:3 as "tread on the shrines of the earth."

and announces judgment. In Amos, the hymn or doxology to God the Creator follows immediately Amos's injunction: "Prepare to meet your God, O Israel" (4:12). God will be wearing an Assyrian face.

Bethel and Gilgal also figure in the context of a second doxology, Amos 5:8–9. Whereas in 4:4–5 the people of Israel are urged, mockingly, to come to Bethel and Gilgal, in 5:4–5 Amos counsels the reverse: "Do not seek Bethel, and do not visit Gilgal or cross over to Beer-Sheba, for Gilgal will go into exile and Bethel will come to nothing." Following the announcement of Gilgal's and Bethel's disastrous futures, Amos indicts "those who turn justice to wormwood and throw righteousness to the ground" (v. 7). The indictment seems to continue in verses 10–13, addressing those—the elite in Israel—who pervert justice to exploit and oppress the poor. Between verse 7 and verses 10–13 intervenes a hymnic celebration of Yhwh as "the one who made the Pleiades and Orion" constellations (v. 8; joined also in Job 9:9 and 38:31) associated with the new year and change of seasons.[23] While Israel turns (*haphak*) justice to wormwood, the God who made the cosmos and rules the seasons also governs day and night: "who turns [*haphak*] deep darkness into morning and day into night" (Amos 5:8). The waters of the sea, too, are at the Creator's command—whether for irrigation or for destruction (vv. 8–9). Destruction is the theme of verse 9: God the Creator of verse 8 brings destruction to the strong, and it comes upon the fortress.

While the doxology of Amos 5:8–9 does not fit organically between verses 5–7 and verses 10–13—the genres are dramatically different—it does fit its context dramatically. The doxology enlists testimony to God the Creator in punctuating the judgment announced against Israel, "the house of Joseph" (*bet yoseph*), and Bethel (*bet-'el*), "the house of God" (vv. 5–6), and then against those who use their office to oppress the poor and deny them justice (vv. 10–13). In its out-of-context eruption of praise, it calls to mind the reported memory of my great-grandfather's brother Ludwig. Especially moved one Sunday morning, in a church on the Oklahoma prairie, Ludwig stood, interrupted the sermon, and said in his adopted Low German tongue, "*Breeda, Ekj wella mal bäde*": "Brothers and sisters, I want to pray now." Perhaps the doxology (vv. 8–9) did not have its origin in the prophet's similarly spontaneous offering of prayerful praise. The text offers it even so, in the midst of—and in confirmation of—Amos's announcement of God's catastrophic judgment against Israel (vv. 16–17).

We may entertain the notion of Amos 5:8–9 as a spontaneous burst of praise in the midst of a judgment speech, but we can hardly do other than read 8:7–9:4,

23. Paul, *Amos*, 168.

7–10 as an eruption of lethal divine anger. Systemic injustice and oppression of the poor (8:4–6) have generated God's anger, which threatens annihilation: "Those who remain I will kill with the sword; not one of them shall flee; not one of them shall escape" (9:1); "the eyes of the Lord God are on the sinful kingdom, and I will destroy it from the face of the earth" (v. 8). "Sinful kingdom" here means Israel—the Northern Kingdom—subsequently called "the house of Jacob" (v. 8) and "the house of Israel" (v. 9). The threat of annihilation is mitigated, finally, awkwardly, in verse 8: "I will destroy it [the sinful kingdom] from the face of the earth—except that I will not completely destroy the house of Jacob."[24] Instead of annihilation, there will be a "sifting process" that identifies for execution "all the sinners of my people" (vv. 9–10).[25] Amos describes these "sinners" as those "who say, 'The disaster [*hara'ah*] shall neither overtake us nor come near us'" (v. 10).

Mays associates Israel's belief in their immunity to disaster with their conception of and expectations concerning the day of the Lord (Amos 5:18–20). Amos's audience, Mays says, knew that Yhwh brought "terrors" on this day.[26] But the day of the Lord "was a hard and fast scheme for them—always catastrophe for the enemies of the nation, a dogma therefore of their invulnerability." Amos's audience may have arrived at a version of this "scheme" naturally if "the day of the Lord" originated in—or early involved—a New Year's festal celebration of Yhwh's kingship and (thus) victory over the forces of chaos: a celebration of Yhwh as Creator and thus also King.[27] As Mays writes of Amos 9:8–10, here Amos "speaks of a sin of belief, the sin of excepting oneself from Yahweh's judgment and therefore from his sovereignty."[28] The broadest expression of Yhwh's sovereignty is as Creator, and it is as Creator—and as *Un*creator—that Yhwh challenges Israel's sense of invulnerability and exceptionalism in the face of its corrupting injustice and faithlessness.[29]

Preceding the third doxology in chapter 9, Amos 8:9–10 portrays Yhwh as *Un*creator. Sovereign over the natural world as its Creator, God rules the day and

24. On the exceptive clause with *'ephes ki*, see Joüon, #173a. In none of the other three examples there cited (Num. 13:28; Deut. 15:4; Judg. 4:9) does *'ephes ki* introduce an exception to an absolute claim that immediately precedes; hence, my description of the exceptive clause here as awkwardly following the preceding prophecy of complete annihilation.

25. Paul, *Amos*, 286–87.

26. Mays, *Amos*, 163—so also the quotations that follow in this paragraph.

27. See, e.g., Müller, "Der finstere Tag Jahwes." For the close association of Yhwh as Creator and Yhwh as King (and Defender), see my *Zion, the City of the Great King*, 147–58. Heather L. Bunce discusses the day of the Lord in the Book of the Twelve in her essay "Day of the Lord."

28. Mays, *Amos*, 163.

29. Commenting on the doxologies in Amos, David Peterson writes that, with each of them, "the prophet affirms that God creates as well as destroys." "World of Creation," 208.

night, light and darkness. Here in chapter 8, in response to the rapacious greed and the exploitation of the poor on the part of Israel's elite, Yhwh promises to darken the day and overturn Israel's festivals:

> I will make the sun set at noon,
> and I will darken the earth in broad daylight.
> I will turn your festivals into mourning
> and your songs to dirges.
> I will bring on all loins sackcloth
> and on every head baldness.
> And I will make it like the mourning for an only child. (vv. 9–10)

As in Amos 5:8, where God the Creator turns deep darkness into morning and day into night (discussed above), so here Yhwh rules the sun and governs darkness and light. That governance moves immediately and seamlessly to overturning Israel's festivals: as darkness to morning and day to night, so Yhwh (over)turns Israel's celebrations into occasions of ritual mourning—like the mourning for an only child: a *yachid* (8:10). Reference to a specific only child (*yachid*) occurs twice in the Old Testament: in the story of the binding (or sacrifice) of Isaac in Genesis 22 and in the account of the sacrifice of Jephthah's daughter in Judges 11. Within the Book of the Twelve, Zechariah 12:10 describes one who has been pierced, evoking mourning as for an only child (*yachid*) and a firstborn.[30] Amos here describes Yhwh as Creator, sovereignly intervening in natural and solar arrangements of God's own design to transform Israel's festivals—putatively celebrating the God now transforming them—into occasions of the most profound and desperate grief. Grief as for an only child.

Amos 9:5–6, the third and final doxology describing Yhwh as Creator, follows God's threat to annihilate Israel and precedes an exception to that threat, an exception in 9:8b that I mentioned earlier. At its beginning the doxology describes "the Lord [*'adonai*] Yhwh of hosts" at whose touch "the earth melts, and all its inhabitants mourn" (9:5a). In Micah, too, the earth melts at Yhwh's treading on its high places (Mic. 1:3–4), but the verb there (*masas*) differs from Amos's in 9:5—*mug*, which frequently conveys the sense of melting in fear, as in "melt in fear, O Philistia" (Isa. 14:31). Yhwh's touching the earth causes it to melt and its inhabitants to mourn. The picture here echoes that of Amos 8:8, where the earth (*ha'arets*) will tremble in fear of God's judgment, and all of its

30. The LXX translates *yachid* with *agapētos*—"beloved." In Judg. 11:34, the LXX describes Jephthah's unnamed daughter as *monogenēs*—"only begotten" and "beloved." This language will inform the Gospel of John in the New Testament.

people will mourn. Both 8:8 and 9:5 depict the earth responding by rising and falling or sinking like the Nile, perhaps calling to mind an earthquake or a flood as God's judgment.[31] Amos 9:6 continues, however, describing God as Creator:

> Who builds in the heavens his upper chambers,
> but whose vault he founds on the earth—
> who calls to the waters of the sea,
> and pours them out upon the earth.
> Yhwh is his name. (9:6)[32]

In Amos 9:5 Yhwh touches the earth, bringing about dramatic effects. Verse 6 serves to make God's relationship or contact with the earth more than episodic. Assuming that "upper chambers" and "vault" both name, in parallel, Yhwh's abode, verse 6 affirms that it was on the earth that Yhwh, the Creator, laid the foundations (*yasad*) of the divine abode. In the translation of verse 6 above, I contrasted Yhwh's building the upper chambers—God's heavenly dwelling—with Yhwh's laying the foundations of this dwelling on the earth. While that grammatically defensible translation could suggest a contrast or opposition, I intend it to stress a continuity instead: not only a continuity but an identity of God the Creator in the heavens and on the earth. That is to say, God does reign in heaven, in the upper chambers, but this reign has its foundation on the earth. A later community perhaps reflected this idea in praying for God's will to be done on earth as it is in heaven. Isaiah 57 also affirms that the exalted God dwells in a high and holy place but with the broken or contrite and low in spirit at the same time (v. 15).

Amos 9:5–6, in its context—like 4:13 and 5:8–9—with its praise of God the Creator certifies not only that the judgments Amos announces have divine juridical authority but that this authority has its ultimate source in God the Creator. It also immediately precedes the affirmation that, while Yhwh may have known only Israel from among all the earth's families (3:2), the range of the Creator's concern and active involvement extends internationally (9:7). In 1:3–2:3, Yhwh announced a series of judgments against nations in Israel's immediate and more distant environment, judgments that then fell also on Judah and Israel. Now, in 9:7, Yhwh denies any possible claim by Israel of exclusive divine concern and engagement. The unique relationship that justifies Yhwh's holding Israel to account for their sins, according to 3:2, does not stand in contradiction of the claim that the defining event of Israel's existence and identity—the exodus

31. James Luther Mays points to Amos 2:13, 3:14–15, and 9:1 as possibly alluding to earthquake (*Amos*, 145), while Gavin Cox proposes a flood. "'Hymn' of Amos."

32. For text-critical and lexical discussion, see Paul, *Amos*, 280.

from Egypt—was but one of the migrations Yhwh brought about, for which the Philistines and Arameans serve as examples. With respect to the limitless range of Yhwh's active involvement with the nations, the people of Israel are like the Ethiopians to Yhwh, far distant though they may be.[33] This active "involvement," whether in judgment or otherwise, Amos attributes to God the Creator.

While judgment stands out as the dominant tone of Amos, the book also, finally, looks forward to a transformed future: to a time when the land God previously afflicted with famine, drought, and plague (Amos 4) becomes so agriculturally fecund that the seasons of reaping overtake those of preparation and planting, and the mountains and hills flow with the fresh fruit of the vine (9:13). This will be Yhwh's—the Creator's—doing (v. 12), and it will include God's restoration of Israel as a flourishing community (v. 14).[34]

Amos's doxologies incorporate and provide the theological foundation for the international reach of Yhwh's agency, and also for Yhwh's action against Israel in the body of the book from the middle of chapter 2 through the first verses of chapter 9 and decidedly *for* Israel in 9:11–15. All the nations, including even Assyria—more distant and more powerful than the nations named in 1:3–2:3 and 9:7—exist within the dynamic, encompassing space of Yhwh's creating, and they are subject, like the earth itself, to Yhwh's "touch" (*naga'*, 9:5). Yhwh's particular and exclusive (3:2) covenantal relationship with Israel is an event within that encompassing and dynamic space. The space is encompassing because whatever shape it may take and whatever "entities" and events it may include exist and take place within the dimensions of God's creating. The encompassing space is dynamic because, while it does not and could not encompass God, its "entities" exist and take place in relation to one another in the active presence of God. This encompassing and dynamic space is constituted as such by the Yhwh attested as God the Creator in the poetry and prose of Amos and the college of prophetic witness in which Amos is included. Above, I referred to Fretheim's claim that creation theology is the key to understanding Amos. His claim has more than a little merit.

Jeremiah (and Ezekiel?)

While the term *covenant* appears but once in Amos, in connection with Tyre (Amos 1:9), both the term and what it signifies play a significant role in Jeremiah.

33. The Ethiopians are referred to "for the remote distance of their land from Israel." Paul, *Amos*, 282.

34. Amos 9:11–15 and its unexpected promise that "the booth of David" will be restored have provoked much discussion. See, e.g., Goswell, "David in the Prophecy of Amos"; Mays, *Amos*, 163–68; Paul, *Amos*, 290–95.

The first words spoken in Jeremiah 11—a chapter saturated with covenant—are spoken by Yhwh to the prophet: "Hear the words of this covenant" (v. 2). "Yhwh the God of Israel" then instructs Jeremiah to tell the people of Judah and Jerusalem's inhabitants, "Cursed is one who does not heed the words of this covenant" (v. 3). Because Israel and Judah broke the covenant God made with them, disaster is threatened (vv. 10–11). Covenant—both the term and the concept—also appears later in Jeremiah in a positive context: the context of restoration. There Yhwh promises a new covenant in Jeremiah 31:31–34, a passage familiar to readers of the New Testament from the quotation of it in Hebrews 8:8–12—the longest New Testament quotation of an Old Testament passage. I will return to the later chapters of Jeremiah after brief comment first on Jeremiah 11 and its covenant logic and then on passages in which God the Creator acts as judge.

In Jeremiah 11, Israel and Judah breaking the covenant God made with them is the basis for God's judgment against them. This general charge of covenant breaking is defined in other general terms for disobedience (v. 8) and then more specifically as following and serving other gods (v. 10). Concern about and judgment of Israel's and especially Judah's infidelity to Yhwh pervade Jeremiah, including its vivid description of adultery in chapter 3. As Jeremiah 22:9 expresses the matter, "They abandoned the covenant of Yhwh their God and bowed down to other gods and served them." The language and concept of covenant—whether on analogy with a treaty relationship between suzerain and vassal[35] or on analogy with marriage—fit well God's demand in Jeremiah for exclusive loyalty and fidelity on the part of Judah. This demand cohered with and was entailed by Jeremiah's assumption that only Yhwh is God: the objects of Judah's infidelity—and before theirs, Israel's—are but "stone and wood" (3:9). Jeremiah, then, denies the reality of any putative deity who is not Yhwh.

It follows in Jeremiah that all divine responsibilities are appropriated to Yhwh. While in other conceptions of divinity responsibilities and prerogatives—including receiving sacrifices—could be and were distributed or shared among different deities, Jeremiah recognizes and insists on only Yhwh. The language of an exclusive covenant serves this insistence, and it provides rhetorical and theological resources for Jeremiah's strong announcements of God's judgment. At the same time, however, Jeremiah's insistence on Yhwh alone means that Yhwh attracts all other divine responsibilities—later theological traditions, postbiblical ones, would call them attributes or offices—including that of Creator. It comes

35. George Mendenhall long ago introduced to wider biblical scholarship Hittite suzerain-vassal treaty texts and proposed their illumination of large swaths of the Bible in terms of covenant. "Covenant Forms in Biblical Tradition."

as no surprise, then, that Jeremiah's insistence on Yhwh as Lord of the covenant stands alongside and coheres with the book's testimony to God the Creator.[36]

God the Creator and Judgment

Jeremiah's early employment of creation language and imagery occurs in the context of judgment—God's judgment—whose scope is cosmic. Jeremiah 4:23–26 reports the prophet's vision of the world brought to un-creation. Four times, at the head of each verse, Jeremiah says, "I saw." What he saw or looked upon was, first, the earth as "waste and void," the NRSV's translation of *tohu wabohu*, a term occurring only here and in Genesis 1:2.[37] Jeremiah's initial gaze also includes the sky—the heavens—whose luminaries fail to provide light. The darkness that covered the deep in Genesis 1:2 is now unrelieved. Jeremiah next observes, in 4:24, that the mountains are quaking and the hills shaking (*qalal*), challenging the assurance of Psalm 93:1 that the world will not be shaken (*mut*). While Genesis 2:5 observed that there was "no man [*'adam*] to work the soil," Jeremiah sees that there is no one at all (*'en ha'adam*)—an earth empty even of birds, empty of all that God had made (Jer. 4:25). Finally, Jeremiah sees that the fertile land is a desert and all the cities have been torn down (v. 26). The picture here Walter Brueggemann describes as "the step by step subtraction from the 'very good' creation of Genesis."[38] Devastation is total: in William McKane's words, "a collapse of cosmic order and an invasion by the powers of chaos."[39] The agent ultimately behind these powers, according to Jeremiah 4:27–28, is Yhwh.[40] Jeremiah envisions God the Creator acting in judgment, undoing what God created: God *de*creating the world.

The American poet Wallace Stevens borrowed the term *decreation* from the French philosopher and Christian mystic Simone Weil.[41] For both Stevens and

36. While interpreters have long drawn connections between Jeremiah and the covenant theology of Deuteronomy, and related Jeremiah also to Hosea, scholars in the latter decades of the twentieth century also pointed to theologically significant connections between covenant and creation. See, as an example, Rendtorff, *Canon and Theology*. Patrick D. Miller ("Creation and Covenant") helpfully describes the contributions several scholars made to the reconsideration—or rehabilitation in biblical scholarship—of the relationship between covenant and creation. See also Brueggemann, "Jeremiah"; Perdue, *Collapse of History*, 141–48.

37. In chap. 1, I translated *tohu wabohu* in Gen. 1:2 as "wildness and waste." I believe "waste and void" better fits the context of Jer. 4:23–26.

38. Brueggemann, "Jeremiah," 156.

39. McKane, *Critical and Exegetical Commentary on Jeremiah*, 107.

40. These latter verses present several textual issues, discussed in McKane (*Critical and Exegetical Commentary on Jeremiah*, 109–10) and Holladay (*Jeremiah 1*, 166–68). The MT at the conclusion of Jer. 4:27—the NRSV translates it as "yet I will not make a full end" (*kalah lo' 'e'eseh*)—is especially nettlesome, since it seems to contradict the total devastation described in vv. 23–26.

41. Lindroth, "Simone Weil and Wallace Stevens."

Weil, despite differences between them, the world of appearances produces an illusory god. Both Stevens and Weil, James Lindroth wrote, present decreation "in terms of the shedding of appearances" and resisting "the pull exerted by the world of appearances . . . leading to spiritual life, to being, to God."[42] In Jeremiah 4, the prophet envisions God erasing all the appearances—even those of God's own creating. As the LXX renders verse 23, Jeremiah looked, "and there was nothing," no appearances at all. In chapter 10, Jeremiah mocks those—"the nations"—whose artisans make illusory gods of the appearances. Speaking in Aramaic instead of Hebrew, God tells Jeremiah, "Thus you shall say to them, 'The gods who did not make the heavens and the earth shall perish from the earth and from beneath these heavens'" (v. 11).[43]

While God's judgment of Israel is not yet relieved—Jeremiah 11, discussed briefly above, goes on to cite covenant-grounded reasons for Israel's disaster—Jeremiah 10 praises Yhwh the incomparable (v. 6) and true God (v. 10), praise that issues in a polemical paean to God the Creator (vv. 12–16). The paean's polemics are directed against the illusions that the nations call gods. Earlier, Jeremiah had named things these illusory deities cannot do (vv. 4–5). Illusions cleared away, Jeremiah then turns to praising God the Creator, the subject of active verbs—naming all that God *does*—in verses 12–13, 16.[44] Yhwh is the God who

> made the earth by his power,
> establishing the world by his wisdom.
> And by his understanding he stretched out the heavens. (v. 12)

Here Jeremiah echoes the Psalms and Isaiah, as well as Wisdom. The following verse celebrates God's power as Creator (v. 13), and in verse 16 Jeremiah describes God as the one "who forms all things."

God's forming or fashioning things (the verb is *yatsar*) begins in Genesis 2:7, when God forms a man from the dust. It extends as far as God's fashioning, fixing, the seasons (Ps. 74:17), and it includes Jacob/Israel, whom Yhwh created and formed (Isa. 43:1). In Jeremiah 10:12–16, God's forming, God's creating,

42. Lindroth, "Simone Weil and Wallace Stevens," 45.

43. The Aramaic here comes as a surprise. Apart from Dan. 2:4–7:28 and portions of Ezra 4 and 7, only in Gen. 31:47 and here in Jer. 10:11 does the MT include Aramaic text. For discussion of the matter, see Holladay, *Jeremiah 1*, 324–25, 334–35. Garnett Reid argues that Jer. 10:11 is the "architectural axis" of 10:1–16 and that its Aramaic suits the Babylonian audience the passage implies. "'Thus You Shall Say to Them.'"

44. Walter Brueggemann contrasts things the gods cannot and did not do with those Yhwh did or continues to do in *Commentary on Jeremiah*, 102–4.

extends to everything (*hakkol*, v. 16). It repairs the world devastated according to Jeremiah 4:23–26. And it extends in particular to Jacob/Israel. For Jeremiah, God—Yhwh—the Creator cannot be abstracted from God as Jacob's portion and Israel as Yhwh's heritage (10:16). The Creator is at the same time, and indissolubly, the God of Israel. Amos's international expansion of Yhwh's judicial power implied—or it expressed—a conception of God as Creator that Amos had made explicit in the context of God's judgment of Israel. Jeremiah shares and expands on the notion of Yhwh's judicial reach—the oracles against the nations in Jeremiah 46–51 certify the claim—but in Jeremiah, God the Creator assures that Israel's endurance and the world's are not dissoluble from God's.

God the Creator and Restoration

Among Jeremiah's most striking rhetorical and theological innovations is the prophet's employment of *covenant* in service of an expansive promise of Judah's and Israel's restoration and Yhwh's irrevocable commitment to them. The concept of covenant—with the term *berit*—does appear elsewhere in the Prophets in a positive sense, with the promise of salvation for and the restoration of Israel: in Hosea 2:20[2:18] and Ezekiel 34:25, for example, which promise peace, and in Isaiah 55:3, where God promises an everlasting covenant (*berit 'olam*) on the precedent of God's promises to (2 Sam. 7) and covenant with (Ps. 89) David. *Covenant*, in passages like these, since it refers to a promise of God made solely on God's initiative and which God simply announced to Israel, is not something Israel has the capacity to "break"—not to mention the logical impossibility: you cannot break a promise I made to you.[45] This Israel has indeed done to God's covenant as Jeremiah employs the concept in Jeremiah 11: Israel and Judah "broke" (*hepheru*, v. 10) the covenant God made with the ancestors—the covenant Moses mediated at Sinai. That covenant, or that kind of covenant, provides no grounds for hope or restoration after it has been broken . . . after its conditions or terms—its "words" (v. 6)—have been violated. In that case, the covenant's "words"—that is, in this instance, its sanctions—follow (v. 8). And the covenant's sanctions mean catastrophe for Judah (v. 11).

Jeremiah, in chapter 31, refers to the same covenant—the covenant Jeremiah 11 recalled, which the ancestors "broke" (31:32). Now, though, God promises a "new covenant," not like the old one God made with the ancestors "when I brought them out of the land of Egypt" (v. 32). The novelty of this "new covenant" is not its content, its stipulations—what Jeremiah 11 calls its "words"

45. Yhwh, on the other hand, retains the freedom to amend promises, even everlasting (*'olam*) ones, as with Eli the priest at Shiloh (1 Sam. 2:30).

and what, in chapter 31, Yhwh refers to as "my instruction" (*torah*, v. 33). The content of the promised new covenant is identical to that of the old, which was inscribed on stone tablets and deposited beside the ark (Deut. 31:9, 26). What defines the new covenant as *new* is the place of its deposit—"within them"—and the site of its inscription: "on their hearts" (Jer. 31:33). Yhwh's *torah* will be interior to the people of Israel, constituent within them, so that instruction in the law will be neither necessary nor sensible (v. 34).

The promise of this new covenant is a part of God's larger promise of restoration in Jeremiah 30–33, often called Jeremiah's Book of Comfort. The new covenant, which includes God's preemptory (prevenient, in some understandings) forgiveness of Israel's sins, prior to any repentance on Israel's part, makes possible not only the restoration of Israel as a people, a polity, and a place but the affirmation of God's enduring bond with Israel, despite "all they have done" (31:37)—all they had done that constituted covenant grounds for Judah's defeat and the forced migration, the exile, of Judah's elite and the destruction of Jerusalem. Jeremiah relentlessly, and in anguish (20:7–10), rehearsed the grounds for God's strong judgment of a nation without apparent capacity to respond with either obedience or repentance. Now, after extreme judgment, Jeremiah promises God's unilateral pardon (*salach*; cf. Exod. 34:9) of Israel's guilt (their sin) and Israel's reconstitution as a people whose obedience will flow from what Yhwh has deposited within them and inscribed on their hearts.

The promise of a new covenant and the (re)affirmation of Yhwh's bond with—enduring faithfulness to—Israel has as its guarantee and guarantor God the Creator. The God who appointed the sun for light by day and the regular order of the moon and the stars (Jer. 31:35) guarantees that Israel's existence as Yhwh's people is as sure as the cosmic order of Yhwh's creation.

And Yes, Ezekiel

Even readers innocent of Hebrew will notice relationships, especially in vocabulary, between Genesis 1–3 and Ezekiel. As perhaps the clearest example, Ezekiel 28:13, 31:9–18, and 36:35 mention Eden in a way that calls Genesis to mind. Scholars have taken note of other connections, such as Ezekiel's use of the Hebrew term *bara'* (to create) in 28:13, which compares with its use in Genesis 1:1 to say that "God created the heavens and the earth."[46] Regardless of these

46. Nevader draws on previous scholars in her list of verbal or thematic connections between Gen. 1–3 and Ezekiel ("Creating a *Deus Non Creator*," 56). Thomas Wagner provides a different list in "'Ungeklärte Verhältnisse,'" 214. Wagner's list considers all of Gen. 1–9.

and other comparisons, whether Ezekiel depends on or draws from a creation tradition remains a matter of debate. Madhavi Nevader mounts a strong argument against the assumption that Ezekiel depends on and sponsors a creation tradition, but in the Latin part of her essay's title—*Deus Non Creator* (God Is Not the Creator)—I believe her to be mistaken.[47]

God acts as Creator in Ezekiel in at least two ways. Most dramatically, God brings about—from dry bones; that is, from virtually nothing—a new creation, a new creature, a new Israel animated by God (Ezek. 37:14). And this new creation accompanies another: God's creation of a new heart (36:24–38). God promises, "I will give you a new heart, and a new spirit I will put within you [*beqirbekem*]. And I will remove the heart of stone from your body and give you a heart of flesh" (v. 26). God's action will involve surgically removing Israel's old, inanimate heart of stone in order to replace it with one of God's fashioning. All of this Moshe Greenberg describes as "a unilateral act of God."[48]

Jeremiah complains repeatedly about Israel's stubborn heart, their evil heart (e.g., Jer. 18:12), and even their "uncircumcised heart" (9:25). Deuteronomy urges the people to circumcise their heart (Deut. 10:16), and Ezekiel urges them to get a new heart and a new spirit (Ezek. 18:31). Deuteronomy concedes Israel's incapacity for their own cardiac circumcision and promises that God will perform the surgery (Deut. 30:6). Ezekiel concedes Israel's incapacity to acquire a new heart or new spirit, and God promises to create a new heart and install it and create a new spirit in Israel—*God's own spirit*, it turns out, in a resurrected, re-created Israel (Ezek. 37:14). In a similar way, Jeremiah concedes Israel's incapacity to heed God's instruction—Yhwh's *torah* (Jer. 6:19; 9:12)—and God promises, "I will put my *torah* within them" (31:33). In all three texts—Deuteronomy, Ezekiel, and Jeremiah—God acts unilaterally, in sovereign freedom. And God acts not to deny the sins by which Israel was judged and exiled but to restore Israel, on nothing but God's own initiative, as people given Yhwh's *torah* in what the NJPS translates as "their innermost being" (Jer. 31:33). In Ezekiel 36:26, it is the new spirit, along with a new heart, that God promises to place in Israel's innermost being (*beqereb* in both texts) as a condition—which God alone can meet and promises to meet—of Israel's enduring restoration.

Scholars have identified other references to creation in Ezekiel—for example, in chapters 38–39, where Paul E. Fitzpatrick sees a cosmogony redolent of ancient combat myths.[49] And Safwat Marzouk draws instructively on ancient

47. Nevader, "Creating a *Deus Non Creator*."
48. Greenberg, *Ezekiel 21–37*, 375.
49. Fitzpatrick, *Disarmament of God*, 82–113.

creation-related texts, including those I discussed in chapter 4, in interpreting the "monstrification" of Egypt in Ezekiel.[50] Even so, Ezekiel's relation to a creation is contested: "For Ezekiel," Nevader claims, "creation itself is contested."[51] This may be the case. And she is surely correct that the *Enuma Elish*—often titled "The Babylonian Creation Epic"—is not a creation epic. Undeniably, though, that epic includes a description of Marduk as creator, a description essential to its "apology for Marduk's supreme rule over the natural and divine worlds." Ezekiel depicts God acting as Creator—as the Re-creator of Israel. While Marduk's supreme rule as creator was won in combat, in Ezekiel, Yhwh as Creator is the presupposition and the assurance of Israel's restoration.

Conclusion

Amos, like Isaiah, assumes that Yhwh is the Creator and King whose rule extends internationally. Both books also make explicit reference to God the Creator. The same is true of Jeremiah. Ezekiel's testimony on the latter point is more muted. The instances of *bara'*—"to create"—in 28:13, 15 are both in the passive and describe the king of Tyre as having been created. If we are to understand that God created Tyre's king, Ezekiel makes nothing of the point. Amos and Jeremiah both invoke God the Creator in their indictments of Israel and their announcements of Israel's punishment. Ezekiel describes Yhwh's action as Creator, perhaps employing the *Chaoskampf* motif—depicting Pharaoh and Egypt as symbolic of chaos and Yhwh's conquest of them,[52] then describing God's triumph in chapters 38–39.[53] But it is definitely in Israel's, and Judah's, restoration and reconstitution—in their re-creation—that God acts as Creator. Of course, the topographical and geographical rearrangements that Ezekiel describes in chapters 40–48 could be brought about only by one able to create them.[54]

At the beginning of this chapter, I described the devastation that Janice wreaked on our symmetrical and apparently well-ordered fescue lawns to create a radically different, more properly natural and hospitable, and less artificially defined space and environment. Amos confronted an apparently well-ordered world—the Jeroboam he addresses in Amos 7 enjoyed a long, rich reign—but one whose well-ordered symmetry was fraught with injustice and,

50. Marzouk, *Egypt as a Monster*, 16–29, 70–76.

51. This quotation and the ones following in this paragraph are from Nevader, "Creating a *Deus Non Creator*," 68.

52. Marzouk, *Egypt as a Monster*, 200.

53. Fitzpatrick, *Disarmament of God*.

54. On Ezek. 47, see Tuell, "Rivers of Paradise."

thus, idolatry.[55] In discussing Jeremiah 4:23–26, then, I referred to Yhwh's "decreating" the world. This strange work of God the Creator comes in response to Israel's and especially Judah's sins, which Jeremiah describes at length. But it is also in announcing Israel's *re*-creation that Jeremiah, like Isaiah, speaks of God the Creator. Unlike Yhwh's decreating, however, God's re-creating—in Ezekiel as well—responds to nothing outside of God. Like God's creation of the world in the beginning, it is creation *de nihilo*, as Augustine said—creation from (virtually) nothing (see chap. 2 in this book on Gen. 2). As I wrote above, God *re*-created Israel when it was virtually nothing—nothing but dry bones. Dry bones can do nothing; at least, they can do nothing to which God should respond. God the Creator determined at time's beginning to say, "Let there be light." God the Creator determined later in time to say to Israel's dry bones, "I am putting *ruach* into you, and you shall live" (Ezek. 37:5). The world's existence and Israel's are at the initiative of the Creator.

The Creator's initiative, as Isaiah, Amos, Jeremiah, and Ezekiel depict it, God exercised in the context of domestic and international conflict. The same is true of the following chapter's subjects, Zechariah and Daniel, which describe Yhwh's interventions as Creator in an enigmatic and apocalyptic mode.

55. An act or practice or system of injustice amounts to an elevation of self in defiance of God.

9

Rearranging the World

GOD THE CREATOR IN ZECHARIAH AND DANIEL

A late friend of mine, a former teacher and then colleague named Chris, was a young man living in Holland when German troops occupied his city, Haarlem, near the beginning of World War II. Like many other young men in the Netherlands, Chris received notice that he should report to the train station at an appointed time. The train took him to Germany, to Berlin, where the Nazis forced him to work as a slave. Sometime after arriving in Berlin, Chris fell gravely ill. His keepers took him from his barracks to a hospital. But before he had recovered from his illness, scores of wounded German troops were returned to Berlin from the Russian front. The hospital quickly dismissed Chris, who wandered, on foot and in his pajamas, back to his barracks; he found that Allied planes had bombed them out of existence. Someone eventually found Chris, near death, and took him to another hospital. There, in the bed next to his, lay a young Polish boy who had been beaten severely in a concentration camp. On the night the boy died, the Allies again bombed Berlin. From his window, Chris watched the bombs explode and the city erupt in flames. He thought to himself, "This is how I shall die; this is how the world will end."

Although Chris's father was the pastor of Haarlem's largest Reformed church, the *Nieuwe Kerk* or New Church, Chris had never taken an interest in theology. But that night, in that fiery, apocalyptic explosion of death and destruction,

Chris felt a powerful call to be a theologian. He wanted, and needed, to try to understand what the Bible says about God's final triumph over those powers of evil and death that he had seen occupying Haarlem, that he now saw displayed before him, witnessed lying next to him, and felt in his own body. Chris did not die that night. Remarkably, he recovered from his illness and somehow—Chris never knew exactly how—found himself on a train bound for Haarlem, where he spent the rest of the war hiding in his parents' attic, studying Greek and Hebrew. After the war, Johann Christiaan Beker did become a theologian, and he wrote significant works on the theology—the *apocalyptic* theology—of Paul the apostle.[1]

Introduction

"Apocalyptic" can describe a type of literature, a theology (or eschatology), a social group or movement, or some combination of the three. Precise definition of the term has proved elusive, in part because of its use in academic and popular contexts and in reference to ancient texts (*texts* in the broadest sense of the term), current ones, and ones from every other time and many places.[2] Any proffered defining criteria of *apocalyptic* will be circular to some degree since they will be drawn from texts or other phenomena that are taken to constitute defining instances of it. The philosopher William P. Alston gave respectability to this kind of inevitable and necessary question-begging by calling it "epistemic circularity."[3] In English, *apocalypse* is the transliteration of the Greek word *apokalypsis*, meaning "revelation" or "unveiling." Modern use of the term has its origin in the New Testament book of Revelation: "The Apocalypse." In that book, God *reveals* certain things to John the island of Patmos. God's revelation—more precisely, the revelation of Jesus Christ, which God gave to him and thereby to John—involves many mysterious images and symbols, all of which work to disclose God's ultimate triumph over reality-distorting powers that seemed then (they have seemed that way since) to hold the world in their grip. So firm is the grip of those powers that liberation from it and from them could come about only through divine intervention, and even intervention of

1. Beker, *Paul the Apostle*; *Paul's Apocalyptic Gospel*. I offer a fuller account of Chris Beker's story in "Suffering and Hope." The article is based on my conversations with Beker, in Princeton, and was reprinted as the foreword to his book *Suffering and Hope*.

2. See the illustrative and instructive survey of Becker and Jöris, "Toward a Scientific Designation." Michael A. Stead surveys some of the literature directly relevant to Zechariah in *Intertextuality of Zechariah 1–8*, 6–8. Cf. also Boda, *Book of Zechariah*, 689–91.

3. Alston, "On Knowing That We Know," 34.

the most dramatic sort: a new creation—a new Jerusalem, and a new heaven and a new earth (Rev. 21:1), which would be the creation of an enduring peace. In chapter 7 of this book, on God the Creator in Isaiah, I postponed discussion of Isaiah 65 until now, because the chapter serves as an introduction—a precursor—to the apocalyptic mode of Zechariah and Daniel.[4]

Isaiah 65

The latter chapters of Isaiah, 56–66, assume a setting in the province of Judah under Persian administration. Persia followed Babylon, which followed Assyria, in the succession of empires dominating the world, so far as it was known west of the Hindu Kush. Nebuchadnezzar of Babylon had forced Judah's upper echelon to migrate to Babylon following his defeat of Judah (in 597) and destruction of Jerusalem (in 586; 2 Kings 25). According to the testimony of Ezra 1:1–8 and 2 Chronicles 36:22–23, Cyrus the Great, founder of the Persian Empire, claimed to have been commissioned by God to rebuild the temple in Jerusalem, testimony that echoes Isaiah's (Isa. 44:28).[5] To fulfill this commission, Cyrus encouraged exiles—Jews—to return to devastated Jerusalem and Judah and to engage in the work of reconstruction.

Jews who migrated from Babylon to Judah—Yehud[6]—did not "return" to an empty land.[7] I put *return* in quotation marks because no one exiled from Judah in 597 or 586 or 582 was likely to be included in a migration westward to Yehud late in the sixth century BCE. Life in the two locations—Babylon and Yehud—continued, and it continued with communication between the Babylonian and Judean communities. Ezekiel delivers an oracle to the Jews in Babylon reporting and condemning what those in Yehud—"those living on the devastated places of the land [*ha'adamah*] of Israel"—have been saying (Ezek. 33:24). And Jeremiah addresses the Jewish community in Babylon by letter,

4. The focus will be on Zech. 1–6 below, where I make further comments on Zechariah and apocalyptic. I comment on all of Zechariah in "Book of Zechariah."

5. Cyrus himself boasted that he "restored the images of the gods" to their places—images that Nebuchadnezzar had taken to Babylon ("Cyrus Cylinder Translation," Livius, July 13, 2020, https://www.livius.org/sources/content/cyrus-cylinder/cyrus-cylinder-translation/). In Judah's case, according to Ezra, in place of a divine image, temple vessels were restored (Ezra 1:7–8; cf. 2 Chron. 36:18).

6. *Yehud*, used in scholarly literature with reference to the Babylonian and then Persian province, is a transliteration of the Aramaic term for Judah (Hebrew: *yehudah*). Aramaic was the diplomatic language employed by Babylonian and Persian administrations of the province.

7. On Jews in Judah following Babylon's conquest, see the essays in Lipschits and Blenkinsopp, *Judah and the Judeans*.

condemning what "prophets" had been promising them (Jer. 29:1–11). Conflict between the Judean and Babylonian communities had its mirror in conflicts within Yehud itself. Isaiah 63, after recounting God's graciously leading Israel (vv. 7–9) and Israel's subsequent "rebellion" (v. 10), appeals to God to "see from heaven and observe from your divine abode" (v. 15). What God is here urged to observe is a community within Yehud—a part of the Jewish community—not acknowledged as legitimately part of Israel or the progeny of Abraham (v. 16).[8] Later, in 66:5, the prophet, addressing the community—those who "tremble" at Yhwh's word (also 66:2; cf. Ezra 9:4; 10:3)—refers to their family or community members (*brothers*) who hate them and exclude or expel them.

It is not possible to identify all the issues that may have been dividing the Jewish community in Persian-administered Yehud or to reduce them to one. In Isaiah, however, the division is absolute between those who forsake Yhwh (Isa. 65:11) and those Yhwh calls "my servants" (vv. 13–15). In Isaiah 63 and 64, the community's complaint that Abraham/Israel has excluded them includes the plea, "But you, O Yhwh, are our father" (63:16; 64:7[64:8]). Repeatedly, the community refers to "all of us" (*kullanu*)—for example, "*all of us* are the work of your hands" (64:7[64:8]). The community protests its exclusion from Abraham/Israel, appealing to "all of us" as the work of God's hands and "our father"—appealing to God as the Creator of them all, as in Malachi 2:10: "Have not *all of us* one *father*? Did not one God create us?"[9] Isaiah implicitly and Malachi expressly appeals to God the Creator—and God's formation, creation, of one people—as the source and ground of hope. In Isaiah 65, that hope turns to the anticipation of a new creation. In Isaiah 65:16c–18, Yhwh announces that "the former troubles are forgotten . . . they are hidden from sight":

> For see, I am creating [*bara'*] new heavens
> and a new earth;
> The former things will not be remembered,
> and they will no longer come to mind.
> But rejoice and be glad forever
> in what I am creating [*bara'*],
> for see, I am creating [*bara'*] Jerusalem as gladness
> and her people as joy.

8. The community speaking in Isa. 63:16 complains that "Abraham does not *know* us, and Israel does not *recognize* us." The verbs here give the complaint a technical sense. It's not that Abraham/Israel doesn't know the identity of these people or cannot recognize them; rather, Abraham/Israel excluded them.

9. The italicized words appear in both Isa. 63–64 and Mal. 2:10.

God here announces not a military intervention in judgment of injustice and idolatry, as earlier in Isaiah, but the creation of a new reality, using the word *bara'*, as in Genesis 1:1. The new heavens and the new earth God is now creating relieve the community—God's servants and "chosen ones" (Isa. 65:15, 22)—of the "former troubles." No enemies, foreign or domestic, are vanquished; rather, the conditions of life are reordered and threats of exploitation or conquest eliminated (vv. 20–23). In this new creation, the peaceable vision of Isaiah 11 is realized: wolf and lamb dine together in peace, and the lion eats straw like the ox (65:25; 11:6–8). That wolves and lions share the same fare as lambs and oxen is not a matter of taming the former and feeding them vegetables, as if vultures could naturally adapt to a salad diet. It is a matter of re-creating them as different creatures. This Yhwh promises as part of the new heavens and the new earth of God's creating.

In Isaiah 65, Yhwh first laments the absence of response to Yhwh's persistent offerings of divine presence and help. "I was ready to be found by those who did not seek me. I said, 'Here I am! Here I am!' to a nation that did not call on my name" (v. 1). At the end of the chapter, as part of Yhwh's new creation, Yhwh takes the initiative: "Before they call, I will answer" (v. 24). This "before," extended on God's own initiative as Creator, echoes that in Jeremiah and Ezekiel, as explained in the preceding chapter of this book: before Israel-in-exile repented or called on God's name, God announced the community's restoration as God's people forgiven (Jer. 31:31–34) and their restoration to life in the land of Israel (Ezek. 37:1–14).

Neither Isaiah 65 nor the larger corpus of which it is a part—framed by the extension to eunuchs and foreigners of inclusion in the Zion/Jerusalem community (Isa. 56:1–8; 66:19–23)—is in an apocalyptic mode. The promise that God will create a new heavens and a new earth did foreshadow, however, its incorporation in apocalyptic literature, including in *the* Apocalypse (Rev. 21:1).[10] Zechariah, too, like Isaiah 65 (and 66) and the latter chapters of Jeremiah and Ezekiel, places emphasis on God's initiative as Creator—Creator not of a new heavens and a new earth but of a new world.

Zechariah

Zechariah, like Isaiah, stands broadly within the Zion tradition, with its attention to Jerusalem as a city and Zion as both a city—the site of God's dwelling—and

10. Isaiah 24–27 has been called "the Isaiah Apocalypse" or something similar. Marvin A. Sweeney denies that the passage is an apocalypse because it "does not portray the end of time" (*Tanak*, 281), which begs the question. Christopher B. Hays offers a substantial argument for why Isa. 24–27 should not be considered an apocalyptic text. *Origins of Isaiah 24–27*.

a literary and theological symbol.[11] The symbolism of Zion can be articulated in unexpected ways. Isaiah 54:5, for example, depicts Yhwh as both the husband and the Creator—the maker (*ʿosayik*)—of personified Zion. Earlier, Isaiah 40 cast Zion/Jerusalem as an evangelist, a "herald of good tidings" (v. 9), to Judah's cities. Those good tidings consisted, in a summary way, of just this: "Here is your God!" The God of Judah's cities had been absent, in what Isaiah calls a "brief moment" of abandonment (54:7), but now he returns in power, victorious (40:10). That victory, correlated with the fall of Babylon, from which Isaiah urges Israel-in-exile to depart (52:11), seemed if not Pyrrhic then fraught with intercommunal conflict, as I noted above. Zechariah, too, acknowledges the victory. Isaiah, prophet and poet—the two are one, especially in the case of Isaiah—employed "Zion" in a radical way to express the fractured yet permanently enduring and intimate relationship of Yhwh to Israel. In Zechariah, however, the angel of Yhwh raises an insistent question: "O Yhwh of hosts, how long?" (Zech. 1:12).

Two realities prompt the angel's question. First is the reality that, the Zion tradition notwithstanding, the temple remains a desecrated ruin, Jerusalem is a disaster site, and the only perceptible king has a Persian name, Darius, and rules an empire vaster than Assyria's or even Babylon's rulers imagined. Within that empire, the tiny Persian province of Yehud—occupying an area roughly the size of London but with a population of perhaps twelve thousand souls—and the city of Jerusalem, with its "few hundred people," languished.[12] The second reality prompting the question "How long?" is the memory of God's promise of seventy years: "This whole land shall become a desolate waste, and these nations," Judah included, "shall serve the king of Babylon for seventy years" (Jer. 25:11). And when the seventy years have ended, "I will fulfill my good promise to you" (29:10). Zechariah's "How long?" follows an evidently unfulfilled divine promise, and Zechariah—or the angel of Yhwh—addresses it to the Lord of hosts.

Uniquely among the prophets, Haggai's and Zechariah's words are dated precisely. Zechariah 1:1, 7 and 7:1 situate the material following them to a specific year, month, and—except for 1:1—day in the reign of Darius, king of Persia. The dates correlate to the years 520 (in chap. 1) and 518. The year 520 had particular significance. Darius, perhaps a usurper, claimed the imperial throne in Persia in 522 following the sudden death of Cambyses, son of and imperial successor

11. Konrad Schmid describes features of the Zion tradition in *Historical Theology*, 412–24. I discuss Zion as a theological symbol in *Zion, the City of the Great King*.

12. The Society for Old Testament Study estimates Yehud's geographical area to be roughly 750 square miles ("Yehud," Society for Old Testament Study, accessed July 13, 2022, https://www.sots.ac.uk/wiki/yehud/). The population estimates are from Finkelstein, "Territorial Extent and Demography," 44–45.

to Cyrus. But Darius could not secure his reign until he had defeated several rival contenders, a feat he accomplished in 520. Darius celebrated his eventual victory by causing an account of it to be inscribed, in three languages, more than ninety meters (or three hundred feet) above ground, on the rock face of a mountain named Behistun (or Besitun). The inscription faced the road leading from Babylon to Ecbatana, two of the four capital cities of Persia (in addition to Susa—the imperial center—and Persepolis). No one on the road, or on the ground, could read the inscription, of course, or make out any of its cuneiform signs. Darius was publishing it to the world on behalf of Ahura Mazda, the deity venerated by Darius and Cyrus in Persia.[13] In 520, Darius had suppressed all opposition, and the world was quiet but by no means at "peace," contrary to the NRSV (Zech. 1:11).

Visions of the Night: Zechariah 1–6

In 520, "in the twenty-fourth day of the eleventh month, the word of the Lord came to Zechariah" (Zech. 1:7). This is a typical revelation formula in the Prophets, usually followed by "and the prophet said, 'Thus says the Lord . . .'" In Zechariah's case, rather than proclaiming the word of the Lord, the prophet says, "I saw in the night, and there was a man" (v. 8). Thus begins the first of Zechariah's night visions—formally, reports about the visions. The setting of the first vision is at night, and the episodes proceed without a change of scene. Zechariah 4:1, for example, assumes that it is still night: Zechariah is awakened, "as one is roused from sleep." The nighttime setting plays a literary and theological role in these visions: it is night, and Zechariah cannot see clearly, in a triple sense. First, since it's dark, he cannot make out just what he is seeing—and what he barely sees is among myrtle trees in "the deep darkness."[14] Second, he cannot make sense of what he is seeing. Third, in the first vision, the intention and the faithfulness of God are imperceptible, and the situation of Yehud is itself dark.[15]

What Zechariah sees in his visions combines the mundane and the supramundane. For that reason, and because it is night, the prophet requires an intermediary: someone who can reveal to him what he is seeing and what it means.

13. The text of Darius's inscription is accessible online at https://www.livius.org/articles/place/behistun/behistun-3/. Darius expresses his intention that it be published "to the world" at iv.60. He summarizes his securing of the throne at iv.52.

14. The Hebrew term *metzulah* ("deep") often refers to watery depths (Exod. 15:5; Jon. 2:4[2:3]). Here it emphasizes the (deep) darkness in which the vision is set.

15. Here and in what follows, I draw on material explored in my earlier essay "Peace as the Visionary Mission."

In Zechariah 1:8, the prophet sees a man mounted on a red horse in front of horses of three other colors, a mundane sight, though also a bit alarming, since horses, unsuited to domestic purposes at that time, were instruments of battle (e.g., Ps. 33:17; cf. Zech. 9:9).[16] Zechariah, wondering about these horses, one with a rider, poses his question—"What are these?"—to a figure he addresses as "my lord," or simply "Sir." The text identifies the one who then answers as "the angel talking with me" (1:9). This supramundane, heavenly being accompanies Zechariah through the series of visions as an interpreting angel.[17] The visions generally follow this pattern:

1. The prophet reports a vision: "I saw [or the angel shows him] . . ."
2. He describes a sign: "and there before me was/were . . ."
3. He asks, "What is this / are these?"
4. The angel identifies the sign: "This is / these are . . ."
5. The angel interprets the sign.

In Zechariah 1:8–11, what the angel identifies and interprets turns out to be anything but ordinary horses. They have returned, it is revealed to Zechariah, from patrolling "throughout the earth,"[18] as Yhwh had appointed them to do. They have returned from their global reconnoitering to report that "the whole earth is settled and quiet" (v. 11).

The scene (Zech. 1:8–11) has a quality both liminal and numinous, with mythic imagery suggestive of both Eden and the temple, and darkness shrouding the presence of Yhwh (cf. 1 Kings 8:12). Zechariah's access to this shrouded presence is mediated through his interpreting angel, the angel of Yhwh, and the angel "standing among the myrtles" (Zech. 1:11). Perhaps two of the angels are the same, and perhaps all three of them are one. Regardless, what Zechariah is given to understand is mediated—revealed to him by at least one heavenly intermediary. And the angel of Yhwh—whose identity often merges with Yhwh's own and here gives voice to Zechariah and Yehud—protests, "How long?" The people of Yehud still suffer Yhwh's anger, even after seventy years.

16. While the Hebrew text (like the LXX and the Targum) at Ps. 33:17 has simply "horse," the NRSV adds an interpretive—correct, but redundant—adjective and renders it as "war horse."

17. I use "interpreting angel" in "Book of Zechariah." Mark Boda consistently translates *mal'ak* as "messenger." The Hebrew word is patient of either translation. "Angel" makes clear the supramundane—"heavenly"—character of the one interpreting what the prophet struggles to see and understand. Boda is explicit about the heavenly character he describes as "messenger." *Book of Zechariah*, 127–28.

18. For the translation, see Boda, *Book of Zechariah*, 116; *IBHS*, #11.2.5.

Yhwh's response follows immediately. Zechariah is told to proclaim two oracles (Zech. 1:14–17). They announce Yhwh's intention to act out of zeal for Jerusalem and Judah. They also address the matter of Yhwh's anger, redirecting it. The angel of Yhwh notes that Yhwh has been angry (*za'am*) at Jerusalem and Judah for seventy years (v. 12). Now Zechariah is to announce that, having been "a little angry" in the past, Yhwh is now "very angry" (*qetseph gadol . . . qatsaphti*) at the nations because "surely they increased the disaster" (v. 15).[19] Here, as elsewhere in the book,[20] Zechariah echoes Isaiah 10:5–15: Yhwh acknowledged that Assyria was the rod of God's anger (*za'am*), but Assyria had in mind greater destruction and conquest than Yhwh had intended (10:7, 15). Abruptly, if momentarily, attention in Zechariah turns from the nations to Jerusalem, and more precisely to Yhwh's startling announcement: "I am returning to Jerusalem with compassion" (Zech. 1:16).[21] The temple will be restored, cities will be prosperous . . . in short, Yhwh will once again comfort Zion and choose Jerusalem (v. 17).

The announcement of Yhwh's return in compassion to the comfort of Zion and the reaffirmation of Jerusalem as God's chosen echo other biblical texts and generally resemble prophetic speech. But the literary context preceding and following this announcement elevates the visions into a different register. As I mentioned above, the prophetic speech follows a vision of horses who have patrolled—reconnoitered—the earth, at Yhwh's instruction, and have reported to the angel of Yhwh the distressing news that the world remains quiet (*shaqat*, Job 1:11). This is, literally, fantastic—horses as Yhwh's instruments of reconnaissance. "The sons of God" we have encountered before in Genesis 6. And they appeared in Job, where "the sons of God" reported to Yhwh after patrolling the earth (1:6–7; 2:1). In its first vision report, Zechariah bears resemblance to those texts, but here in Zechariah we see not divine beings but world-traveling horses, with at least one rider (Zech. 1:8).

Framing the series of visions in chapters 1–6 are the one just considered—Zechariah 1:8–13, with oracles following in verses 14–17—and the final vision, Zechariah 6:1–8. In Zechariah 6, once again horses of different colors appear but this time with chariots. The scene in chapter 1 was quiet and dark; the four

19. Literally, "they were allies of the disaster" (Ollenburger, "Book of Zechariah," 753n27). The translation above is from Boda, *Book of Zechariah*, 142–43.

20. Michael A. Stead provides an exhaustive treatment of Zechariah's use of presumably earlier texts, as suggested by his book's title, *Intertextuality of Zechariah 1–8*.

21. I understand the verb here—*shabti*—as a performative perfect, both announcing and initiating an action (Joüon, #112f, g; Ollenburger, "Book of Zechariah," 754n28). Boda offers further discussion of the grammar in *Book of Zechariah*, 143.

horses, returned from patrolling throughout the earth and now stationary among the myrtles, reported that all was quiet. The scene in chapter 6 is alive with movement and suggestions of light. The horses, powerful ones (*'amutsim*, v. 3), and chariots—the imagery is obviously martial—"burst like the sun"[22] from "between two mountains" of bronze (v. 1). Comparisons with ancient material outside and within the Old Testament abound.[23] But the picture in verse 1 calls to mind "the horses, at the entrance to the temple, which Judah's kings had dedicated to the sun, . . . and the chariots of the sun" (2 Kings 23:11), as well as the bronze pillars that stood before the temple (1 Kings 7:15–22). Zechariah's interpreting angel, identifying what Zechariah sees clearly in the light, says of the horses that, "having presented themselves to the Lord of the whole earth," they are now proceeding as "the four winds of heaven" (Zech. 6:5; cf. 2:10[2:6]). The horses dedicated to the sun and the chariots of the sun—both images likely cast in metal—were removed from the temple, according to the verse that mentions them. But it seems plausible that Zechariah draws from those images, or similar ones, to depict the horses and chariots as if bursting forth from the temple, from between two bronze mountains (recalling the bronze pillars), like the sun. The interpreting angel, after describing "these" as going out universally—"the four winds of heaven" (6:5)—names only two winds, two directions: north and south (v. 6).[24] The horses and chariots need not go east because that—Zion, Jerusalem, the not-yet-rebuilt temple—is their place of departure.

In the framing visions (Zech. 1:8–13 and 6:1–8), horses patrol the whole earth:

> These [horses] are the ones Yhwh sent to patrol throughout the earth. (1:10)

> They [the horses] sought to patrol the earth, and [the interpreting angel] said, "Go, patrol throughout the earth." And they patrolled throughout the earth. (6:7)

But in Zechariah 6, the horses and chariots heading north have a specific purpose, a purpose already accomplished: "They have set my spirit at rest in the northland" (v. 8). "My spirit" refers to Yhwh's capacity to accomplish what human might or power cannot, as Yhwh has already said: "Neither by might nor by power, but by my spirit, says the Lord" (4:6). The same terms—might (*chayil*)

22. Ollenburger, "Book of Zechariah," 782.
23. See Boda, *Book of Zechariah*, 356–67.
24. The NRSV has "to the west country" in v. 6, noting that the Hebrew has "after them," which is likely correct. See Boda, *Book of Zechariah*, 372.

and power (*koach*)—appear together in Psalm 33:16, where God declares that by these neither will a king be saved nor a warrior delivered.[25]

In Zechariah 6:8, Yhwh's powerful spirit rests in the northland—Babylon—to accomplish the deliverance for which the angel of Yhwh longed and which no king or warrior could deliver. Deliverance, in this case, means the release to Zion of Israel-in-exile; the denial by "the Lord of the whole earth" (4:14) of Darius's claim to be "king of kings" and "king of all lands";[26] the disempowerment of those nations that had scattered or winnowed Judah, Israel, and Jerusalem (2:1–4[1:18–21]); the reconstruction and unlimited expansion of an unwalled Jerusalem protected by Yhwh's fire; and, finally, the presence of Yhwh dwelling in Zion's midst along with nations that have joined themselves to Yhwh (*nilwu . . . 'el-yhwh*, 2:15[2:11], similar to Isa. 56:6) and become Yhwh's people (Zech. 2:5–16[2:1–12]).

Zechariah envisions the reordering of the world, a world ordered to God's design and intention. Zechariah's first vision longs for, anticipates—and in the following oracle (1:14–17), God promises—a reordering intervention. The final vision, in chapter 6, *envisions* the accomplishment of that reordering. The scope of these framing visions extends to the whole earth. But in the sequence of visions, the scope is dynamic: it moves from the whole earth, in the first vision, to Judah and Jerusalem in the second (2:1–4[1:18–21]), to the city of Jerusalem in the third (2:5–9[2:1–5]), and to a subject as particular as Joshua the high priest in the fourth (3:1–10). In a courtroom scene that departs from the structure of the other visions, the *satan*—the prosecuting attorney in God's court (cf. Job 1:6–12)—brings accusations against Joshua. This elicits Yhwh's rebuke of the *satan* and the removal of Joshua's guilt—his *'awon*—whatever it may have been (Zech. 3:2–4).[27] As a consequence, Joshua gains sanction as a priest. More significantly, Yhwh promises to remove the guilt, or the punishment—the *'awon*—of the land, of Yehud, "in one day" (3:9). After the reinvestiture of Joshua, the focus of Zechariah's visions narrows to the small point of a remarkable lampstand or menorah (4:1–14): the promise of God's powerful presence—"but by my spirit" (4:6)—in the midst of a ruin.

25. Ollenburger, "Book of Zechariah," 770. Stead says that the horses in Zech. 6:8 "go out bent on conquest" (*Intertextuality of Zechariah 1–8*, 214n72). I agree, except that the conquest has been achieved—within the framework of the visions.

26. See Darius's Behistun Inscription, i.1. "Behistun (3)," Livius, April 21, 2020, https://www.livius.org/articles/place/behistun/behistun-3/.

27. Lamentations is unsparing in its charges against the priests and the prophets—their guilt, their sins, their iniquity (*'awon*, 4:13). It would be unsurprising if Joshua, as the grandson of the last high priest before Babylon's destruction of the temple (Seraiah, executed by Nebuchadnezzar), and as a leader of the first group to move from Babylon to Yehud, would be counted among the guilty priests.

Having moved and narrowed from the whole earth to Judah, to Joshua the priest, and to the lampstand, precisely there—at the smallest, most particular point and moment—Zechariah's first visions (chaps. 1–4) pivot. They expand their scope from Joshua the priest and the lampstand of God's announced presence to the province of Judah in a twofold expurgation: first of thievery and deceit (5:1–4) and then of venerated objects, or subjects, other than Yhwh (vv. 5–11), whatever or whoever they have been. These latter objects are compressed into one female image (suggestive of Asherah or Astarte, perhaps),[28] packaged, and carried to Babylon for veneration, carried to Shinar (v. 11)—that is, the Shinar of Genesis 11 and Babel's tower. Babylon, from which "Zion" is urged to escape (Zech. 2:11[2:7]), lies in the north country, the destination of the horses and chariots that have set Yhwh's liberating spirit at rest.

Zechariah's visions thus exhibit a serial movement from the whole earth to Judah, to a person and an object in Jerusalem, and then again to Judah and the whole earth. The movement from periphery to center and back can be represented this way:

1:7–17 The ends of the earth
  2:1–4[1:18–21] Judah
    2:5–9[2:1–5] Jerusalem
      3:1–10 Joshua the priest
      4:1–14 A lampstand and Zerubbabel
  5:1–11 Judah
6:1–8 The ends of the earth[29]

At the visions' extremes—the first vision and the last—the scope of the visions extends to the four winds: the horses, with or without riders and chariots, patrol throughout the earth. At the center of this earth stands the lampstand, the menorah (Zech. 4:2), in anticipation of a reconstructed temple whose founding is imminent (v. 9). Just there, where the visions' focus is narrowest and most particular, they refer to Yhwh as "Lord of the whole earth" (v. 14). And from this most particular point, the temple in Jerusalem, the "eyes of Yhwh range over the whole earth" (v. 10),[30] watching over God's domain from the particular site where God is most intensely present.

28. Ollenburger, "Book of Zechariah," 779. Diana Edelman offers a graphic argument for Asherah in "Proving Yahweh Killed His Wife."

29. Ollenburger, "Peace as the Visionary Mission," 108.

30. Second Chronicles 16:9 uses the same verb and verb form as Zech. 4:10 to describe Yhwh's ranging throughout the earth in support of those devoted to Yhwh (except that the verb is feminine [*meshotetot*] in 2 Chronicles). Note also Yhwh's seven eyes in Zech. 3:9.

Conclusion

Zechariah 1–6 describes in dramatic, visionary fashion the re-creation of the world. At the most dramatic moment of this envisioned and reported rearrangement, this re-creation, Zechariah commands universal silence (2:17[2:13]), not only or primarily because what is envisioned in the first two chapters contradicts what could be reasonably imagined but because—also barely imaginable in the circumstance—Yhwh is awakened, roused to action. With the world at rest under the visible dominion of Darius (1:7), Yhwh asserts the Creator's prerogative to reorder reality and to restore its proper order. That restoration and re-creation is envisioned, announced, and initiated in spite of, and in the face of, compelling empirical, disconfirming evidence: piles of temple rubble and unchallenged Persian imperial domination, for example. Zechariah's visions, in their announcement of Yhwh as Lord of the whole earth, contrary to evident fact, echo Isaiah's proclamation of Yhwh as God the Creator (Isa. 40) while Babylon's lord and world creator, Marduk, reigned supreme and had Yhwh symbolically under his feet (see chap. 7 in this book). These visions, I have suggested, assume an apocalyptic mode.

Indicative of Zechariah's apocalyptic mode in the visions is, first, precisely their visionary character. What Zechariah *sees* is revealed to him by the interpreting angel. Their formal character as *revelation* is, arguably, the defining characteristic of apocalyptic texts.[31] Zechariah 1:7–6:8 can be read as a revelation mediated to the prophet, analogous to the revelation mediated to John (Rev. 1:1). Second, apocalyptic literature may protest current arrangements, political or cosmic, by disclosing an alternative future, or a future rearrangement, one impinging on the present, as in Zechariah. Third, Zechariah gathers up all of imperial history, as Judah, Israel, and Jerusalem suffered it, compressing it into a single moment and a single image: four horns, now disarmed, robbed of their power to do harm (Zech. 2:1, 4[1:18, 21]). Daniel, discussed below, expands on Zechariah's model by compressing imperial history into a physical image, composed not of horns but of metals. Finally, the drama that Zechariah's visions narrate takes place in one night, compressing time in a way that joins complaint ("How long?") with an announcement of triumph (6:8). In a night, Zechariah is given to see the entire event of Judah's restoration, even while the event remains to the future as a matter of promise and hope—eschatological hope not for the end of the world but for the end of imperial succession and the establishment of proper *lordship* in and over history (4:14). This hope and this establishment

31. The claim itself involves a redundancy, of course, since "revelation" is simply a translation of *apokalypsis*. On the subject, see Rowland, *By an Immediate Revelation*.

would be realized on the prerogative, initiative, and action of God alone. In this respect, but in an apocalyptic mode, Zechariah shares with Isaiah a vision of Yhwh's exclusive prerogative—the prerogative of God the Creator.[32] That prerogative God has exercised in the disruptive intervention Zechariah envisions.

The only human exercising agency in these chapters is Zerubbabel, of David's royal line, envisioned as builder of the new temple (Zech. 4:9–10). The mundane details of a new temple are not out of place in the middle of expansive visions of re-creation. Jon D. Levenson, observing the connection between the creation account in Genesis 1:1–2:3 and the account of tabernacle construction in Exodus 25–40, refers to a "homology" of "temple and created world."[33] Echoes of that homology—that illustrative similarity—appear here. The new temple announced in Zechariah 4 figures centrally in the world's re-creation because its site (Zion, in Jerusalem) is the site of Yhwh's focal presence after all, and it is the destination of Jews urged to abandon Babylon for Judah—for Yehud—and of non-Jews devoting themselves to Yhwh. Zechariah's visions of God's reordering the world extend to the four winds, and they have their focus in a lampstand in Zion.

Daniel

Zechariah 9–14, though differing from chapters 1–6 (or 1–8) in several respects, continues in an apocalyptic mode, evident especially in chapter 14 with its vision of a final, cataclysmic battle between Yhwh and the nations. Daniel, however, is the Old Testament's sole apocalyptic text. Like Zechariah, Daniel sees the world disordered and envisions a disruptive and creative intervention by God. In Daniel's case, as in other apocalyptic literature from regions of antiquity near to Daniel's, the world's *dis*order is reflected in its subjection to alien Hellenistic rule—and especially the imposition of Greek culture—in the wake of Alexander's victories that brought Persian imperial power to an end.[34]

An Image of the Future: Daniel 1–6

Imperial history and its bearing on Israel and Judah play a role in the narratives of Daniel 1–6, which feature Daniel and his companions, faithful

32. On Yhwh's exclusive prerogative in Isaiah, see chap. 7 and my *Zion, the City of the Great King*, 147–58.

33. Levenson, *Creation and the Persistence of Evil*, 82, 86. I commented earlier, in this book's first chapter, on the relationship of world and temple in Gen. 1.

34. On Daniel and its apocalyptic context, see J. Collins, *Apocalyptic Imagination*.

Jews elevated to leadership in a foreign court, like Joseph in Pharaoh's court and Esther in the Persian court. In the case of Daniel and his friends, lethal measures directed against them by successive rulers are divinely thwarted, and kings come to acknowledge Yhwh's sovereignty in and over the world (Dan. 2:46–47; 3:28–29; 4:31–34[4:34–37]; 6:26–27[6:25–26]). The Hellenistic Greeks—those who competed for control of Palestine and Jerusalem after the death of Alexander—differ. In Daniel 10 and 11, each of the nations is championed by its heavenly prince; chief among the princes is Michael, prince of the Jews (10:13, 20–21). The cosmic relations and conflicts among the princes in heaven are reflected in the international conflicts on earth. Finally, though, "a contemptible person" (*nibzeh*, 11:21) arises to seize the Greek throne—a ruler for whom there is no heavenly prince counterpart. This ruler "will exalt and magnify himself above every deity, and he will speak wondrous [incredible] things against the God of gods"—that is, Yhwh (v. 36). This ruler acknowledges not even the deities of his own tradition; he worships only power: "the god of fortresses" (v. 38). The text is here transparent in its reference to Antiochus IV, who titled himself Epiphanes—"God manifest"—and who, as an evangelist for Hellenism, suppressed Judaism in Jerusalem in 168 or 167 BCE (v. 31). Against the self-exalting power of this ruler there is no human defense, only hope in God's reordering the world.

Daniel's apocalyptic visions focus climactically on the final, irredeemable Hellenistic ruler, but the visions also include him in a history of imperial succession that, in chapter 2, Daniel compresses into a material image. This kind of historical compression was anticipated in Zechariah 2:1–4[1:18–21], as I noted above. In Zechariah, the unnamed empires who oppressed Judah and Jerusalem are disempowered—de-horned (2:4[1:21]). In Daniel, imperial history comes to an end. Daniel describes the humanoid image that embodies this history from its head to its toes; he associates its descending body parts with metals of declining value, from gold, silver, and bronze to a mix of iron and clay, and he represents imperial history's decline from Babylon to Greece, the empire finally being divided among ten toes, with the "contemptible person" as the last toe.

The association of empires with metals of different value has precedent in the late eighth-century BCE poet Hesiod. In his *Opera et dies* (*Works and Days*), he describes a kind of world history by way of four ages, declining from gold and silver to bronze and iron (109–76).[35] Daniel resembles Hesiod in this respect, and he inverts a sequence traditional farther east, in which Persia was greater than Babylon, as Babylon had been greater than Assyria—empires that had

35. Hesiod includes an intervening age, an age of demigods (*hemithio*; *Opera et dies*, 160).

preceded Persia's, which surpassed them both.[36] But imperial history reaches its end in Daniel 2: a stone is cut out from the mountain—cut out "not by [human] hands" (*la' biyadin*)[37]—and it smashes the image's feet, bringing the entire image, and the imperial history it represented, crashing to an end (vv. 34, 45). The empire-crushing stone then becomes a great mountain that fills the earth (v. 35), a guard against any further empire. Imperial history is ended, but there will be in its place the final kingdom: "the God of heaven" will establish a kingdom, a kingdom-shattering kingdom without end (v. 44).[38]

During the Neo-Assyrian, Neo-Babylonian, and Persian periods of hegemony (eighth through fourth centuries BCE), Aramaic was the language of imperial administration, including the administration of Judah/Yehud (e.g., 2 Kings 18:26; Isa. 36:11).[39] It appears in the text of the Bible, in Ezra, which begins and ends in Hebrew but changes to Aramaic in passages involving communication with Persian authorities (portions of Ezra 4–7). Daniel, too, begins and ends in Hebrew, but the text changes to Aramaic in the middle of 2:4, where "the Chaldeans" address the king Nebuchadnezzar.[40] The book continues in Aramaic through the end of chapter 7, an apocalyptic dream; like Daniel 2, it involves a series of empires stripped of their dominion. The court tales involving Daniel and his Jewish companions in "conversation" with the powers that threaten them or, remarkably, seek their wisdom are thus told in the language of imperial power whose efforts to enlist them in its project (1:3–8) they were determined, as faithful Jews, to reject.

Two apocalyptic scenarios, then—Daniel 2 and 7—form an envelope around the court tales, locating them within God's reordering of the world. In this

36. J. Collins, *Daniel*, 167–68. Carol Newsom considers the possibility of a Zoroastrian background in Newsom and Breed, *Daniel*, 76. See also her discussion on pp. 80–81.

37. The NRSV and some other translations have "not by human hands" in v. 34. Neither the MT nor the LXX includes "human," though the text clearly implies that the stone's excavation was not a human achievement.

38. Newsom argues that Dan. 2 has in view not the end of imperial history but its continuation in "the earthly sovereignty of a revived kingdom of Israel" (Newsom and Breed, *Daniel*, 83). This seems to me most unlikely. Nothing in the text suggests anything like a king of Israel to follow the non-Israelite kings named in the book. And nothing in Daniel hints at a hope of revived sovereignty for Israel—sovereignty of Yhwh, yes, but Yhwh's sovereignty and Israel's are uncoupled.

39. Aramaic's history extends from well before the eighth century into modernity. Gzella, *Aramaic*.

40. Chaldeans as an ethnic or political group were earlier located in territory south of Babylon but came to control the Babylonian Empire (Hess, "Chaldea"; cf. Dan. 9:1). In Dan. 2, however, they are a group of royal advisers included among the king's diviners and sages (v. 2). By "the text" here, I mean principally the MT. Manuscripts of Daniel among the DSS also attest the combination of Hebrew and Aramaic in Daniel. J. Collins, *Daniel*, 2–3.

reordering, God reconfigures "dominion" (*sholtan*), removing it from imperial powers and donating it to "the people of the holy ones of the Most High" (7:27). Their kingdom, like God's dominion, will have no end (6:26; 7:27). This will be entirely the doing of God the Creator.

The End of Imperial History: Daniel 7–12

Daniel's vision—his revelatory, apocalyptic dream—in chapter 7 presents God as Creator. God's dominion has been confessed in the court tales: Nebuchadnezzar confesses that Yhwh's dominion is an everlasting one and that God's kingdom endures through the generations (4:31[4:34]). And in Daniel's recounting of Nebuchadnezzar's dream (2:31–35) and his interpretation of it (vv. 36–45), the stone that brings down the statue becomes the kingdom of God, which the God of heaven will establish. In these instances, God as Creator is already implied. In Daniel 2, the imperial succession represented by the statue represents visually a world disordered—increasingly disordered—and then reordered, "not by [human] hands." In chapter 7, it is not another's dream but Daniel's own that he reports, describing beasts arising from "the great sea" that "the four winds of heaven" have stirred up (v. 2). "The great sea" refers to the Mediterranean in other biblical texts (e.g., Josh. 1:4; 9:1). Daniel 7's reference to "the great sea" may have a split reference: to the Mediterranean, on the one hand, and to Canaanite mythological tradition, on the other. That tradition is reflected in Psalm 74:13–15, with the Sea/River, the dragon, and Leviathan (see chaps. 4 and 5 of this book).[41] Those forces of chaos Yhwh defeated primordially, but their historical embodiments continued to disorder the world in their exercise of imperial power. As Yhwh "shattered . . . Sea" and "crushed the heads of Leviathan" (vv. 13–14), so will Yhwh disempower the empires.

Daniel 7 envisions the same kingdoms that chapter 2 represented with metals of declining quality but casts them as grotesque beasts that could not possibly be tamed like Leviathan (Ps. 104:26). This grotesquerie—"violations of the natural order that God set up in creation," as Robert R. Wilson writes[42]—reaches its nadir with the terrifying fourth beast with ten horns, corresponding to the ten toes of the statue in Daniel 2. But in Daniel 7, even from the ten horns one more stands out: "a little one" (v. 8), a slur against Antiochus Epiphanes (see above). With the mention of this little one, the scene changes from beasts emerging from the churning sea to a courtroom, where the Ancient of Days (*'attiq yomin*) will sit, enthroned, for judgment (v. 9). Coming "with the clouds of heaven" to the

41. J. Collins describes the tradition at length in *Daniel*, 286–95.
42. Wilson, "Creation and New Creation," 202.

Ancient of Days is "one like a human being" (*kebar 'enash*, v. 13). To him, everlasting kingdom and dominion is given (v. 14). As noted above, the same everlasting kingdom and dominion is ascribed to God (6:26) and also to "the people of the holy ones of the Most High" (7:27). This "one like a human being" receives no narrative definition in Daniel's dream but is a mediating figure in the judgment and termination of serial imperial reigns and the assignment of dominion to the people of the holy ones of the Most High. By "mediating figure," I mean that he shares in the divinity of the Ancient of Days, while the everlasting kingship and dominion granted him devolves upon the people—not as the divinization of people subject to imperial oppression but as their inclusion in the divine work of salvation, of liberation, and thus of God's triumph on behalf of peace.

The picture of God as the Ancient of Days in heavenly court and of the mediating human figure—"the son of man"—coming with the clouds of heaven elicits comparison with Canaanite mythological traditions mentioned earlier in this section. God as the Ancient of Days with white hair—hair "like pure wool" or "lamb's wool"[43] (Dan. 7:9)—compares with the Ugaritic texts' portrayal of El as the gray-bearded father of the gods.[44] And the human figure coming with the clouds resembles the epithet of Baal as "rider on the clouds." Jason Bembry goes so far as to suggest that "'one like a son of man' and 'the Ancient of Days' [mirror] the relationship of Baal and El in the Ugaritic narrative poetry."[45] Daniel here reflects and puts to use mythological material whose origin lies more than a millennium in the past in a culture that predated Israel's existence. That mythological material—part of Israel's broad context and its own historical memory, employed also in Isaiah 27:1, which depicts God's final triumph over Leviathan[46]—serves Daniel's acknowledgment that the oppressive situation of faithful Jews is part of a cosmic disorder, for which human measures can provide no remedy.

While Daniel 7, joined with chapter 2, frames the court tales, it also introduces the apocalyptic visions that extend through chapter 12. The visions in chapters 8 and 10–11 portray historical conflict from the time of the Medes and Persians (8:3) through Alexander the Great (v. 5) to Antiochus Epiphanes (vv. 23–25; 11:36–39). These chapters devote the greatest attention to battles and competing claims to sovereignty between the Seleucids and the Ptolemies following the death of Alexander.[47] They reflect the same kind of violent succes-

43. J. Collins, *Daniel*, 301.

44. J. Collins, *Daniel*, 301. On the Canaanite mythological background to Dan. 7, see also Wilson, "Creation and New Creation."

45. Bembry, *Yahweh's Coming of Age*, 107.

46. The text and imagery of Isa. 27:1 mirror those in the Ugaritic Baal Cycle (*KTU* 1.5 i.1–4).

47. For details, see Grabbe, *History of the Jews*. On the relation of Dan. 8 to chaps. 10–11, see Newsom and Breed, *Daniel*, 328.

sion, in their competition for empire, that Daniel 2 and 7 represent as a series of metals or beasts, each empire worse than the preceding. But as I noted above, these historical conflicts are set within, yet also participate in, a larger cosmic conflict—one in which God will be the decisive participant. This is the hope of the Jews, left unmentioned as the people caught in the vice between Greek forces to the north and those to the south.

In between, in Daniel 9, between the compressed visionary history in chapter 8 and the more expansive one in chapters 10–11, Daniel speaks for the Jews in his own voice. He speaks a penitential prayer reminiscent of Ezra's in Nehemiah 9. Daniel appeals to the righteousness of God alone (*hatsedaqah*, Dan. 9:7, 16), confessing no righteousness on Israel's part (v. 10) that could provide grounds for appeal (v. 18). In his penitential prayer, Daniel appeals to God to "let your light shine again on your desolated [*shamem*] sanctuary" (v. 17; cf. 11:31; 12:11). Concern for the site of God's presence—God's sanctuary—in the midst of God's people stands at the center of the historical and cosmic conflicts envisioned before and after Daniel's prayer.[48] Daniel 9:1–19 stands in the middle of a sequence of revelations, just as visions surround Zechariah 4. Daniel prays in the context of the desolation of the Jews and of Jerusalem (Dan. 9:18), while Zechariah sees a lampstand, the promise of God's presence, in the midst of temple rubble. In Zechariah and Daniel, the future envisioned has its center and foundation in the faithfulness of God, even after seventy years (Zech. 1:12; 7:5; Dan. 9:2).

Conclusion

The world did not end while Johann Christiaan Beker watched, from a hospital, the bombing of Berlin during World War II. We continue to enjoy and suffer history, including its wars. Zechariah and Daniel do not envision the end of the world, but they do envision the end of history. Zechariah 1–6 and Daniel, prophecies in an apocalyptic mode, envision the end of history (but not of time) in a particular sense. In so far as history is constituted as imperial history in its cycles, history has been brought to an end. In the Zecharian and Danielic visions, history as generated and determined by military power and conquest—by mutant beasts and destructive horns—has been terminated, and with it history as forced migration, enslavement, and tyranny. War, the narrative anchor of imperial history's plot, has become in these visions otiose: a useless and impossible

48. I am indebted to my former student Rev. Ryan D. Harker and his seminar paper "Renewal of Covenant." Cited with permission.

relic of the past, as in Isaiah 2:2–4 // Micah 4:1–3, where nations pound their armaments into farm implements under the "*torah* that proceeds from Zion and the word of Yhwh from Jerusalem" (Isa. 2:3).

At the same time, however, Zechariah and Daniel envision the beginning of history. Zechariah's "But now" (8:11) announces a disjunction between the past and the new beginning coming to pass. That new beginning is brought about by God's impossible (except for God; v. 6) creation of a future lived in freedom from forces hostile to *shalom* and, so, hostile to creation and the Creator. For Daniel, this means freedom even from the tyranny of death (12:2). That freedom Isaiah 65 prefigured in the context of announcing God's creation of a new Jerusalem and a new heavens and a new earth.

In 1895, Hermann Gunkel compared the creation account in Genesis 1 with the consummation or end time in the New Testament book of Revelation. He argued that "what transpired in the primeval time [*Urzeit*] will repeat itself in the end time [*Endzeit*]."[49] This gave rise to the idea that the eschatological future, at the end of time, resembles or recapitulates the conditions of Eden. Neither Zechariah 1–6 nor Daniel 2–7 has in view the end of time; neither do they, or Isaiah, see the future as the return of Eden. But they do see or dream the world's re-creation, envisioning a world, this world, in which God the King and Creator reigns *visibly*, uncontested, on behalf of *shalom*, reordering the world and including the peace of Jerusalem.

49. Gunkel, *Schöpfung und Chaos*, 370.

10

God the Creator beyond the Old Testament

The previous nine chapters of this book discussed a variety of biblical texts from Genesis to Daniel. In this chapter I will first draw attention to two more Old Testament texts that portray God acting as Creator. Second, and as this chapter's title hints, I will turn to Jewish and, especially, Christian literature beyond the Old Testament. As I explained in the introduction, my use of the term *Old Testament* is intentional and in the interest of honesty: as a Christian, I read the canonical Hebrew and Aramaic books as the first and larger part of a Bible that includes the New Testament. My particular interest here lies in the way some of this literature "beyond the Old Testament" refers to or describes God as Creator. That will involve reference to a selection of Jewish texts that Roman Catholics call deuterocanonical and Jews and Protestants traditionally regard as apocryphal. And I will pursue this interest in God the Creator briefly—and even further beyond my academic license—into and beyond the New Testament. I intend also to return, even more briefly, to a matter of controversy in biblical scholarship and theology, introduced at the beginning of chapter 2—creation out of nothing (*ex nihilo*).

First come two Old Testament texts, Exodus 1–15 and Zephaniah. I turn in this chapter to Exodus, and especially chapter 15, because of the resonance in the New Testament of its testimony to God the Creator. Zephaniah provides a canonical precedent for the appropriation of Genesis 1–11 in some subsequent Jewish literature. My selection of texts does not establish a developmental or providential teleology. I intend it to provide examples of the "history of effects"—the *Wirkungsgeschichte*—or the reception history of certain texts in the Old Testament or the Tanakh in which God the Creator is a subject.[1]

Exodus

Terence E. Fretheim has been especially vigorous in pointing to creation theology in the book of Exodus. Responding to previous interpreters' predominant emphasis on "redemption" in Exodus, Fretheim writes, "A creation theology provides the *cosmic purpose* behind God's redemptive activity on Israel's behalf. While the liberation of Israel is the focus of God's activity in Exodus, it is not the ultimate purpose. The deliverance of Israel is ultimately for the sake of all creation (see 9:16)."[2]

In the verse to which Fretheim points, Exodus 9:16, God says to Moses, "I have let you continue [or live] in order to show you my power and in order to declare my name in all the earth." Fretheim sees God's power and ownership of the earth exhibited throughout the plague narrative in Exodus 7–12. He associates both of these with a theology of creation. "The *most basic perspective* within which the plagues are to be understood is *a theology of creation*."[3] In speaking of creation, Fretheim draws attention to the natural world and the way nature has become distorted. Regarding the plagues, he writes, "Continuity with the natural is sufficient to show that it is creation that is adversely affected. . . . But even more, God has entered into the willfulness of their [the Egyptians'] intent, driving their obduracy inexorably to their final ruin."[4] This obduracy, Fretheim continues, and the Egyptians' "anticreation activity [turn] the creation against them."[5] Fretheim understands creation's response to the Egyptians here in terms of a "moral order" that the Egyptians have violated—a moral order of which

1. The term *Wirkungsgeschichte* is Hans-Georg Gadamer's (*Truth and Method*, 300–307). The German term can also be translated as "effective history." On reception history, see Knight, "*Wirkungsgeschichte*."

2. Fretheim, *God and the World*, 110 (italics original). I would say, with reference to the verse Fretheim cites, that the deliverance of Israel is ultimately for God's sake—and if so, then also for Israel's, since God has previously bound God's own identity, revealed as Yhwh, with Israel's (Exod. 6:2–6).

3. Fretheim, *Exodus*, 106 (italics original).

4. Fretheim, *Exodus*, 159–60.

5. Fretheim, *Exodus*, 160.

"God is the broker."[6] Of course, God is the Creator of that moral order—which is to say, with no little redundancy, the Creator of creation—in virtue of which God is its broker. God is the agent of the plagues as the Creator to whom elements of the natural world respond in unnatural judgment and in answer to Pharaoh's question "Who is Yhwh, that I should obey Yhwh?" (5:2).

Exodus 15:1–21, the Songs of Moses and of Miriam, celebrates God's glorious triumph at the sea in Israel's exodus from Egypt. The two songs are framed by Moses's opening exclamation and Miriam's concluding one: "Horse and rider [Yhwh] threw into the sea" (vv. 1, 21). In between, the poem celebrates God's victory. In verse 4, the horses and riders are Pharaoh's, so the poem is set in the context of God's deliverance of Israel from slavery in Egypt. The battle described in the poetry poses asymmetrical forces against each other: one (Pharaoh) has chariots and an army (v. 4) and a sword (v. 9). Yhwh's right hand is the countervailing weapon (v. 6), along with—and remarkably—the sea itself, responding to Yhwh's fury and breath by overwhelming the enemy (vv. 7–8, 10).[7] This turn of events is remarkable, since texts we examined in the Psalms and Isaiah (chaps. 5 and 7)—as well as the older Canaanite literature they echo (in chap. 4)—cast the sea as the aquatic embodiment and force of chaos. In Exodus 15, however, God enlists the sea as the instrument of salvation and destruction: Israel's salvation and the destruction of a hostile military power. The sea is here an instrument of God's creative agency:

> Pharaoh's chariotry and his army [Yhwh] cast into the sea. (15:4)
>
> The deeps [*tehomot*] covered them. (15:6)
>
> You blew with your wind; the sea covered them. (15:10)

The sea's ingestion of military might—"horse and rider"—and Israel's deliverance at the sea do not end the matter of God's creating. In celebrating the redemption of Israel (Exod. 15:13), the people process past the nations toward God's own mountain, the royal dwelling place that Yhwh had made (*pa'al*) and established (*hekin*, v. 17). The latter verb is the one Psalm 8 uses to describe God's establishing—i.e., creating—the sun and the moon, and it is the verb Psalm 24:2 uses in declaring that God created the world. In this context, the last words of Exodus 15:16 describe Israel as the people God created. The verb in this

6. Fretheim, *Exodus*, 160. Fretheim also associates creation with a moral order in commenting on Amos; see chap. 8 earlier in this book.

7. I draw here from my earlier essay "Peace and God's Action."

instance, *qanah*, occurs also in Genesis 4:1, Deuteronomy 32:6, and Proverbs 8:22 with the sense of "create" or "(pro)create."[8] Deuteronomy 32:6 expands on the declaration—in the form of a rhetorical question—that Yhwh is Israel's Father by defining this "begetting" in terms of Yhwh's having created (*qanah*) and made (*'asah*) and established (*kun*) them. Malachi 2:10 makes explicit the connection between Israel's having one Father and Yhwh having created them (*bara'*). The semantic affiliations among the terms in these canonical (con)texts support the conclusion that Exodus 15:6, like Malachi 2:10, describes Israel as God's creation.

Exodus 1–15 portrays God the Creator as active in the distortions of the natural world—in the plagues, as instruments of revelation and persuasion—and active in electing an often counter-creation power, the sea, on behalf of the Israel of God's creation and their salvation. This will not be the last time in this chapter we witness the sea and its power under divine control.

Zephaniah

The book of Zephaniah identifies the prophet as "son of Cushi" (1:1), suggesting that he may have been of African descent.[9] While the book itself lies at some remove from Exodus and the events it recounts, those events, too, are situated in Africa, in the days of Pharaoh. Zephaniah refers to circumstances centuries later, "in the days of King Josiah" (v. 1). But in both Exodus and Zephaniah, God performs a strange work. If in the Exodus plague narrative God acts in horrific mutations of the natural world of God's own creation, in Zephaniah 1, God acts directly against the world: "I will completely sweep away everything from the face of the ground" (v. 2). The distorted order of the natural world in Exodus 7–12 God directed to Pharaoh on God's own behalf and on behalf of Israel. In the total destruction God announces in Zephaniah 1, God acts in judgment of Judah and Jerusalem (v. 4), by way of undoing creation (vv. 2–3).

Zephaniah's language in 1:2–3, in which Yhwh promises to sweep away humans and animals, birds and fish—and to "cut off humanity [*ha'adam*] from the face of the ground" (v. 3)[10]—seems to allude to Genesis 1 and 2, and even to the Genesis flood narrative (cf. Gen. 6:7; 7:4; 8:8). This has been the argument of

8. William H. C. Propp provides an extensive technical discussion of the translation in *Exodus 1–18*, 539–41. He translates the end of Exod. 15:16 as "the people you have gotten." David E. Bokovoy acknowledges "two, albeit distinct nuances typically associated with biblical *qnh*"—"to acquire" and "to create"—in "Did Eve Acquire?," 21.

9. Bennett, "Book of Zephaniah," 671; Sweeney, *Zephaniah*, 49.

10. Adele Berlin refers to this sequence as "the list of the doomed." *Zephaniah*, 81.

several scholars since at least 1980.[11] Some of these scholars have noted that the list of beings swept away or "cut off" in Zephaniah 1:2–3 inverts the order of beings God created in Genesis 1.[12] As has not been much noticed, the elimination of *ha'adam* ("humanity" in contemporary English translations of Zeph. 1:3) is crucial to Zephaniah's poem of un-creation by way of its allusion to Genesis—in this instance, to Genesis 2. My discussion of Genesis 2 in this book's second chapter began with remarks about the description of the earth in 2:5 as "virtually nothing," defined by lack, including, finally, the lack of an *'adam*, a human, to work the ground. Mending that lack—forming *ha'adam*—was God's initial act as Creator (2:7). Zephaniah 1:2–3 announces God's intention to reduce the earth once again to virtually nothing.

Destruction is not the last act that Zephaniah ascribes to God the Creator, and neither is 1:2–3 the only place in the book that alludes to Genesis 1–11. At the beginning of Zephaniah 3, the prophet pronounces doom or "woe" to Jerusalem for the city's corruption (vv. 1–4). Verse 5 shifts attention to Yhwh, who addresses Jerusalem in verses 6–13.[13] Verse 8 announces Yhwh's determination "to gather nations, to assemble kingdoms" for the purpose of pouring out divine indignation. In Yhwh's anger and passion, "the whole earth will be consumed." Abruptly, in verse 9 Yhwh's intentions for the nations, and ultimately for Jerusalem (vv. 11–12), become positive and transformative: "For then I will change the [languages] of the peoples to pure speech, so that all of them may call upon the name of Yhwh and serve him with one accord." Verse 10 then promises that "my worshipers, the Daughter of my dispersed ones," will bring Yhwh offerings. In these verses, Zephaniah 3:9–10, scholars have seen allusions to Genesis 11:1–9, the story of Babel. On the plains of Shinar, the people—"the whole earth"—spoke one language (*saphah*) with a shared vocabulary. God confused (*balal*) their language so that they could no longer communicate with each other, and God scattered (*puts*) them over all the earth (Gen. 11:1, 9). In Zephaniah 3:9–10, God assembles the nations and transforms their language into a pure speech (*saphah barur*), and the Yhwh worshipers who have been scattered (*puts*) will come to Jerusalem. The dispersal, the scattering, God brought about in Genesis 11, defending creation against unlimited human power (v. 6), is here in Zephaniah 3 turned around.

11. See DeRoche, "Zephaniah 1:2–3." On the basis of allusions to Gen. 1–11, and certain verbal parallels, DeRoche says that Zephaniah "is proclaiming . . . *the reversal of creation*" (106, italics original). James D. Nogalski provides discussion of DeRoche's argument and objections to it but generally supports and expands on DeRoche's claims in "Zephaniah's Use of Genesis 1–11."

12. E.g., besides DeRoche, Melvin, "Making All Things New (*Again*)," 276.

13. On Zeph. 3:5 belonging with vv. 6–12, see Sweeney, *Zephaniah*, 169–70.

"It is as if the story of Babel were being reversed and all the peoples reunited in the worship of the Lord," writes Adele Berlin.[14] In other words, confused language becomes pure—suited to the worship of Yhwh—and the diverse and dispersed are (re-)gathered. God the Creator here performs a new work, which is also a work of repair, promising to bring about, to perform, that work of new creation.

God the Creator in Second Temple Judaism—Some Samples

Zephaniah's apparent use of Genesis 1–11 in announcing God's judgment and salvation sets a precedent for Jewish literature beyond those Hebrew and Aramaic texts that constitute the Jewish Tanakh and underlie the Old Testament.[15] An early such text, 1 Enoch's Book of Watchers (1 En. 1–36) from the third century BCE, expands on Genesis 6:1–4. In Enoch, the Watchers—angels—married mortal women and taught humans to make weapons, among other things, and "corrupted the earth with their violence, murder and adultery."[16]

The Watchers and the corruption they wrought also feature in the book of Jubilees, a work of the second century BCE that rewrites Genesis.[17] In Jubilees, the Watchers "violated the natural order" in order to "mate with the daughters of men," which amounted to "a cosmic breach."[18] These two texts, in Enoch and Jubilees, draw upon the adumbrated story of divine breach of creation in Genesis 6:1–4 in identifying the origin of the earth's corruption.[19] Jubilees 2 describes God's creation of the world in six days, with the Sabbath on the seventh day, just as in Genesis 1:1–2:3. God also creates sea monsters (cf. 1:21), which Jubilees describes as "the first corporeal beings" of God's creation. Consistent with the book's title and its narrative structured by multiples of seven, Jubilees 3:15 notes that Adam and Eve were in Eden seven years. But Jubilees expands on Genesis, introducing angels and demons. On the first day, God creates "ministering spirits" (2:2): seven categories of angels and "all of the spirits of his creatures which are in heaven and on earth." Demons, or evil spirits descended from the fallen Watchers (10:1–5), corrupt the earth and both humans and animals (4:2–3;

14. Berlin, *Zephaniah*, 14.

15. I will not here consider Sirach and its extensive references to creation and the Creator. See, though, Reiterer, "'Alles hat nämlich der Herr gemacht.'" Neither will I refer to the Dead Sea Scrolls, on which see Wold, "Genesis 2–3."

16. Hahne, *Corruption and Redemption*, 40.

17. Wintermute, "Jubilees." Quotations of Jubilees in the text are Wintermute's translation.

18. Wintermute, "Jubilees," 48.

19. I have referred to this "breach" expressly in the second and third chapters of this book on Gen. 2–3 and 11.

5:1–4).[20] Accounts of the flood and of Babel follow. Between them, Jubilees reports that God gave orders to bind the evil spirits. But their chief, Mastema—Satan—persuaded God, addressed as Creator, to preserve one-tenth of the evil spirits (10:7–9). Evil, demonic power was not fully banished from the earth.

The style and spirit of Jubilees, as well as its purpose, are far removed from those of Zephaniah, despite their common use of Genesis 1–11 and statements of God creating. Jubilees rewrites Genesis in some large part to stress the importance of obedience to the law.[21] Zephaniah draws on Genesis to announce God's utter judgment and salvation, first reversing parts of the creation stories in Genesis 1 and 2 and finally reversing the confusion of tongues in Genesis 11.

Like Jubilees, Tobit, an early Jewish tale of faithfulness—God's and Tobit's—also knows about angels and demons, or at least one demon. Asmodeus, their chief, is referred to twice as "the wicked demon" (Tob. 3:8, 17) in the book's only mention of demons. But in Tobit, "the wicked demon Asmodeus" serves as the oblique side of God's own agency. Tobias, Tobit's son, had been set on marrying a woman, Sarah, who had already married seven men, each of whom Asmodeus, dwelling within Sarah's body, had killed before the marriage was consummated (3:8; 6:15). The demon prevented Sarah from marrying the wrong man (6:13) and preserved her for Tobias.[22] The angel Raphael restores Tobit's sight—he had become blind (2:9–10)—and frees Sarah from the wicked demon Asmodeus (3:17).

Tobit offers prayers—the prayers are prayed by Tobias and Sarah on their wedding night and upon arising the next morning—in Tobit 8:5–7 and 8:15–17. The first blesses God and calls on "the heavens and all your creation" to bless God (v. 5). The prayer then turns to remember that God made Adam and Eve, from whom God made all of humanity (v. 6), referring finally to Genesis 2:18 ("not good is the man's being alone" [Tob. 8:6]). Tobit does not otherwise refer expressly to God as Creator, or to Genesis. But in the story of Tobit, "God is able to restore the world order which was thrown off balance."[23] In this regard, Tobit echoes testimony from the earliest and latest texts of the Old Testament, but it does so in a way that has captured the imagination of artists like Rembrandt and helps account for its continued use in Amish weddings.[24]

20. Dale Basil Martin helpfully discusses angels and demons/evil spirits in Jubilees in "When Did Angels Become Demons?," 667–69.

21. Wintermute, "Jubilees," 38.

22. Frölich, "Creation in the Book of Tobit," 40–41.

23. Frölich, "Creation in the Book of Tobit," 48.

24. Rembrandt portrays the blind Tobit in *The Blindness of Tobit* (1651): https://www.metmuseum.org/art/collection/search/359805. My oral sources of information about Amish weddings are Amish.

I will mention briefly two more Second Temple Jewish texts that speak of God the Creator: Judith and the Wisdom of Solomon.[25] Unlike 1 Enoch, Jubilees, and Tobit, these two books do not recall Genesis 1–11, or parts of it, in speaking of or addressing the Creator, though both of them depend on and expand biblical texts. The book of Judith tells the story of its eponymous heroine as a faithful Israelite challenging her fellow Israelites to exercise trust in God in the face of an Assyrian invasion. Nebuchadnezzar, "king of the Assyrians" (Jdt. 1:7), had determined to destroy the nations west of Assyria, including Judith's people. Leading the campaign would be Holofernes, Nebuchadnezzar's general. Bravely, shrewdly—also deceitfully—and with confidence in the susceptibility of the male gazer (10:14–15), Judith manages to find her way into Holofernes's camp and his tent, beheads him, and carries his severed head to her people. The book of Judith's references to God the Creator come almost exclusively in "confessional speech directed *to* God."[26] Judith prays: "Please, please [*nai, nai*], God of my ancestor, God of Israel's inheritance, Lord [*despotēs*] of heaven and earth, creator of the waters, king of all your creation [*ktisis*], hear my prayer. And make my deceitful words a wound and a bruise on those who have planned cruel things against your covenant, against your sacred temple, Mount Zion, and against the house your children possess" (9:12–13).

Apart from Judith's imploring God to make her lies effective in bringing harm to the enemy,[27] her prayer is entirely consistent with biblical precedent, including in its invocation of God as King and Creator in conjunction with Zion (see chap. 5 above). Judith elsewhere invokes or prays to God the Creator, who is at the same time, and because of that fact, also Lord of history. As Barbara Schmitz writes, the references to creation theology in Judith "serve to confirm the sovereignty of God and his powerful and effective action in history—so creation theology stands in service of a theology of history."[28] Later, Christian theologians would speak of creation and providence.

The Wisdom of Solomon shares neither the epexegetical character of Jubilees nor the narrative form of Jubilees and Judith. But in its splendidly poetic

25. Second Temple Jewish texts were those written during Second Temple Judaism. This refers, strictly speaking, to Judaism of the period 515 BCE to 70 CE. But the term is used typically in referring to Judaism in the Hellenistic and Roman eras. Shayna Sheinfeld discusses the matter, along with issues about defining Judaism in this era and its literature, in the introduction to *Gender and Second-Temple Judaism*.

26. Schmitz, "'Dir soll Deine ganze Schöpfung dienen,'" 51 (italics added).

27. Judith's character in the book of Judith is the reverse of Rahab's in Josh. 2. The prostitute Rahab acts against her city's interests in concealing Israelite spies, while Judith plays the seductress in order to assassinate Holofernes on behalf of her people.

28. Schmitz, "'Dir soll Deine ganze Schöpfung dienen,'" 59.

chapters, Wisdom acknowledges that God has made everything, including humankind (1:14; 9:1–3). Earlier, in chapter 2 of this book, I referred to Wisdom's statement in 11:17 that God's "all-powerful hand . . . created the world out of formless matter [*ex amorphous hules*]." This verse has figured in discussions about creation out of nothing (*ex nihilo*), a subject on which David Winston comments in his commentary on Wisdom and one to which I will return below.[29] The question whether God created the world out of nothing arises in connection with other texts as well, including both 2 Maccabees and, in the New Testament, Paul's Letter to the Romans. Further, Wisdom 2:23—depending on its interpretation—elicits comparison with certain statements in both the Old Testament and the New. Michael A. Knibb translates 2:23 as "God created human beings for incorruption, and made them the image of his own nature."[30] God created us, Wisdom says, as an *icon* of God in God's eternity or nature or "unique identity" (CEB). In turning next to the New Testament, I will begin with the matter of the icon.

God the Creator in the New Testament

Wisdom's affirmation that God created us as the (or an) icon of God reaffirms what Genesis 1:27 says in Greek. In the LXX of Genesis, God created humankind "*according to* the icon of God" (*kat eikona theou*), as if there had been a divine icon to serve as a model for God's creation of humankind. The LXX thus qualifies Wisdom's bolder declaration. Lying behind texts like Wisdom 2:23 and 9:9, which locate personified Wisdom "with God" and testify to her presence when God made the world, is Proverbs 8:22–31, discussed in chapter 6. Together with Proverbs 3:19, Wisdom 7:22 and 9:1–2 and Sirach 1:4 and 24:9[31]—including Genesis 1:27 LXX—form some of the scriptural resources for the first three verses of John's Gospel, which affirm that the Word, the *logos*, was with God and was God (1:1) and that all things came into being through the Word (*panta di autou egeneto*, v. 3). The claims of John 1:1–3 bring the *logos*, the Word, into close—the closest possible—association with God the Creator, even sharing the Creator's identity ("and was God"). John's opening words, "In the beginning," mirror those of Genesis 1:1, which commences the poetic narrative of God's

29. Winston, *Wisdom of Solomon*, 38–40.

30. Knibb, *New English Translation of the Septuagint*. Winston: "God created man for immortality, and made him an image of his own proper being" (*Wisdom of Solomon*, 112, and see 121). The NRSV understands the crucial word in Wis. 2:23 (*adiotētos*) differently: "made us in the image [*eikona*] of his own eternity."

31. Carter, *John*, 137. I owe this reference to Swartley, "Creation and the Gospel of John," 119.

making the world. The text does not say expressly that the Word was the agent (or co-agent) of the world's creation, but it does insist that nothing came into being without him or apart from him (*chōris autou*, John 1:3).

While John 1:1–3 describes the Word as rich with divinity, verse 14 establishes its humanity: "The Word became flesh and lived among us" (NRSV). Even while the Word was a human neighbor, the Word's "glory" was evident to the people. It was a glory "full of grace and truth," and that of a father's only child: *monogenēs*, "only begotten" in the KJV. This is a reaffirmation of an intimate relation between God the Creator and the Word—one of virtual or shared identity—and an ominous foreshadowing. Only two specific individuals are described in the Old Testament as "only" children (in Hebrew, *yachid*; in the LXX, *monogenēs*): Isaac (Gen. 22) and the unnamed daughter of Jephthah (Judg. 11), both of them objects of sacrifice by their fathers. John's Gospel signals in its prologue (1:1–14) that the "Word who was with God" and through whom everything was made is the one of whom the Gospel goes on to tell: the one whom Roman soldiers crucified.

In a different genre, the New Testament Letter to the Colossians—attributed to Paul in 1:1–2—makes similar claims. Echoing again the wisdom of Israel (Prov. 8) and early Judaism (Wis. 9, for example), Colossians 1:15 declares that "he"—the "beloved Son" of the Father (vv. 3, 13)—is "the image [*eikōn*] of the invisible God, the firstborn of all creation" (NRSV).[32] The following verse makes the even stronger claim that "in him all things were created" (v. 16). "All things" here encompasses a comprehensive totality: things in heaven and on earth, things visible and invisible, dominions and powers—all "created through him and for him" (v. 16). The text does not quite identify Christ himself as *the Creator* of all things, though he existed before "all things" (v. 17).[33] But neither does it take care to distinguish Christ from God the (Father and thus) Creator.[34] Of course, the matter at point in Colossians 1 is not speculation about creation. The point is to establish that the firstborn of all creation is at the same time the firstborn from the dead (v. 18). The phrase "from the dead" suggests something ominous and unexpected in reference to one in whom and through whom and for whom (v. 16) everything was created, who existed before all things (v. 17)—one in whom God's fullness (*plērōma*) made its home (v. 19). Yet the "all things" created in Christ stood in need of

32. Juraj Feník and Róbert Lapko offer an argument and evidence for Christ as firstborn, meaning primacy rather than (primarily) sovereignty here, in "Reign of Christ in Colossians."

33. McKnight, *Letter to the Colossians*, 151.

34. I referred in chap. 9 to Old Testament texts referring to God as Father and thus Creator: Isa. 64:7[64:8]; Mal. 2:10.

reconciliation to God, a reconciliation God determined to achieve by "making peace through the blood of his [Christ's] cross" (v. 20). The identification of Christ with the Creator serves to identify Christ as the Redeemer. Oda Wischmeyer writes, "Paul's cosmology is in the final analysis Christology." What she says of Paul could apply also to Colossians, except that Paul's cosmology is also soteriology.[35]

God the Creator achieved primordial and subsequent peace through the destruction or disarmament of powers hostile to God's created order, whether dragons or armies, as I described in chapter 5. This peace-achieving strategy is by no means the only one God employs in the Old Testament (Isa. 32:15–18; 52:1–8; 52:13–53:12). And in Exodus 15, as we saw earlier in this chapter, one of those hostile powers—the sea—retains its character as a hostile power but one responsive to God's determination to rescue Israel from Pharaoh's army. In discussing Exodus 15 above, I noted that the sea would again make an appearance in this chapter. Its appearance here does not mark a departure from the subject of the preceding paragraph: the close identification of Jesus Christ with the Creator in the New Testament.

The first two chapters of Mark's Gospel narrate some extraordinary claims about Jesus, including "[you are] the Holy One of God" (1:24). This came from the mouth of a demon, but it was not wrong: Peter makes the same statement (in his case, as a confession) in John 6:69. And in Mark 2:28, Jesus declares himself—the Human One (Son of Man)—to be lord of the Sabbath. The Greek is emphatic, as if to say that the Human One is Lord (*kyrios*), and this extends even to the Sabbath. Returning to the demon in Mark 1, Jesus meets its declaration, perhaps intended to gain control of Jesus,[36] with a rebuke: "He rebuked it, saying, 'Silence'" (1:25). Later, in Mark 4, after teaching large crowds "beside the sea" (v. 1, the Sea of Galilee) and explaining things to his disciples, Jesus requested passage to the other side (v. 35). A great wind arose, producing high waves and imperiling the lives of the disciples, who found Jesus asleep. Roused from slumber, Jesus "rebuked the wind and said to the sea, 'Silence! Be still!'" (v. 39). Calm followed, and the disciples asked, "Who then is this, that even the wind and the sea obey him?" (v. 41). In Mark 1:25, Jesus rebukes an instance of chaotic power. In Mark 4:39, Jesus rebukes not the sea but the wind, but both wind and sea—the ancient symbol and embodiment of a hostile, chaotic force—obey him. They respond to Jesus's rebuke (*epitimaō*) just as did rider and horse in Psalm 76:7[76:6] and as did the Red Sea when God purposed to lead

35. Wischmeyer, "Kosmos und Kosmologie bei Paulus," 99. Thomas R. Yoder Neufeld, writing on Ephesians, might add anthropology and social ethics to the list. See his "*Creatio ex Detrito*."
36. A. Collins, *Mark*, 169.

Israel through it (106:9). In narrative fashion rich with allusion, Mark identifies Jesus with the Creator who disempowered Leviathan on behalf of creation—the order of God's creation.[37]

The Gospel of Mark evinces an extraordinarily high Christology. Among other things, Mark portrays Jesus exercising the kind of power over the sea that God demonstrated in Exodus 15, which is not less than the power of the Creator, power exercised in the service of liberation from slavery and salvation from the power of death.

Paul, Romans, and Creation from Nothing

In this chapter I commented on Exodus and Zephaniah and then illustrated some of the ways those texts provide material or precedent for later Jewish and Christian literature. I also pointed to Proverbs 8:22–31, which provided resources for some Second Temple Jewish texts to talk about Wisdom and the Creator. Both Genesis 1 and Proverbs 8 lie behind the Gospel of John. And the language and imagery of Colossians draw from and are part of a reservoir of Old Testament, Jewish, and perhaps earliest Christian literature.[38] Returning finally to the beginning, and Exodus 15, a brief discussion of the Gospel of Mark brought us to this point, to the apostle Paul. A discussion of creation in Pauline literature could fill volumes. I will limit myself to a few comments on Romans 8 and then Romans 4.

Romans 8

Since it expressly mentions creation, Romans 8:18–25 receives a great deal of attention in discussions of creation in Paul or of Paul's cosmology.[39] The passage attributes no specific action to God, but it comes near the end of Romans 5–8, in which, according to Ryan D. Harker, Paul says that "through the cross of Christ, God defeats the powers of sin and death" and enables "those in Christ to 'fulfill the righteous requirement of the Law' by walking 'according to the Spirit,' God's eschatological gift of new creation."[40] Conflict language is frequent in Romans,

37. As Darrin W. Snyder Belousek says, "Mark depicts Jesus doing what the Psalms depict Yhwh doing: just as Yhwh rebuked the sea and it obeyed Yhwh's command, so also Jesus rebukes the wind and sea which obey Jesus's command" ("'Who Then Is This?,'" 111). Adela Yarbro Collins refers in this context to Job 9:13, 26:12, Pss. 74:13, 89:10, Isa. 27:1, and 51:9 (*Mark*, 262). Matthew and Luke also include the story (Matt. 8:23–27 // Luke 8:22–25).

38. If David Winston is right that Wisdom was composed in the period 37–41 CE (*Wisdom of Solomon*, 23), Colossians and all of Paul's letters were composed after Wisdom and before 2 Esdras.

39. See, e.g., Gaventa, "Neither Height nor Depth."

40. Harker, "Redeeming Creation in Romans," 150, 151.

with God preeminently in conflict with the powers of sin and death, but God encounters other enemies as well—namely, us, "the ungodly" for whom Christ died (5:6). Justified by faith, we now have peace with God through Christ, Paul says in 5:1, because "while we were enemies, we were reconciled to God through the death of his Son" and "will be saved by his life" (v. 10 NRSV). The death of Jesus Christ and his resurrection to life by the power of God are, as one, the action of God the Creator, who has created a new community (8:34). Even in that community, while enjoying "the first fruits of the Spirit," Paul says, we "groan inwardly," awaiting "the redemption of our bodies" (v. 23 NRSV). In that groaning, we join creation itself: "We know that the whole creation has been groaning in labor pains until now" (v. 22 NRSV).

Paul, who wrote of being sold into bondage, slavery, to sin (Rom. 7:14), now describes the hope that the creation will be freed from "enslavement to decay into the glorious freedom of God's children" (8:21). Paul here establishes a remarkable community of the human and the nonhuman, each groaning in hope. More remarkable, perhaps, is the likelihood, for which Laurie J. Braaten argues, that in 8:22 "the entire creation is groaning in lament because of an ongoing history of human sin and accompanying divine judgment."[41] As the earth mourns and its creatures languish—in a kind of reversal of creation—because of human sin in Hosea 4:2–3, so also does creation mourn and languish in Romans 8.[42] We are joined with creation in a common groaning and hope, even as our human sin continues to be responsible for creation's pain, its mourning, its groaning. As Harry Alan Hahne expresses it, "There is solidarity between humanity and the natural world, both of which groan for deliverance from the corruption of the physical world."[43]

God its Creator remains creation's hope and guarantee because neither can creation be separated from the love of God (Rom. 8:39). Creation hopes, longs for, waits, and groans, as do we. It cannot, I suppose, exercise faith, which is ours to do.

Romans 4

Romans 4 continues Paul's discussion of justification and faith (from 3:28), of which Paul cites Abraham as the exemplar. Abraham demonstrated his faith by believing God's promise of something physically impossible: that he, with his century-old body "as good as dead" (*nenekrōmenon*), and the barren Sarah (4:19) would produce a child. But Abraham believed, Paul says, in the God "who

41. Braaten, "All Creation Groans," 153.
42. Braaten, "All Creation Groans," 142–43. See also my comments on Zephaniah above.
43. Hahne, *Corruption and Redemption*, 207.

makes the dead alive and calls nonexisting things into existence [*hōs onta*]" (v. 17). This statement certainly describes God the Creator. Does it also describe God creating *ex nihilo*—out of nothing? Comparisons have been drawn with 2 Maccabees 7, in which a Jewish mother, having seen six of her seven sons killed for refusing the king's command to eat pork, encourages the seventh to consider the earth and the heavens and the things in them and to understand that "not out of things that existed did God make them" (2 Macc. 7:28). Does this describe creation out of nothing?

Jonathan A. Goldstein, commenting on this verse and reviewing Greek, Jewish, and Christian literature, concludes that *creatio ex nihilo* is not in view here and that the mother is articulating a strong view of God's creative power, extending to resurrection from the dead. She encourages her seventh son to accept death "so that in [God's] mercy I may recover you with your brothers" (2 Macc. 7:29).[44] Barbara Schmitz more recently expressed a similar view, pointing to the close connection between creation and resurrection: in the mother's speech (vv. 27–29), she says, "An analogy is drawn according to which hope in life after death is carried over to theological reflection on creation."[45] In Romans 4, Paul does not directly address resurrection from the dead. But as Paul points out, Abraham's body was "as good as dead" and incapable of producing another child (v. 19). It is to God's power that Paul points as the basis for Abraham's believing and the content of that belief. As Robert Jewett says, commenting on Romans, the framework of verse 17 "is the divine Creator whose power to overcome death and nothingness abides forever."[46] Here again, creation—God acting as Creator—is brought into close relationship with resurrection from the dead, or in Schmitz's terms, life after death. How close does this come to creation *ex nihilo*?

My remarks at the beginning of chapter 2 recommended reflection on what we might mean by *nothing*. I then suggested that Genesis 2:5 (similarly to 1:2) presents the earth as being virtually nothing, or as good as nothing, in anticipation of God's act of creating. Even if the earth was something like a *nihil*, does the text have in mind creation *ex nihilo*? People in the past reflected on how odd it is to say of something that it was created out of nothing. In chapter 5, I referred to Picasso's artistic creation of a bull's head. In that example, we know exactly what it means to talk of Picasso creating a work of art *out of* handlebars and a bicycle seat. Then saying that God created the world out of nothing, created the heavens and the earth *ex nihilo*, looks to be analogous—as if *nothing* names the unique substance out of which God made the world. But this cannot be right.

44. Goldstein, *2 Maccabees*, 307–11.
45. Schmitz, "Geschaffen aus dem Nichts?," 74.
46. Jewett, *Romans*, 344–45.

George S. Hendry addresses the problem in an article with the arresting title "Nothing."[47] Hendry notes that English lacks the ability to distinguish "nothing" in the absolute sense from its use with a relative sense. Greek, however, can convey this distinction by using *mē ontos*—to describe something not existing in a proper form—and *ouk ontos*, with reference to something "absolutely non-existent."[48] Romans 4:17, which uses *mē onta* (in the accusative case), would not then be making a claim about absolute nonexistence. Of course, neither Paul nor any part of the Bible, whether the Tanakh or the Christian Bible (deuterocanonical books included), offers a judgment about absolute or relative nothing, or about the possibility—or not—of "preexistent matter" (see chap. 2). But this does not conclude the discussion. I offer two further comments on creation *ex nihilo*.

First, returning to Paul, his statement in Romans 4:17 has to do with God's faithfulness in keeping promises and God's power to keep them, even when that power is exercised in relation to something "as good as dead"—and not merely as good as dead but death itself. In 1 Corinthians 15, death is the last enemy, to be vanquished by Christ, and this in a chapter on the resurrection of the dead rich with allusions to Genesis 1–3.[49] Ephesians says that we were dead in our trespasses, but God made us alive in Christ (2:5). Further, God was at work "fashioning 'us' into his creation (*poiēma*; 'work of art' [NJB]), created . . . in and through the Messiah for good works prepared ahead of time for us to walk in (2:10; cf. 3:12)."[50] Creation, justification, and resurrection here come together "as one and the same divine action."[51] D. H. Bertschmann, in an essay on John Barclay's work on Paul, refers to Barclay's notion of "disruptive divine grace as *creatio ex nihilo*, creation out of nothingness: 'Incongruous grace is thus the mark of the God who creates *ex nihilo*.'"[52] In these terms, *creatio ex nihilo* is not simply or primarily a doctrine about the absolute origin of matter but about God's power, faithfulness, and self-sufficiency, as Theophilus of Antioch remarked in the second century.[53]

Second, the Greek understandings of the world that formed the context in which Christians beyond the New Testament began to think about creation out

47. Hendry, "Nothing." See also Young, "'Creatio ex Nihilo,'" 146.

48. Knox, *Changing Christian Paradigms*, 191. Knox is quoting Chadwick, *Early Christian Thought*, 47.

49. S. Cook, *Apocalyptic Literature*, 174.

50. Yoder Neufeld, "*Creatio ex Detrito*," 161.

51. Käsemann, *Commentary on Romans*, 123.

52. Bertschmann, "*Ex Nihilo* or *Tabula Rasa*?," 31. The embedded quotation is from Barclay, *Paul and the Gift*, 455.

53. *Theophilus to Autolycus*, Early Christian Writings, accessed July 15, 2022, http://www.earlychristianwritings.com/text/theophilus-book2.html.

of nothing held the natural world to be eternal. This necessarily placed a limit on God that made God a being among beings; it made God subject to certain presuppositions. Creation *ex nihilo*, Otto Weber writes, expresses the truth that "God bears the ground and the presuppositions of his creative activity in himself. . . . His activity requires no presuppositions outside his own being."[54] In commenting on Genesis 1–11, among other places, I pointed to the stress certain Old Testament texts place on the crucial distinction between Creator and creature. Stories in Genesis 1–4, narrated as episodes of rivalry with God, deflect into intra-creature rivalries issuing in conflict and, finally, violence. It is consistent with the narratives in Genesis 1–11, I believe, that God and creatures do not exist in a contrastive and competitive relationship, and mythical assumptions to the contrary challenge creation itself; they stand in denial of creation. God's interruptions in history, even in prehistory, are entirely consistent with the point.

The action God takes against chaotic and hostile forces, as various Old Testament texts portray that action, should be understood not as divine interventions from outside into a world independently constituted but as expressions of God's constant involvement in the world and God's determination on behalf of the world's continued existence, and its continued existence as God's world on God's behalf and on behalf of God's creation.[55] *God's creation*, in this case, includes the world and its constituents, nonhuman and human alike, and—because we are talking about God—it includes Israel.

Creatio ex nihilo—creation out of nothing at all—describes creation as God's gift. It describes creation as God's free, uncompelled act of love, a necessity only but truly within God's own self and determination *pro nobis et pro mundo*—for our sake and for the world's. "To put it provocatively," Rowan Williams writes, "God creates 'in God's interest' (there could be no other motive for divine action); but that 'interest' is not the building-up of the divine life, which simply is what it is, but its giving away. For God to act for God's sake *is* for God to act for our sake."[56] As far as I can tell, all the biblical texts discussed in this chapter and previous ones confirm this claim.

Creation is God's gift. Among God's lesser but still inexpressibly great gifts are the ancient writings of the prophets, sages, and apostles who bear witness to God the Creator.

54. O. Weber, *Foundations of Dogmatics*, 501.

55. For deeper consideration of these matters, see, e.g., Robinette, "Difference Nothing Makes"; G. Anderson, "Creation." May, *Creatio ex Nihilo*, provides a thorough historical account of the doctrine's origin.

56. Rowan Williams, *On Christian Theology*, 74 (italics original).

Bibliography

Acocella, Joan. "How to Read 'Gilgamesh.'" *New Yorker*, October 7, 2019. https://www.newyorker.com/magazine/2019/10/14/how-to-read-gilgamesh.

Alston, William P. "On Knowing That We Know: The Application to Religious Knowledge." In *Christian Perspectives on Religious Knowledge*, edited by C. Stephen Evans and Merold Westphal, 15–39. Grand Rapids: Eerdmans, 1993.

Alter, Robert. *The Book of Psalms: A Translation with Commentary*. New York: Norton, 2007.

Anderson, Bernhard W. *Contours of Old Testament Theology*. Minneapolis: Fortress, 1999.

———. "A Stylistic Study of the Priestly Creation Story." In *Canon and Authority*, edited by George W. Coats and Burke O. Long, 148–62. Philadelphia: Fortress, 1977.

Anderson, Gary. "Biblical Origins and the Problem of the Fall." *Pro Ecclesia* 10 (2001): 17–30.

———. "Creation: *Creatio ex nihilo* and the Bible." In *Christian Doctrine and the Old Testament: Theology in the Service of Biblical Exegesis*, 41–58. Grand Rapids: Baker Academic, 2017.

Anderson, James. *Monotheism and Yahweh's Appropriation of Baal*. LHB/OTS 617. London: Bloomsbury T&T Clark, 2015.

Anderson, Joel E. "Jonah's Peculiar Re-creation." *Biblical Theology Bulletin* 41 (2011): 179–88.

Aristotle. *Poetics*. Translated with commentary by Richard Janko. Indianapolis: Hackett, 1987.

Assmann, Jan. *Ma'at: Gerechtigkeit und Unsterblichkeit im alten Ägypten*. München: Beck, 1990.

Augustine. *Confessions*. Translated by R. S. Pine-Coffin. New York: Penguin Books, 1962.

"Babylonian and Assyrian Historical Texts." Translated by A. Leo Oppenheim. In *ANET*, 265–317.

Bachmann, Veronika. "Illicit Male Desire or Illicit Female Seduction: A Comparison of the Ancient Retellings of the 'Sons of God' Mingling with the 'Daughters of Men' (Genesis 6:1–4)." In *Early Jewish Writings*, edited by Eileen Schuller and Marie-Therese Wacker, 113–41. Atlanta: SBL, 2017.

Baden, Joel, Hindy Najman, and Eibert Tigchelaar, eds. *Sibyls, Scriptures, and Scrolls: John Collins at Seventy*. 2 vols. Leiden: Brill, 2017.

Ball, C. J. *Light from the East*. London: Eyre and Spottiswoode, 1899.

Baltzer, Klaus. *Deutero-Isaiah: A Commentary on Isaiah 40–55*. Translated by Margaret Kohl. Hermeneia. Minneapolis: Fortress, 2001.

Barclay, John. *Paul and the Gift*. Grand Rapids: Eerdmans, 2015.

Barker, Margaret. *Creation: A Biblical Vision for the Environment*. London: T&T Clark, 2010.

Barr, James. *The Garden of Eden and the Hope of Immortality*. Minneapolis: Fortress, 1993.

Barth, Karl. "The Strange New World within the Bible." In *The Word of God and the Word of Man*, 28–50. Translated by Douglas Horton. Gloucester, MA: Peter Smith, 1978.

Batto, Bernard F. *In the Beginning: Essays on Creation Motifs in the Ancient Near East and the Bible*. Siphrut 9. Winona Lake, IN: Eisenbrauns, 2013.

———. "*Kampf* and *Chaos*: The Combat Myth in Israelite Tradition Revisited." In *Creation and Chaos: A Reconsideration of Hermann Gunkel's* Chaoskampf *Hypothesis*, edited by JoAnn Scurlock and Richard H. Beal, 217–36. Winona Lake, IN: Eisenbrauns, 2013.

Bauckham, Richard. *God and the Crisis of Freedom: Biblical and Contemporary Perspectives*. Louisville: Westminster John Knox, 2002.

Bauer, Georg Lorenz. *Beylagen zur Theologie des Alten Testaments, enthaltend die Begriffe von Gott und Vorsehung, nach den Verschiedenen Büchern und Zeitperioden Entwickelt: Kann als ein zweyter Theil der Theologie des alten Testaments angesehen warden*. Leipzig: Weyand, 1801.

Bauks, Michaela. *Die Welt am Anfang: Zum Verhältnis von Vorwelt und Weltentstehung in Genesis 1 und in der altorientalischen Literatur*. WMANT 74. Neukirchen-Vluyn: Neukirchener Verlag, 1997.

———. "Erkenntnis und Leben in Genesis 2–3: Zum Wandel eienes ursprünglich weisheitlich geprägten Lebensbegriffs." *ZAW* 127 (2015): 20–42.

Baumann, Gerlinde. "Psalm 74: Myth as Source of Hope in Times of Devastation." In *Psalms and Mythology*, edited by Dirk J. Human, 91–103. LHB/OTS 462. New York: T&T Clark, 2007.

Beauchamp, Paul. *Création et Séparation: Etude Exégetique de Genesis 1*. Paris: Gabala, 1969.

Becker, Patrick, and Steffen Jöris. "Toward a Scientific Designation: Apocalypticism in Biblical and Modern Studies—A Comparative Approach." *HBT* 38 (2016): 22–44.

Beker, J. Christiaan. *Paul's Apocalyptic Gospel: The Coming Triumph of God*. Philadelphia: Fortress, 1982.

———. *Paul the Apostle: The Triumph of God in Life and Thought*. Philadelphia: Fortress, 1980.

———. *Suffering and Hope: The Biblical Vision and the Human Predicament*. Grand Rapids: Eerdmans, 1994.

Bembry, Jason. *Yahweh's Coming of Age*. Winona Lake, IN: Eisenbrauns, 2011.

Bennett, Robert A. "The Book of Zephaniah." In *NIB*, 7:659–704.

Berlin, Adele. *Zephaniah*. AB 25. New Haven: Yale University Press, 1994.

Bertschmann, D. H. "*Ex Nihilo* or *Tabula Rasa*? God's Grace between Freedom and Fidelity." *IJST* 22 (2020): 29–46.

Bird, Phyllis A. "'Male and Female He Created Them': Genesis 1:27b in the Context of the Priestly Account of Creation." *HTR* 74 (1981): 129–59.

Blenkinsopp, Joseph. *Creation, Un-creation, Re-creation: A Discursive Commentary on Genesis 1–11*. London: T&T Clark, 2011.

———. *Isaiah 1–39*. AB 19. New York: Doubleday, 2000.

Block, Daniel. "Eden: A Temple? A Reassessment of the Biblical Evidence." In *From Creation to New Creation: Biblical Theology and Exegesis*, edited by Daniel M. Gurtner and Benjamin L. Gladd, 3–32. Peabody, MA: Hendrickson, 2013.

Boda, Mark J. *The Book of Zechariah*. NICOT. Grand Rapids: Eerdmans, 2016.

Bokovoy, David E. "Did Eve Acquire, Create, or Procreate with Yahweh? A Grammatical and Contextual Reassessment." *VT* 63 (2013): 19–35.

Bordreuil, Pierre, and Dennis Pardee. *A Manual of Ugaritic*. Linguistic Studies in Ancient West Semitic 3. Winona Lake, IN: Eisenbrauns, 2009.

Botterweck, G. Johannes. "*yada*'." In vol. 5 of *Theological Dictionary of the Old Testament*, edited by G. Johannes Botterweck and Helmer Ringgren, translated by David E. Green, 448–81. Grand Rapids: Eerdmans, 1986.

Braaten, Laurie J. "All Creation Groans: Romans 8:22 in Light of Biblical Sources." *HBT* 28 (2006): 131–59.

Brett, Mark G. *Genesis: Procreation and the Politics of Identity*. London: Routledge, 2000.

Brown, William P. *The Ethos of the Cosmos: The Genesis of Moral Imagination in the Bible*. Grand Rapids: Eerdmans, 1999.

———. *The Seven Pillars of Creation: The Bible, Science, and the Ecology of Wonder*. New York: Oxford University Press, 2010.

———. "When Wisdom Fails." In Jones and Yoder, "*When the Morning Stars Sang*," 209–23.

Brown, William P., and S. Dean McBride, eds. *God Who Creates: Essays in Honor of W. Sibley Towner*. Grand Rapids: Eerdmans, 2000.

Brueggemann, Walter. *A Commentary on Jeremiah: Exile and Homecoming*. Grand Rapids: Eerdmans, 1998.

———. "Creation in First Isaiah." In Harker and Bunce, *Earth Is the Lord's*, 35–52.

———. "Jeremiah: *Creatio in Extremis*." In Brown and McBride, *God Who Creates*, 152–70.

———. "A Shape for Old Testament Theology, I: Structure Legitimation." *CBQ* 47 (1985): 28–46.

Bührer, Walter. "Göttersöhne und Menschentöchter: Genesis 6:1–4 als innerbiblische Schriftauslegung." *ZAW* 123 (2011): 495–515.

Bunce, Heather L. "The Day of the Lord in the Book of the Twelve." In Harker and Bunce, *Earth Is the Lord's*, 84–98.

Callender, Dexter E., Jr. *Adam in Myth and History: Ancient Israelite Perspectives on the Primal Human*. Harvard Semitic Studies. Winona Lake, IN: Eisenbrauns, 2000.

Carlson, R. A. "The Anti-Assyrian Character of the Oracle in Is. 9:1–6." *VT* 24 (1974): 130–35.

Carr, David M. *Reading the Fractures of Genesis: Historical and Literary Approaches*. Louisville: Westminster John Knox, 1999.

Carter, Warren. *John: Storyteller, Interpreter, Evangelist*. Peabody, MA: Hendrickson, 2008.

Chadwick, Henry. *Early Christian Thought and the Classical Tradition*. Oxford: Oxford University Press, 1966.

Chapman, Cynthia R. "The Breath of Life: Speech, Gender, and Authority in the Garden of Eden." *JBL* 138 (2019): 241–63.

Chen, Y. S. *The Primeval Flood Catastrophe: Origins and Early Development in Mesopotamian Traditions*. Oxford: Oxford University Press, 2013.

Clifford, Richard J. *Creation Accounts in the Ancient Near East and in the Bible*. CBQMS 26. Washington, DC: Catholic Biblical Association, 1994.

———. "The Divine Assembly in Genesis 1–11." In Baden, Najman, and Tigchelaar, *Sibyls, Scriptures, and Scrolls*, 1:276–92.

———. *Proverbs: A Commentary*. OTL. Louisville: Westminster John Knox, 1999.

Clines, David J. A., ed. *Dictionary of Classical Hebrew*. 9 vols. Sheffield: Sheffield Phoenix, 1993–2014.

Cogan, Mordechai. *1 Kings*. AB 10. New York: Doubleday, 2000.

Cohen, S. Marc, and C. D. C. Reeve. "Aristotle's Metaphysics." In *Stanford Encyclopedia of Philosophy*, edited by Edward N. Zalta. Winter 2021 ed. https://plato.stanford.edu/archives/win2021/entries/aristotle-metaphysics/.

Collins, Adela Yarbro. *Mark: A Commentary*. Edited by Harold W. Attridge. Hermeneia. Minneapolis: Fortress, 2007.

Collins, John J. *The Apocalyptic Imagination: An Introduction to Apocalyptic Literature*. 2nd ed. Grand Rapids: Eerdmans, 1998.

———. *Daniel: A Commentary*. Hermeneia. Minneapolis: Fortress, 1993.

Conrad, Edgar W. *Fear Not Warrior: A Study of 'al tîrā' Pericopes in the Hebrew Scriptures*. Brown Judaic Studies 75. Chico, CA: Scholars Press, 1985.

Cook, Joan E. "Everyone Called by My Name: Second Isaiah's Use of the Creation Theme." In Dempsey and Pazdan, *Earth, Wind, and Fire*, 48–56.

Cook, Stephen L. *The Apocalyptic Literature*. IBT. Nashville: Abingdon, 2003.

Cox, Gavin. "The 'Hymn' of Amos: An Ancient Flood Narrative." *JSOT* 38 (2013): 81–108.

Cozens, Simon, and Christoph Ochs. "'Have You No Shame?' An Overlooked Theological Category as Interpretive Key in Genesis 3." *Journal of Theological Interpretation* 13, no. 2 (2019): 186–99.

"Creation Epic, The." Translated by E. A. Speiser. In *ANET*, 62.

Dahood, Mitchell. *Psalms III: 51–100*. AB 17. Garden City, NY: Doubleday, 1968.

Dalley, Stephanie. *The Mystery of the Hanging Garden of Babylon: An Elusive World Wonder Traced*. New York: Oxford University Press, 2015.

———. *Myths from Mesopotamia: Creation, the Flood, Gilgamesh, and Others*. Rev. ed. Oxford: Oxford University Press, 2000.

Danker, Frederick W., Walter Bauer, William F. Arndt, and F. Wilbur Gingrich. *A Greek-English Lexicon of the New Testament and Other Early Christian Literature*. 3rd ed. Chicago: University of Chicago Press, 2000.

Day, John. *God's Conflict with the Dragon and the Sea*. Cambridge: Cambridge University Press, 1985.

Dekker, Jaap. *Zion's Rock-Solid Foundations: An Exegetical Study of the Zion Text in Isaiah 28:16*. Oudtestamentische Studiën 54. Leiden: Brill, 2007.

Dempsey, Carol J., and Mary Margaret Pazdan, eds. *Earth, Wind, and Fire: Biblical and Theological Perspectives on Creation*. Collegeville, MN: Liturgical Press, 2004.

DeRoche, Michael. "Isaiah XLV 7 and the Creation of Chaos?" *VT* 42 (1992): 11–21.

———. "Zephaniah 1:2–3: The 'Sweeping' of Creation." *VT* 30 (1980): 104–9.

Dietrich, F. E. C. *Abhandlungen zur hebräischen Grammatik*. Leipzig: Vogel, 1846.

Dietrich, Jan. "Sozialanthropologie des Alten Testaments: Grundfragen zur Relationalität und Sozialität des Menschen." *ZAW* (2015): 224–43.

Dietrich, Manfried. "Das biblische Paradies under der babylonischer Tempelgarten: Überlegungen zur Lage des Gartens Eden." In *Das biblische Weltbild und seine altorientalischen Kontexte*, edited by Bernd Janowski and Beate Ego, 281–323. FAT 32. Tübingen: Mohr Siebeck, 2001.

Dietrich, Manfried, Oswald Loretz, and Joaquín Sanmartín, eds. *The Cuneiform Alphabetic Texts from Ugarit, Ras Ibn Hani, and Other Places*. 3rd enl. ed. of *KTU*. Münster: Ugarit-Verlag, 1995.

Edelman, Diana. "Proving Yahweh Killed His Wife (Zechariah 5:5–11)." *BibInt* 11 (2003): 335–44.

Ephron, Ronald J. "Royal Ideology and State Administration in Pharonic Egypt." In vol. 1 of *Civilizations of the Ancient Near East*, edited by Jack M. Sasson, 273–77. New York: Scribner, 1995.

Epic of Gilgamesh: A New Translation, The. Edited and translated by A. R. George. London: Penguin Books, 1999.

Errington, Andrew. "God's Practical Knowledge of Creation." *IJST* 23 (2021): 214–34.

Feník, Juraj, and Róbert Lapko. "The Reign of Christ in Colossians: A Reassessment." *CBQ* 81 (2019): 495–516.

Filho, Danilo Marcondes de Souza. "The Maker's Knowledge Principle and the Limits of Science." *Proceedings of the American Catholic Philosophical Association* 76 (2002): 229–37.

Finkelstein, Israel. "The Territorial Extent and Demography of Yehud/Judea in Persian and Hellenistic Periods." *RB* 117 (2010): 39–54.

Fishbane, Michael. "Jeremiah 4:23–26 and Job 3:3–13: A Recovered Use of the Creation Pattern." *VT* 21 (1971): 151–67.

Fitzpatrick, Paul E. *The Disarmament of God: Ezekiel 38–39 in Its Mythic Context*. CBQMS 37. Washington, DC: Catholic Biblical Society, 2004.

Fleming, Chris. *René Girard: Mimesis and Violence*. Malden, MA: Polity Press, 2004.

Flynn, Conrad. "What Star Wars Stole from the Bible." Medium. December 18, 2019. https://medium.com/@conradflynn/what-star-wars-stole-from-the-bible-d47ee60aebe3.

Folger, Tim. "Nothingness of Space Could Illuminate the Theory of Everything." *Discover*, July 17, 2008. http://discovermagazine.com/2008/aug/18-nothingness-of-space-theory-of-everything#.UfniaWR4Z4V.

———. "Virtual Particles." *Science Encyclopedia*. http://science.jrank.org/pages/7195/Virtual-Particles.html.

Fox, Everett. *The Five Books of Moses: Genesis, Exodus, Leviticus, Numbers, Deuteronomy; A New Translation with Introductions, Commentary, and Notes*. Schocken Bible 1. New York: Schocken, 1995.

Fox, Michael V. "The Epistemology of the Book of Proverbs." *JBL* 126 (2007): 669–84.

———. "God's Answer and Job's Response." *Biblica* 94 (2013): 1–23.

———. "The Meaning of the Book of Job." *JBL* 137 (2018): 7–18.

———. *Proverbs 1–9*. AB 18A. New Haven: Yale University Press, 2000.

Freedman, H., and Maurice Simon, trans. and eds. *Midrash Rabbah*. 10 vols. London: Soncino, 1939.

Fretheim, Terence E. *Exodus*. Interpretation: A Bible Commentary for Teaching and Preaching. Louisville: Westminster John Knox, 1991.

———. *God and the World in the Old Testament: A Relational Theology of Creation*. Nashville: Abingdon, 2005.

———. *Reading Hosea–Micah: A Literary and Theological Commentary*. Macon, GA: Smith and Helwys, 2013.

Frölich, Ida. "Creation in the Book of Tobit." In Nicklas and Zamfir, *Theologies of Creation*, 35–50.

Gadamer, Hans-Georg. *Truth and Method*. Translated by Joel Weinsheimer and Donald G. Marshall. 2nd rev. ed. New York: Crossroad, 1989.

Gardiner, Patrick, ed. *Theories of History*. New York: Free Press, 1959.

Gaventa, Beverly Roberts. "Neither Height nor Depth: Discerning the Cosmology of Romans." *SJT* 64 (2011): 265–78.

Giorgetti, Andrew. "The 'Mock Building Account' of Genesis 11:1–9: A Critique of Mesopotamian Royal Ideology." *VT* 64 (2014): 1–20.

Girard, René. *Things Hidden since the Foundation of the World*. Translated by Stephen Bann and Michael Metteer. Palo Alto, CA: Stanford University Press, 1977.

———. *Violence and the Sacred*. Translated by Patrick Gregory. Baltimore: Johns Hopkins University Press, 1977.

Gleason, Kathryn L. "Gardens." In vol. 2 of *The Oxford Encyclopedia of Archaeology in the Ancient Near East*, edited by Eric M. Meyers, 382–85. New York: Oxford University Press, 1997.

Goldingay, John. *The Message of Isaiah 40–55: A Literary-Theological Commentary*. London: T&T Clark, 2005.

———. *Old Testament Theology*. Vol. 1, *Israel's Gospel*. Downers Grove, IL: IVP Academic, 2003.

Goldstein, Jonathan A. *2 Maccabees*. AB 41A. Garden City, NY: Doubleday, 1983.

Gordon, Robert P. "The Ethics of Eden: Truth-Telling in Genesis 2–3." In *Ethical and Unethical in the Old Testament: God and Humans in Dialogue*, edited by Katherine Dell, 11–33. London: T&T Clark, 2010.

———, ed. *The God of Israel*. University of Cambridge Oriental Publications 64. Cambridge: Cambridge University Press, 2007.

Goswell, Greg. "David in the Prophecy of Amos." *VT* 61 (2011): 243–57.

———. "The Order of the Books in the Greek Old Testament." *Journal of the Evangelical Theological Society* 52 (2009): 449–66.

Goulder, Michael. "Deutero-Isaiah of Jerusalem." *JSOT* 28 (2004): 351–64.

Grabbe, Lester L. *A History of the Jews and Judaism in the Second Temple Period*. Vol. 2, *The Coming of the Greeks: The Hellenistic Period (335–175 BCE)*. Library of Second Temple Studies 68. Edinburgh: T&T Clark, 2008.

Granerød, Gard. "A Forgotten Reference to Divine Procreation? Psalm 2:6 in Light of Egyptian Royal Ideology." *VT* 60 (2010): 323–36.

Greenberg, Moshe. *Ezekiel 21–37*. AB 22A. New York: Doubleday, 1997.

Greenfield, Jonas C. "Hadad." In *DDD*, 377–82.

Gunkel, Hermann. *Schöpfung und Chaos in Urzeit und Endzeit: Eine religionsgeschichtliche Untersuchung über Genesis 1 und Ap. Joh 12*. Göttingen: Vandenhoeck & Ruprecht, 1895.

Gzella, Holger. *Aramaic: A History of the World's First Language*. Grand Rapids: Eerdmans, 2021.

Habel, Norman C. *Job: A Commentary*. OTL. Philadelphia: Westminster, 1985.

Hahne, Harry Alan. *The Corruption and Redemption of Creation: Nature in Romans 8:19–22 and Jewish Apocalyptic Literature*. Library of New Testament Studies 336. London: T&T Clark, 2006.

Hamilton, Victor P. *The Book of Genesis, Chapters 1–17*. NICOT. Grand Rapids: Eerdmans, 1990.

Hamori, Esther J. "Echoes of Gilgamesh in the Jacob Story." *JBL* 130 (2011): 625–42.

Harker, Ryan D. "Redeeming Creation in Romans: The Eschatological Role of the 'Children of God' Compared to That of the Land in *2 Baruch*." In Harker and Bunce, *Earth Is the Lord's*, 136–54.

———. "Renewal of Covenant, Renewal of Creation: A Rhetorical Analysis of the Apocalyptic Visions of Daniel." Seminar paper presented at Anabaptist Mennonite Biblical Seminary, Elkhart, Indiana, 2015.

Harker, Ryan D., and Heather L. Bunce, eds. *The Earth Is the Lord's: Essays on Creation and the Bible in Honor of Ben C. Ollenburger*. University Park: Pennsylvania State University Press [Eisenbrauns], 2019.

Hasel, Gerhard. "The Significance of the Cosmology in Genesis 1 in Relation to Ancient Near Eastern Parallels." *Andrews University Seminary Studies* 10 (1972): 1–20.

Hays, Christopher B. *Hidden Riches: A Sourcebook for the Comparative Study of the Hebrew Bible and the Ancient Near East*. Louisville: Westminster John Knox, 2014.

———. *The Origins of Isaiah 24–27: Josiah's Festival Scroll for the Fall of Assyria*. Cambridge: Cambridge University Press, 2019.

Heard, Christopher. "The Tree of Life in Genesis." In *The Tree of Life*, edited by Douglas Estes, 74–99. Themes in Biblical Narrative 27. Leiden: Brill, 2020.

Heidel, Alexander. *The Babylonian Genesis: The Story of Creation*. 2nd ed. Chicago: University of Chicago Press, 1951.

Hendry, George S. "Nothing." *Theology Today* 39 (1982): 274–89.

Hesiod. *Opera et dies (Works and Days)*. In *The Homeric Hymns and Homerica*, translated by Hugh G. Evelyn-White. Cambridge, MA: Harvard University Press, 1914. https://www.perseus.tufts.edu/hopper/text?doc=Perseus%3Atext%3A1999.01.0132%3Acard%3D109.

———. *Theogeny*. Translated by Richard S. Caldwell. The Focus Classical Library. Indianapolis: Hackett, 1987.

Hess, Richard S. "Chaldea." In vol. 1 of *The Anchor Bible Dictionary*, edited by David Noel Freedman, 886–87. New York: Doubleday, 1992.

Hiebert, Theodore. "The Tower of Babel and the Origin of the World's Cultures." *JBL* 126 (2007): 29–58.

———. *The Yahwist's Landscape: Nature and Religion in Early Israel*. New York: Oxford University Press, 1996.

Holladay, William L. *Jeremiah 1: A Commentary on the Book of the Prophet Jeremiah, Chapters 1–25*. Hermeneia. Philadelphia: Fortress, 1986.

Holmstedt, Robert D. "The Restrictive Syntax of Genesis 1:1." *VT* 58 (2008): 56–67.

Hossfeld, Frank-Lothar, and Erich Zenger. *Psalms 2: A Commentary on Psalms 51–100*. Translated by Linda M. Maloney. Hermeneia. Minneapolis: Augsburg Fortress, 2005.

———. *Psalms 3: A Commentary on Psalms 101–150*. Translated by Linda M. Maloney. Hermeneia. Minneapolis: Fortress, 2011.

Huovila, Kimmo, and Dan Lioy. "The Meaning of *Hebel* in Ecclesiastes." *Conspectus* 27 (2019): 35–49.

Hurowitz, Victor (Avigdor). *I Have Built You an Exalted House: Temple Building in the Bible in Light of Mesopotamian and Northwest Semitic Writings*. JSOTSup 115. Sheffield: Sheffield Academic, 1992.

Husson, Valentin. "Building and Dwelling in *Inception*." In *Inception and Philosophy: Ideas to Die For*, edited by Thorsten Botz-Bornstein, 269–78. Chicago: Open Court, 2011.

James, George Wharton. *Indian Blankets and Their Makers*. New York: Dover, 1974.

Janzen, J. Gerald. "On the Moral Nature of God's Power: Yahweh and the Sea in Job and Deutero-Isaiah." *CBQ* 56 (1994): 458–78.

Jeremias, Jörg. *Das Königtum Gottes in den Psalmen: Israels Begegnung mit dem kanaanäischen Mythos in den Jahwe-König-Psalmen*. FRLANT 141. Göttingen: Vandenhoeck & Ruprecht, 1979.

Jericke, Detlef. *Die Ortsangaben im Buch Genesis: Ein historisch-topographischer und literarisch-topographischer Kommentar*. Göttingen: Vandenhoeck & Ruprecht, 2013.

Jewett, Robert. *Romans: A Commentary*. Hermeneia. Philadelphia: Fortress, 2007.

Jones, Scott C., and Christine Roy Yoder, eds. *"When the Morning Stars Sang": Essays in Honor of Choon Leong Seow on the Occasion of His Sixty-Fifth Birthday*. BZAW 500. Berlin: de Gruyter, 2018.

Joüon, Paul, and Takamitsu Muraoka. *A Grammar of Biblical Hebrew*. 2nd ed. Rome: Gregorian and Biblical Press, 2009.

Käsemann, Ernst. *Commentary on Romans*. Translated by Geoffrey W. Bromiley. Grand Rapids: Eerdmans, 1980.

Kautzsch, Emil, ed. *Gesenius' Hebrew Grammar*. Translated by Arther E. Cowley. 2nd ed. Oxford: Clarendon, 1910.

Kawashima, Robert S. "Violence and the City: On the Yahwist's Leviathan." *Near Eastern Archaeology* 78 (2015): 264–72.

Keck, Leander E., ed. *The New Interpreter's Bible*. 12 vols. Nashville: Abingdon, 1994–2004.

Keil, C. F., and Franz Delitzsch. *The Twelve Minor Prophets*. Translated by James Martin. 2 vols. Grand Rapids: Eerdmans, 1949.

Keller, Catherine. "'Be This Fish': A Theology of Creation out of Chaos." *Word and World* 32 (2012): 15–20.

Kennedy, James M. "The Root *G'R* in the Light of Semantic Analysis." *JBL* 106 (1987): 47–64.

Kittel, Rudolf. "Die Zukunft der alttestamentlichen Theologie." *ZAW* 39 (1921): 84–99.

Klaiber, Walter. *Schöpfung: Urgeschichte und Gegenwart*. Göttingen: Vandenhoeck & Ruprecht, 2005.

Knibb, Michael A. *A New English Translation of the Septuagint*. New York: Oxford University Press, 2007. Accessible online at https://ccat.sas.upenn.edu/nets/edition/29-wissal-nets.pdf.

Knight, Mark. "*Wirkungsgeschichte*, Reception History, Reception Theory." *Journal for the Study of the New Testament* 33 (2010): 137–46.

Knox, Crawford. *Changing Christian Paradigms and Their Implications for Modern Thought*. Leiden: Brill, 1993.

Koosed, Jennifer L. *(Per)mutations of Qohelet*. LHB/OTS 429. Edinburgh: T&T Clark, 2006.

Kraftchick, Steven J., Charles D. Myers Jr., and Ben C. Ollenburger, eds. *Biblical Theology: Problems and Perspectives, in Honor of J. Christiaan Beker*. Nashville: Abingdon, 1995.

Kraus, Hans-Joachim. *Psalms 1–59: A Continental Commentary*. Translated by Hilton C. Oswald. Minneapolis: Augsburg, 1988.

Krusche, Marcel. "A Collective Anointed? David and the People in Psalm 89." *JBL* 139 (2020): 87–105.

Kuja, Ryan. "Remembering the Body: Misogyny through the Lens of Judges 19." *Feminist Theology* 19 (2016): 89–95.

Kvanvig, Helge S. *Primeval History: Babylonian, Biblical and Enochic: An Intertextual Reading*. JSJSup 149. Leiden: Brill, 2011.

Kynes, Will. *An Obituary for "Wisdom Literature": The Birth, Death, and Reintegration of a Biblical Corpus*. New York: Oxford University Press, 2019.

Lambert, Wilfred G. *Babylonian Creation Myths*. Mesopotamian Civilizations. Winona Lake, IN: Eisenbrauns, 2013.

Lambert, W. G., and A. R. Millard. *Atra-Ḫasīs: The Babylonian Story of the Flood*. Oxford: Clarendon, 1969.

Lanfer, Peter T. "Solomon in the Garden of Eden: Autonomous Wisdom and the Danger of Discernment." In Baden, Najman, and Tigchelaar, *Sibyls, Scriptures, and Scrolls*, 1:714–25.

Lenzi, Alan. "Proverbs 8:22–31: Three Perspectives on Its Composition." *JBL* 125 (2006): 687–714.

Levenson, Jon D. *Creation and the Persistence of Evil: The Jewish Drama of Divine Omnipotence*. San Francisco: Harper & Row, 1988.

———. *The Hebrew Bible, the Old Testament, and Historical Criticism*. Louisville: Westminster John Knox, 1993.

Levinson, Bernard M. *"The Right Chorale": Studies in Biblical Law and Interpretation*. FAT 54. Tübingen: Mohr Siebeck, 2008.

Lind, Millard C. "Monotheism, Power, and Justice: A Study in Isaiah 40–55." In *Monotheism, Power, Justice: Collected Old Testament Essays*, 153–67. Elkhart, IN: Institute of Mennonite Studies, 1990.

Lindroth, James. "Simone Weil and Wallace Stevens: The Notion of Decreation as Subtext in 'An Ordinary Evening in New Haven.'" *Religion and Literature* 19 (1987): 43–62.

Lipschits, Oded, and Joseph Blenkinsopp, eds. *Judah and the Judeans in the Neo-Babylonian Period*. Winona Lake, IN: Eisenbrauns, 2003.

Lohfink, Norbert. "Der Zorn Gottes und das Exil: Beobachtungen am deuteronomistischen Geschichtswerk." In *Liebe und Gebot: Studien zum Deuteronomium*, edited by R. G. Kratz and H. Spieckermann, 137–55. FRLANT 190. Göttingen: Vandenhoeck & Ruprecht, 2000.

Löning, Karl, and Erich Zenger. *To Begin With, God Created . . . : Biblical Theologies of Creation*. Translated by Omar Kaste. Collegeville, MN: Michael Glazer, 2000.

Machinist, Peter. "How Gods Die, Biblically and Otherwise: A Problem of Cosmic Restructuring." In *Reconsidering the Concept of Revolutionary Monotheism*, edited by Beate Pongrartz-Leister, 189–240. Winona Lake, IN: Eisenbrauns, 2011.

———. "Literature as Politics: The Tukulti-Ninurta Epic and the Bible." *CBQ* 38 (1976): 455–82.

Marglit, Baruch. "The Canaanite Origin of Psalm 29 Reconsidered." *Biblica* 51 (1970): 332–48.

Martens, Elmer A. "Intertext Messaging: Echoes of the Aaronic Blessing (Numbers 6:24–26)." *Direction* 38 (2009): 163–78.

Martin, Dale Basil. "When Did Angels Become Demons?" *JBL* 129 (2010): 657–77.

Marzouk, Safwat. *Egypt as a Monster in the Book of Ezekiel*. FAT 76. Tübingen: Mohr Siebeck, 2015.

Matty, Nazek Kahled. *Sennacherib's Campaign against Judah and Jerusalem*. BZAW 487. Berlin: de Gruyter, 2016.

May, Gerhard. *Creatio ex Nihilo: The Doctrine of "Creation out of Nothing" in Early Christian Thought*. Translated by A. S. Worrall. London: T&T Clark International, 1994.

Mays, James Luther. *Amos*. OTL. Philadelphia: Westminster, 1969.

McBride, S. Dean, Jr. "Divine Protocol: Genesis 1:1–2:3." In *God Who Creates: Essays in Honor of W. Sibley Towner*, edited by William P. Brown and S. Dean McBride Jr., 3–41. Grand Rapids: Eerdmans, 2000.

McCarter, P. Kyle. *2 Samuel*. AB 9. Garden City, NY: Doubleday, 1984.

McCarthy, Dennis J. "'Creation' Motifs in Ancient Hebrew Poetry." In *Creation in the Old Testament*, edited by Bernhard W. Anderson, 74–89. Philadelphia: Fortress, 1984.

McDowell, Catherine L. *The Image of God in the Garden of Eden: The Creation of Humankind in Genesis 2:5–3:4 in Light of* mīs pî, pīt-pî, *and* wpt-r *Rituals of Mesopotamia and Ancient Egypt*. Siphrut 15. Winona Lake, IN: Eisenbrauns, 2015.

McFague, Sallie. *Models of God: Theology for an Ecological, Nuclear Age*. Philadelphia: Fortress, 1987.

McGrath, Alister E. *Christian Theology: An Introduction*. 6th ed. Hoboken, NJ: Wiley-Blackwell, 2016.

McKane, William. *A Critical and Exegetical Commentary on Jeremiah*. Vol. 1, *Jeremiah 1–25*. International Critical Commentary. Edinburgh: T&T Clark, 1986.

———. *Proverbs: A New Approach*. OTL. Philadelphia: Westminster, 1970.

McKnight, Scot. *The Letter to the Colossians*. New International Commentary on the New Testament. Grand Rapids: Eerdmans, 2018.

Melvin, David. "Making All Things New (*Again*): Zephaniah's Vision of a Return to Primeval Time." In *Creation and Chaos: A Reconsideration of Hermann Gunkel's* Chaoskampf *Hypothesis*, edited by Joann Surlock and Richard H. Beal, 269–81. Winona Lake, IN: Eisenbrauns, 2013.

Mendenhall, George. "Covenant Forms in Biblical Tradition." *Biblical Archaeologist* 17 (1954): 50–76.

Mettinger, Tryggve N. D. *The Eden Narrative: A Literary and Religio-historical Study of Genesis 2–3*. Winona Lake, IN: Eisenbrauns, 2007.

———. "The God of Job: Avenger, Tyrant, or Victor." In *The Voice from the Whirlwind: Interpreting the Book of Job*, edited by Leo G. Perdue and W. Clark Gilpin, 39–49. Nashville: Abingdon, 1992.

Metzger, Martin. "Eigentumsdeklaration und Schöpfungsaussage." In "*Wenn nicht jetzt, wann dann?" Aufsätze für Hans-Joachim Kraus zum 65 Geburtstag*, edited by Hans-Georg Geyer, Johann Michael Schmidt, Werner Schneider, and Michael Weinrich, 37–51. Neukirchen-Vluyn: Neukirchener Verlag, 1983.

Meyers, Carol L. "Gender Roles and Genesis 3:16 Revisited." In *A Feminist Companion to Genesis*, edited by Athalya Brenner, 118–41. Feminist Companion to the Bible 2. Sheffield: Sheffield Academic, 1993.

Middleton, J. Richard. "Created in the Image of a Violent God? The Ethical Problem of the Conquest of Chaos in Biblical Creation Texts." *Interpretation* 58 (2004): 341–55.

———. *The Liberating Image: The* Imago Dei *in Genesis 1*. Grand Rapids: Brazos, 2005.

Miller, Patrick D. "Creation and Covenant." In Kraftchick, Myers, and Ollenburger, *Biblical Theology*, 155–68.

———. "The Poetry of Creation: Psalm 104." In Brown and McBride, *God Who Creates*, 87–103.

Miller, Robert D., II. *The Dragon, the Mountain, and the Nations: An Old Testament Myth, Its Origins, and Its Afterlife*. Winona Lake, IN: Eisenbrauns, 2017.

Moberly, R. W. L. "On Interpreting the Mind of God: The Theological Significance of the Flood Narrative (Genesis 6–9)." In *The Word Leaps the Gap: Essays on Scripture and Theology in Honor of Richard B. Hays*, edited by J. Ross Wagner, C. Kavin Rowe, and Katherine Grieb, 44–66. Grand Rapids: Eerdmans, 2008.

———. *The Theology of the Book of Genesis*. Old Testament Theology. New York: Cambridge University Press, 2009.

Moo, Douglas A., and Jonathan A. Moo. *Creation Care: A Biblical Theology of the Natural World*. Biblical Theology for Life. Grand Rapids: Zondervan, 2018.

Müller, Reinhard. "Der finstere Tag Jahwes: Zum kultische Hintergrund von Amos 5, 18–20." *ZAW* 122 (2010): 576–92.

Murphy, Roland E. *Ecclesiastes*. WBC 23A. Dallas: Word. 1992.

———. *The Tree of Life: An Exploration of Biblical Wisdom Literature*. 2nd ed. Grand Rapids: Eerdmans, 1990.

Nevader, Madhavi. "Creating a *Deus Non Creator*: Divine Sovereignty and Creation in Ezekiel." In *The God Ezekiel Creates*, edited by Paul M. Joyce and Dalit Rom-Shiloni, 55–70. LHB/OTS 607. London: Bloomsbury T&T Clark, 2015.

Newsom, Carol. *The Book of Job: A Contest of Moral Imaginations*. New York: Oxford University Press, 2003.

Newsom, Carol, and Brennan W. Breed. *Daniel: A Commentary*. OTL. Louisville: Westminster John Knox, 2014.

Nicklas, Tobias, and Korinna Zamfir, eds. *Theologies of Creation in Early Judaism and Ancient Christianity*. Deuterocanonical and Cognate Literature Studies 6. Berlin: de Gruyter, 2010.

Niehaus, Jeffrey. "In the Wind of the Storm: Another Look at Genesis 3:8." *VT* 44 (1994): 263–67.

Nilson, Tina Dykesteen. "The Creation of Darkness and Evil (Isaiah 45:6C–7)." *RB* 115 (2008): 5–25.

Nogalski, James D. "Zephaniah's Use of Genesis 1–11." *Hebrew Bible and Ancient Israel* 2 (2013): 351–72.

O'Connor, Kathleen. *Genesis 1–25A*. Smyth and Helwys Bible Commentary. Macon, GA: Smyth and Helwys, 2018.

———. "Wild, Raging Creativity: Job in the Whirlwind." In Dempsey and Pazdan, *Earth, Wind, and Fire*, 48–56.

———. "Wisdom Literature and Experience of the Divine." In Kraftchick, Myers, and Ollenburger, *Biblical Theology*, 183–95.

Ollenburger, Ben C. "The Book of Zechariah." In *NIB*, 7:735–840.

———. "Creation and Peace: God and Creature in Genesis 1–11." In *The Old Testament in the Life of God's People: Essays in Honor of Elmer A. Martens*, edited by Jon Isaak, 143–58. Winona Lake, IN: Eisenbrauns, 2009.

———. "Creation and Violence." In *Struggles for Shalom: Peace and Violence across the Testaments*, edited by Laura L. Brenneman and Brad D. Schantz, 26–35. Eugene, OR: Pickwick, 2014.

———. "Isaiah's Creation Theology." *Ex Auditu* 3 (1987): 54–71.

———, ed. *Old Testament Theology: Flowering and Future*. Sources for Biblical and Theological Study 1. Winona Lake, IN: Eisenbrauns, 2004. Revised edition of *The Flowering of Old Testament Theology*.

———. "Peace and God's Action against Chaos in the Old Testament." In *The Church's Peace Witness*, edited by Marlin E. Miller and Barbara Nelson Gingerich, 70–88. Grand Rapids: Eerdmans, 1994.

———. "Peace as the Visionary Mission of God's Reign." In *Beautiful upon the Mountains: Biblical Essays on Mission, Peace, and the Reign of God*, edited by Mary H. Schertz and Ivan Friesen, 97–120. Elkhart, IN: Institute of Mennonite Studies, 2003.

———. "Pursuing the Truth of Scripture." In *But Is It All True? The Bible and the Question of Truth*, edited by Alan G. Padgett and Patrick R. Keifert, 44–65. Grand Rapids: Eerdmans, 2006.

———. "Suffering and Hope: The Story behind the Book." *Theology Today* 44 (1987): 350–59.

———. "We Believe in God . . . Maker of Heaven and Earth." *HBT* 12 (1990): 64–96.

———. *Zion, the City of the Great King: A Theological Symbol of the Jerusalem Cult*. JSOTSup 41. Sheffield: JSOT Press, 1987.

Oswald, Wolfgang. "Das Erstlingswerk Gottes—zur Übersetzung von Genesis 1:1." *ZAW* 120 (2008): 417–21.

———. "Textwelt, Kontextbezug und historische Situation in Isaiah 7." *Biblica* 89 (2008): 201–20.

Paas, Stefan. *Creation and Judgment: Creation Texts in Some Eighth Century Prophets*. OTS 47. Leiden: Brill, 2003.

Patrick, Dale. "Translation of Job 42:6." *VT* 26 (1976): 369–71.

Paul, Shalom M. *Amos: A Commentary*. Hermeneia. Minneapolis: Fortress, 1991.

Perdue, Leo G. *The Collapse of History: Reconstructing Old Testament Theology*. OBT. Minneapolis: Fortress, 1994.

———. *Wisdom and Creation: The Theology of Wisdom Literature*. Nashville: Abingdon, 1994.

Perowne, J. J. Stewart. *The Book of Psalms*. 2 vols. London: George Bell and Sons, 1878.

Peterson, David. "The World of Creation in the Book of the Twelve." In Brown and McBride, *God Who Creates*, 204–14.

Pritchard, James B., ed. *Ancient Near Eastern Texts Relating to the Old Testament*. 3rd ed. Princeton: Princeton University Press, 1969.

Propp, William H. C. *Exodus 1–18*. AB 2. New Haven: Yale University Press, 1999.

Quirke, Stephen. "Creation Stories in Ancient Egypt." In *Imagining Creation*, edited by Markham Geller and Mineke Schipper, 61–86. IJS Studies in Judaica 5. Leiden: Brill, 2007.

Reid, Garnett. "'Thus You Shall Say to Them': A Cross-Cultural Confessional Polemic in Jer 10:11." *JSOT* 31 (2006): 221–38.

Reiterer, Friedrich V. "'Alles hat nämlich der Herr gemacht': Das Telos der Schöpfung bei Ben Sira." In Nicklas and Zamfir, *Theologies of Creation*, 95–136.

Rendtorff, Rolf. *Canon and Theology: Overtures to an Old Testament Theology*. OBT. Minneapolis: Fortress, 1993.

———. *Theologie des Alten Testaments: Ein kanonischer Entwurf*. 2 vols. Neukirchen-Vluyn: Neukirchener Verlag, 1999, 2001.

Ricoeur, Paul. *Freud and Philosophy: An Essay on Interpretation*. Translated by Denis Savage. New Haven: Yale University Press, 1970.

Roberts, J. J. M. "The Enthronement of Yhwh and David: The Abiding Theological Significance of the Kingship Language of the Psalms." *CBQ* 64 (2002): 675–86.

———. *First Isaiah: A Commentary*. Hermeneia. Minneapolis: Fortress, 2015.

Robinette, Brian D. "The Difference Nothing Makes: *Creatio ex nihilo*, Resurrection, and Divine Gratuity." *Theological Studies* 72 (2011): 525–57.

Rose, Christian. "Nochmals: Der Turmbau zu Babel." *VT* 54 (2004): 223–38.

Rowland, Christopher. *By an Immediate Revelation: Studies in Apocalypticism, Its Origins and Effects*. Wissenschaftliche Untersuchungen zum Neuen Testament 473. Tübingen: Mohr Siebeck, 2021.

Sandmel, Samuel. "Parallelomania." *JBL* 81 (1962): 1–13.

Schellenberg, Annette. *Der Mensch, das Bild Gottes? Zum Gedanken einer Sonderstellung des Menschen im Alten Testament und in weiteren altorientalischen Quellen*. Abhandlungen zur Theologie des Alten und Neuen Testaments 101. Zürich: Theologische Verlag, 2011.

———. "Humankind as the 'Image of God.'" *Theologische Zeitschrift* 65 (2009): 97–115.

Schifferdecker, Kathryn. *Out of the Whirlwind: Creation Theology in the Book of Job*. Harvard Theological Studies 61. Cambridge, MA: Harvard University Press, 2008.

Schmid, Hans Heinrich. "Creation, Righteousness, and Salvation: 'Creation Theology' as the Broad Horizon of Biblical Theology." In *Creation in the Old Testament*, edited by Bernhard W. Anderson, 102–17. Issues in the Study of Religion and Theology 6. Philadelphia: Fortress, 1984.

Schmid, Konrad. "The Ambivalence of Wisdom: Genesis 2–3 as a Sapiential Text." In Jones and Yoder, *"When the Morning Stars Sang,"* 275–86.

———. *A Historical Theology of the Hebrew Bible*. Translated by Peter Altmann. Grand Rapids: Eerdmans, 2019.

———. "Loss of Immortality? Hermeneutical Aspects of Genesis 2–3 and Its Early Reception." In *Beyond Eden: The Biblical Story of Paradise (Genesis 2–3) and Its Reception History*, edited by Konrad Schmid and Christoph Riedweg, 58–87. FAT, 2nd ser., vol. 24. Tübingen: Mohr Siebeck, 2008.

Schmitz, Barbara. "'Dir soll Deine ganze Schöpfung dienen' (Jdt 16,14): Schöpfungstheologie im Buch Judit." In Nicklas and Zamfir, *Theologies of Creation*, 51–59.

———. "Geschaffen aus dem Nichts? Die Funktion der Rede von der Schöpfung im Zweiten Makkabäerbuch." In Nicklas and Zamfir, *Theologies of Creation*, 61–79.

Schreiner, Josef. *Sion-Jerusalem: Jahwes Königssitz: Theologie der heiligen Stadt im Alten Testament*. Studien zum Alten und Neuen Testaments 7. München: Kösel-Verlag, 1963.

Schüle, Andreas. "And Behold, It Was Very Good . . . and Behold, the Earth Was Corrupt (Genesis 1:31; 6:12)." In *Theology from the Beginning: Essays on the Primeval History and Its Canonical Context*, 99–119. FAT 133. Tübingen: Mohr Siebeck, 2017.

Seow, C. L. *Job 1–21: Interpretation and Commentary*. Illuminations. Grand Rapids: Eerdmans, 2013.

———. "Qohelet's Eschatological Poem." *JBL* 118 (1999): 209–34.

Seri, Andrea. "The Role of Creation in *Enuma Elish*." *Journal of Ancient Near Eastern Religions* 12 (2012): 4–29.

Seufert, Matthew. "The Presence of Genesis in Ecclesiastes." *Westminster Theological Journal* 78 (2016): 75–92.

Sharp, Carolyn. "Ironic Representation, Authorial Voice, and Meaning in Qoheleth." *BibInt* 12 (2004): 37–68.

Sheinfeld, Shayna. Introduction to *Gender and Second-Temple Judaism*, edited by Kathy Ehrensperger and Shayna Sheinfeld, 1–22. Lanham, MD: Rowan & Littlefield, 2020.

Smith, George. *The Chaldean Account of Genesis, Containing the Description of the Creation, the Fall of Man, the Deluge, the Tower of Babel, the Times of the Patriarchs, and Nimrod; Babylonian Fables, and Legends of the Gods; From the Cuneiform Inscriptions*. New York: Scribner, Armstrong and Co., 1876.

Smith, Mark S. *The Genesis of Good and Evil: The Fall(out) and Original Sin in the Bible*. Louisville: Westminster John Knox, 2019.

———. "Monotheism and the Redefinition of Divinity in Ancient Israel." In *The Wiley Blackwell Companion to Ancient Israel*, edited by Susan Niditch, 278–97. Hoboken, NJ: Wiley-Blackwell, 2016.

———. *The Priestly Vision of Genesis 1*. Minneapolis: Fortress, 2010.

Smith, Mark S., and Wayne T. Pitard. *The Ugaritic Baal Cycle*. Vol. 2. Supplements to Vetus Testamentum 114. Leiden: Brill, 2009.

Smith, Morton. "The Common Theology of the Ancient Near East." *JBL* 71 (1952): 35–47.

Snyder Belousek, Darrin W. "'Who Then Is This?': Jesus the Creator in the Gospel of Mark." In Harker and Bunce, *Earth Is the Lord's*, 101–17.

Soggin, J. Alberto. "'And You Will Be like God and Know What Is Good and What Is Bad': Genesis 2–3." In *Sefer Moshe: The Moshe Weinfeld Jubilee Volume; Studies in the Bible and the Ancient Near East, Qumran, and Post-Biblical Judaism*, edited by Chaim Cohen, Avi Hurvitz, and Shalom M. Paul, 191–94. Winona Lake, IN: Eisenbrauns, 2004.

Sommer, Benjamin. *A Prophet Reads Scripture: Allusion in Isaiah 40–66*. Stanford, CA: Stanford University Press, 1998.

Sparks, Kenton L. *Ancient Texts for the Study of the Hebrew Bible: A Guide to Background Literature*. Peabody, MA: Hendrickson, 2005.

———. "*Enūma Elish* and Priestly Mimesis: Elite Emulation in Nascent Judaism." *JBL* 126 (2007): 625–48.

Speiser, E. A., trans. "The Creation Epic." *ANET*, 62.

Spronk, Klaas. "Rahab." In *DDD*, 864–86.

———. "Shamgar ben Anat (Judg 3:31)—a Meaningful Name." *ZAW* 128 (2016): 684–87.

Stead, Michael A. *The Intertextuality of Zechariah 1–8*. LHB/OTS 506. New York: T&T Clark, 2009.

Steymans, Hans Ulrich. "Gilgamesh und Genesis 1–9." *Biblische Zeitschrift* 54 (2010): 201–28.

Stulman, Louis, and Hyun Chul Paul Kim. *You Are My People: An Introduction to Prophetic Literature*. Nashville: Abingdon, 2010.

"Sumerian King List, The." Translated by A. Leo Oppenheim. *ANET*, 265.

Swartley, Willard M. "Creation and the Gospel of John." In Harker and Bunce, *Earth Is the Lord's*, 118–35.

Sweeney, Marvin A. *Isaiah 1–39, with an Introduction to Prophetic Literature*. The Forms of the Old Testament Literature 16. Grand Rapids: Eerdmans, 1996.

———. *Tanak: A Theological and Critical Introduction to the Jewish Bible*. Minneapolis: Fortress, 2012.

———. *Zephaniah: A Commentary*. Hermeneia. Minneapolis: Augsburg Fortress, 2003.

Tadmor, Hayim. "History and Ideology in the Assyrian Royal Inscriptions." In *Assyrian Royal Inscriptions: New Horizons in Literary, Ideological and Historical Analysis; Papers of a Symposium Held in Cetona (Siena), June 26–28, 1980*, ed. F. M. Fales, 13–33. Orientalis Antiqui Collectio XVII. Rome: Instituto per l'Oriente, 1981.

Timiadis, Emilianos. *The Nicene Creed: Our Common Faith*. Philadelphia: Fortress, 1993.

Trefil, James F. *The Moment of Creation: Big Bang Physics from before the First Millisecond to the Present Universe*. Garden City, NY: Dover, 2004.

Trible, Phyllis. *God and the Rhetoric of Sexuality*. OBT. Philadelphia: Fortress, 1978.

Tuell, Steven. "The Rivers of Paradise: Ezekiel 47:1–12 and Genesis 2:10–14." In Brown and McBride, *God Who Creates*, 171–89.

Tull, Patricia K. "'Who Has Measured the Waters?' Creation in Second Isaiah and Contemporary Imagination." In Harker and Bunce, *Earth Is the Lord's*, 53–66.

Turner-Smith, Sarah G. "Naked but Not Ashamed: A Reading of Genesis 2:25 in Textual and Cultural Context." *Journal of Theological Studies* 69, no. 2 (2018): 425–46.

Ussishkin, David. "Sennacherib's Campaign to Judah: The Events at Lachish and Jerusalem." In *Isaiah and Imperial Context: The Book of Isaiah in the Times of Empire*, edited by Andrew T. Abernethy, Mark G. Brett, Tim Bulkeley, and Tim Meadowcroft, 1–34. Eugene, OR: Pickwick, 2013.

van der Lugt, Pieter. "Who Changes His Mind about Dust and Ashes? The Rhetorical Structure of Job 42:2–6." *VT* 64 (2014): 623–39.

Van der Toorn, Karel, Bob Becking, and Pieter W. van der Horst, eds. *Dictionary of Deities and Demons in the Bible*. 2nd rev. ed. Grand Rapids: Eerdmans, 1999.

Van Leeuwen, Raymond C. "Cosmos, Temple, House: Building and Wisdom in Ancient Mesopotamia and Israel." In *From the Foundations to the Crenellations: Essays on Temple Building in the Ancient Near East and Hebrew Bible*, edited by Mark J. Boda and Jamie Novotny, 399–421. Alter Orient und Altes Testament 366. Münster: Ugarit-Verlag, 2010.

———. "Creation and Contingency in Qoheleth." In *The Identity of Israel's God in Christian Scripture*, edited by Don Collett, Mark Gignilliat, and Ephraim Radner, 143–59. Resources for Biblical Study. Atlanta: SBL, 2020.

Veijola, Timo. *Verheissung in der Krise: Studien zur Literatur und Theologie der Exilszeit anhand des 89. Psalms*. Helsinki: Suomalainen Tiedeakatemia, 1982.

Vincent, Jean Marcel. "Recherches exégétiques sur le Psaume XXXIII." *VT* 28 (1978): 442–54.

von Rad, Gerhard. *Genesis: A Commentary*. OTL. Philadelphia: Westminster, 1972.

———. "The Royal Ritual in Judah." In *The Problem of the Hexateuch and Other Essays*, 222–31. Translated by E. W. Trueman. London: SCM, 1984.

———. *Wisdom in Israel*. Translated by James D. Martin. Nashville: Abingdon, 1972.

Voth, H. R. *Traditions of the Hopi*. Chicago: Field Columbian Museum, 1905. http://www.sacred-texts.com/nam/hopi/toth/.

Wagner, Thomas. "'Ungeklärte Verhältnisse': Die priesterliche Urgeschichte und das Buch Ezechiel." *Kerygma und Dogma* 59 (2013): 207–29.

Walsh, Carey. "The Beasts of Wisdom: Ecological Hermeneutics of the Wild." *BibInt* 25 (2017): 135–48.

Waltke, Bruce K., and Michael O'Connor. *An Introduction to Biblical Hebrew Syntax*. Winona Lake, IN: Eisenbrauns, 1990.

Walton, John H. *Genesis 1 as Ancient Cosmology*. Winona Lake, IN: Eisenbrauns, 2011.

Watson, Rebecca S. *Chaos Uncreated: A Reassessment of "Chaos" in the Bible*. BZAW 341. Berlin: de Gruyter, 2005.

Weber, Beat. "'They Saw You, the Waters—They Trembled' (Psalm 77:17B): The Function of Mytho-Poetic Language in the Context of Psalm 77." In *Psalms and Mythology*, edited by Dirk J. Human, 104–25. LHB/OTS 462. New York: T&T Clark, 2007.

Weber, Otto. *Foundations of Dogmatics*. Vol. 1. Translated by Darrell L. Guder. Grand Rapids: Eerdmans, 1981.

Welker, Michael. *Creation and Reality*. Translated by John F. Hoffmeyer. Minneapolis: Fortress, 1999.

Wenham, Gordon J. *Genesis 1–15*. WBC 1. Waco: Word, 1987.

———. "Sanctuary Symbolism in the Garden of Eden Story." *Proceedings of the World Congress of Jewish Studies* 9 (1986): 19–25.

Westermann, Claus. *Genesis 1–11: A Continental Commentary*. Translated by John J. Scullion. Minneapolis: Augsburg, 1984.

Whitely, Peter M. *The Orayvi Split: A Hopi Transformation*. Part 2: The Documentary Record. New York: Anthropological Records of the American Museum of Natural History, 2008. http://digitallibrary.amnh.org/bitstream/handle/2246/5954/A087%20part%202.pdf?sequence=10.

Williams, Ronald J. *Hebrew Syntax: An Outline*. 2nd ed. Toronto: University of Toronto Press, 1976.

Williams, Rowan. *On Christian Theology*. Challenges in Contemporary Theology. Oxford: Blackwell, 2000.

Wilson, Robert R. "Creation and New Creation: The Role of Creation Imagery in the Book of Daniel." In Brown and McBride, *God Who Creates*, 190–203.

Winston, David. *The Wisdom of Solomon*. AB 43. Garden City, NY: Doubleday, 1979.

Wintermute, Orval S. "Jubilees." In vol. 2 of *Old Testament Pseudepigrapha*, edited by James H. Charlesworth, 35–142. New York: Doubleday, 1985.

Wischmeyer, Oda. "Kosmos und Kosmologie bei Paulus." In *Weltkonstruction: Religiöse Weltdeutung zwischen Chaos und Kosmos von Alten Orient bis zum Islam*, edited by Peter Gemeinhardt and Annette Zgoll, 87–101. Orientalische Religionen in der Antike 5. Tübingen: Mohr Siebeck, 2010.

Wold, Benjamin G. "Genesis 2–3 in Early Christian Tradition and 4QInstruction." *Dead Sea Discoveries* 23 (2016): 329–46.

Wolde, Ellen van. *Reframing Biblical Studies: When Language and Text Meet Culture, Cognition, and Context*. Winona Lake, IN: Eisenbrauns, 2009.

———. *Stories of the Beginning: Genesis 1–11 and Other Creation Stories*. Ridgefield, CT: Morehouse, 1997.

———. *Words Become Worlds: Semantic Studies of Genesis 1–11*. Leiden: Brill, 1994.

Wolterstorff, Nicholas. *Divine Discourse: Philosophical Reflections on the Claim That God Speaks*. Cambridge: Cambridge University Press, 1995.

Wright, N. T. "The Meaning of Jesus." *Books & Culture*, March/April 1999.

Yee, Gale. "The Theology of Creation in Proverbs 8:22–31." In *Creation in the Biblical Traditions*, edited by Richard J. Clifford and John J. Collins, 85–96. CBQMS 24. Washington, DC: Catholic Biblical Association, 2004.

Yoder, Perry B. *Shalom: The Bible's Word for Salvation, Justice, and Peace*. Newton, KS: Faith & Life Press, 1987. Repr., Eugene, OR: Wipf & Stock, 2017.

Yoder Neufeld, Thomas R. "*Creatio ex Detrito*: Creation and Peace in Ephesians." In Harker and Bunce, *Earth Is the Lord's*, 155–70.

Yon, Marguerite. *The City of Ugarit at Tell Ras Shamra*. Winona Lake, IN: Eisenbrauns, 2006.

Young, Frances. "'Creatio ex Nihilo': A Context for the Emergence of the Christian Doctrine of Creation." *SJT* 44 (1991): 139–51.

Zevit, Ziony. *What Really Happened in the Garden of Eden?* New Haven: Yale University Press, 2013.

Zimmerli, Walther. *Old Testament Theology in Outline*. Translated by David E. Green. Atlanta: John Knox, 1978.

Scripture Index

Note: Bracketed references denote ET versification, where it differs from the MT.

Old Testament

Genesis

Jeremiah

Lamentations

Ezekiel

Daniel

Hosea

Joel

Amos

Jonah

Micah

Nahum

Habakkuk

Zephaniah

Zechariah

Subject Index